THE GERMAN SHEPHERD DOG

POPULAR DOGS' BREED SERIES

THE GERMAN SHEPHERD DOG

JOSEPH SCHWABACHER
AND
THELMA GRAY

Revised by Madeleine Pickup

Popular Dogs
London Sydney Auckland Johannesburg

Copyright © Thelma Gray and Popular Dogs Publishing Co. Ltd
1967, 1969, 1971, 1973, 1976, 1978, 1982, 1986, 1990

Appendices A, G and H copyright © The Kennel Club 1982, 1986

Popular Dogs Publishing Co. Ltd
20 Vauxhall Bridge Road, London SW1V 2SA

An imprint of Random Century

Random Century Australia (Pty) Ltd
20 Alfred Street, Milsons Point, Sydney 2061, Australia

Random Century New Zealand Limited
191 Archers Road, PO Box 40–086, Glenfield, Auckland 10

Century Hutchinson Group South Africa (Pty) Ltd
PO Box 337, Bergvlei 2012, South Africa

First published (as *The Popular Alsatian*) 1922
Revised edition 1924, 1926, 1936, 1950
Reprinted eight times
Revised edition (*The Alsatian*) 1967, 1969, 1971, 1973, 1976, 1978, 1982
Revised edition (*The German Shepherd Dog*) 1986
Reprinted 1988

Revised edition 1990
Set in Garamond by BookEns, Saffron Walden, Essex
Printed and bound in Great Britain by
Mackays of Chatham plc, Chatham, Kent

British Library Cataloguing in Publication Data

Schwabacher, Joseph
    The German shepherd dog.–Rev. ed.
    1. German shepherd dog
    I. Title   II. Gray, Thelma   III. Pickup,
    Madeleine   IV. Schwabacher, Joseph.
    Alsatian
    636.7′3   SF429.G37

ISBN 0 09 1745004

Contents

Illustrations

Guide dog and owner off-duty

Druidswood Octavia
Owned by Mrs M. Pickup

Actionnaire of Druidswood
Owned by Mrs M. Pickup

IN THE TEXT

PREFACE

It feels a little strange sifting through a book written by two well-known breeders, both of whom I knew from 'lang forbye' and, in Thelma's case, from our teenage years when 50 years' friendship was born, a friendship which continued in friendly rivalry until her much lamented death in Australia in 1984. We shared, as will most readers of this book, a deep love and admiration for our great breed; and I know that it ranked number one among her wide range of breeds in which her successes were world-renowned. She was immensely proud that her Champion Sergeant of Rozavel was also C.D. and was trained and handled by herself.

I am not required to make many alterations to an excellent and well-written book; but I have brought it a little more up to date, particularly where products are used in the feeding and health chapters. The list of Champions has also been extended, and a few new photographs added. I hope that it will make for additional usefulness and enjoyment of an already favourite book, and serve as a memorial for the two original authors who did so much to bring our breed through the difficult years.

1986

M.P.

Author's Introduction

I was still at school when my parents bought a Mattesdon-bred German Shepherd Dog puppy. Gretchen was not a very good specimen, something we did not appreciate at the time, nor had she been well reared. But she was gentle and intelligent and we loved her.

London, where we lived, and its parks, which offer the only open spaces where dogs can run and play, was a notorious centre of canine infection in those bad old days when there were no preventative injections against distemper. Gretchen contracted the disease at a very early age. After weeks of patient nursing and the efforts of the late President of the Royal Veterinary College, Sir Frederick Hobday, our close neighbour and friend who continued to attend our pets long after he had relinquished normal general practice, she died.

We were all heart-broken, but during her short life Gretchen had turned me into a German Shepherd Dog devotee, and, with her successors, imbued me with a love and admiration for the breed, now of 40 years' duration and showing no signs of diminishing.

For some little time we all felt too sad to attempt to replace Gretchen, and in any case it was necessary to let some months go by to be sure that no infection lingered in the house, but eventually my mother bought a magnificent dog from Mrs Moore-Brabazon, of the Cabra prefix, and we kept him for many years. It was soon after we got him that I began to take an interest in German Shepherd Dog pedigrees, shows, and the like, and learned something about leading breeders at home and in Germany. I soon became familiar with the kennel name Secretainerie, made famous by the late Joseph Schwabacher.

He lived in Germany, and in those days it never occurred to

me that he might settle in England and that I would come to regard him as a friend and adviser. As things turned out, I already had a well-established and sizable kennel of German Shepherd Dogs with a couple of Champions to my credit when this did, in fact, come to pass.

Hitler dominated Germany, and Mr Schwabacher had the great misfortune to find himself incarcerated in one of the most notorious concentration camps, where he suffered terrible privations and ill-treatment. He was more fortunate than most of his companions, however, because he succeeded in escaping to Britain, where, as a refugee with very limited means, he faced up to the difficult task of making a new life in a new country at a time when he was far from young. He seldom spoke of his experiences, and with characteristic reticence does not refer to his personal tragedies in his book.

His great love had been the German Shepherd Dog, and naturally as soon as he was able to make some connections with his favourite breed he did so. This was not very easy for him because he had left not only his relations but his dogs in Germany. but in one respect he was very fortunate indeed.

For in 1942, quite coincidentally, an import arrived in the form of a son of one of his own bitches – Franze Secretainerie. The dog, named Ingosohn of Errol, was sired by the German Grand Champion, Ingo v. Piastendamm, and while it was not an outstanding specimen, it had a lot of good points and, as things turned out, a great deal to offer the breed in Britain.

Owing to his difficult circumstances, Mr Schwabacher was unable to found a kennel without financial assistance, but he eventually succeeded in finding a backer and partner, and then embarked on an elaborate breeding project.

In this, the immediate post-war period, it was difficult to buy good bitches. Breeding had been restricted and top-class stock in most breeds was hard to find. Mr Schwabacher had to take what he could get, and as a result quite a number of his foundation broods were not of a very high standard. This inevitably meant that not all of the animals emerging from the newly established-in-Britain Secretainerie kennel did credit to such a well-known affix. Mr Schwabacher himself was often disappointed with the results of his breeding programme, but he had no illusions about the excellence of one particular line which he sponsored and which resulted in that acknowledged all-time pillar of the breed, Ch. Avon Prince of Alumvale.

It was unfortunate that the Secretainerie kennel was being maintained at a time when the available inoculations against distemper and kindred virus diseases were found to have become largely ineffectual, long before the introduction of the highly successful egg-adapted-type vaccines which generally provide reliable protection today. Rearing a large number of litters at a time is inclined to be risky, and this policy brought recurrent disastrous epidemics which decimated Mr Schwabacher's young stock and brought serious financial reverses. Eventually he could carry on no longer and he closed the breeding kennels, confining his activities to a few bitches placed with other people on breeding-terms arrangements of one kind or another, selecting individuals who were anxious to follow his methods and take his advice.

Although this new venture worked quite well, Joseph Schwabacher's attempts to build up a great kennel under the Secretainerie name were largely abortive, so that his experience of mating, breeding and whelping was mainly confined to that portion of his life which he devoted to dogs in Germany.

Breeding is conducted rather differently there, where there are very few 'kennels' in the accepted sense of the word, most breeders keeping one or two bitches themselves and farming out a few more with local friends or relatives.

It is for this reason that I have completely re-written the sections dealing with mating, breeding and rearing. I feel that with a lifetime of raising German Shepherd Dogs behind me, under the conditions general in Britain, and with 10 generations of Rozavel German Shepherd Dogs in unbroken line, I may be in a better position to help newcomers to acquaint themselves with methods known to be successful in this country.

Therefore Chapters I and II from the previous edition have been incorporated and are now Chapter 1: much of it is Mr Schwabacher's work with some additions of my own, and this is also the case with Chapter 3 which I have left predominantly as he devised it.

Chapters 4 and 5 are entirely Joseph Schwabacher's work;

they are admirable and I do not feel I could improve them. Chapters 2, 7, 8, 9, 10 and 11 are entirely my own work, and I have added a Glossary of Terms.

When I became acquainted with Joseph it was towards the latter part of his life. He was ageing noticeably, and probably due to his experiences in the concentration camp – I believe it was Buchenwald – he did not enjoy good health. We had many sessions together when we traced obscure pedigrees, some of which I have kept, written in his spidery foreign handwriting, and I often sought help and information about the German dogs in modern pedigrees. He loved to be consulted on any matter appertaining to German Shepherd Dogs, and I always found him kind and helpful.

He knew a great deal about the breed, and could be very critical. He not unnaturally had a very good opinion of the standard of the breed in Germany, which he was apt to compare, sometimes unfavourably, with the quality of the German Shepherd Dogs bred in Britain. His outspokenness alienated some of the well-established breeders, who resented a foreigner, however well qualified, telling them what to do and what not to do.

In consequence Joseph Schwabacher had friends and enemies and was a controversial figure of his time. Yet everything he said or did was based on a great love for the German Shepherd Dog breed. Looking back, I feel that people may, not unnaturally, have been a little oversensitive so soon after the Second World War, and less able to accept a German in their midst than might have been the case a few years later. We were all gathering ourselves together after the holocaust of the war, and I feel that we did not appreciate Mr Schwabacher as we should have done.

I can see him now, sitting at the ringside of any important Championship Show, and I remember him taking tea on our lawn on one of those rare, sunny summer afternoons, with half a dozen German Shepherd Dogs panting at our feet. The conversation was all about dogs all the time, and I welcomed his candid criticisms even if I did not always agree. He died very shortly after, but I think he would have considered me a suitable writer to revise and re-write his book. He knew that I loved the breed and have always hoped, through my breeding plans, to contribute something to its good.

I hope he would have approved of my efforts in connection with this book, so much of which he has written. This, and the many beautiful dogs descended from those he was instrumental in producing during his time in Britain, are his memorials.

1967   T.G.

Since the sixth edition appeared in 1967, I have in subsequent impressions made a few minor revisions to the text and brought the appendices up to date five times. I have also replaced and added some photographs.

1978   T.G.

I

The Ancestry of the German Shepherd Dog

'THREE thousand years are looking down upon you!'

Thus exclaimed the Emperor Napoleon as he rallied his legions in the shadows of the pyramids of Egypt. We, in turn, look back to the year 1400 B.C. when we study the picture of the dog sculptured in limestone which is now in the Egyptian museum in the Louvre, Paris. The statue was found at Lycopolis, the ancient capital of Upper Egypt, and could easily have had a modern German Shepherd Dog as its model. Writers like to trace back the histories of various breeds of dogs for thousands of years, and sometimes profess to discover recognisable types carved in stone or pictured on papyrus, such pictures appearing rather nondescript to unbiased eyes. Because we believe that a type of dog truly resembling the German Shepherd Dog really did exist thousands of years ago we illustrate as a means of comparison the picture of a modern statue executed by Frau Dillon, a Swabian sculptress. Sculpted from life, the dog looks exactly like the museum-piece!

It goes to prove that the German Shepherd Dog is a dog of natural build, free from man-made exaggerations, at least when bred to the right type. The pictures could portray the same dog. We may well exclaim: 'Three thousand years are looking down on the German Shepherd Dog!'

The dog was almost certainly the first domestic animal. Its bones have been found among the remains of the last Palaeolithic hunting races of mankind, hunters who retreated with their dogs into North America, whilst the pastoral and agricultural peoples of the Neolithic Age advanced from the lands east of the Caspian Sea.

Palaeontological evidence shows that a wild dog existed in the northern part of the Eurasian continent at the close of the last glacial period. An examination of the skeletal remains of this animal, found at the beginning of the present century near Moscow, shows that it was quite distinct from contemporary jackals and wolves. This prehistoric dog was named, in honour of its discoverer, Canis Poutiatini. The skull shows a less-powerful jaw than that of the wolf, and the flesh-tearing incisor teeth are markedly less well developed. This wild dog was the primitive ancestor of all hunting and sheep-herding types.

At Olmutz, in Moravia, in the mounds among the marshes of North Holland and Friesland, and at Anau in Turkestan (in strata deposited about 8,000 years ago) significant discoveries have been made, dating back to the Bronze Age. In both places skeletal remains found were of dogs and of a domesticated type of sheep, proving that even in those remote times the dog was already serving man and guarding flocks. In 1540 the Castle of Steinau, belonging to the Counts of Hanover, was reconstructed and during the alterations digging took place on ground which had been reserved as a burying place for the hunting and yard dogs. The remains of the dogs exhumed, some dating from the thirteenth century, were thrown into a cave, where they were subsequently discovered and examined. As a result, a comparison of the bones from the Steinau Hohle with those of the modern shepherding dogs on the one side, and with those of the Bronze Age and Canis Poutiatini on the other, establishes without doubt the continuity of descent of the modern German Shepherd Dog.

With the extensive development of arable farming, particularly in the rich wheat and root-growing districts of central and northern Germany, where there are no numerous dividing hedges as in the English countryside, a type of dog was required to circle the flocks and prevent them straying off the pastures and on to the cultivated land.

From a crossing of the best dogs of the northern state of Württemberg with those of the central states of Frankonia and Thuringia the modern German Shepherd Dog was developed.

The German Shepherd Dog is a member of an enormous family, one that is widely distributed and found in almost every corner of the globe. The names of this 'family' are legion, but they all have been bred, promoted, devised – use what words you will – to herd sheep in one way or another.

Man has long needed sheep. For wool to clothe him, for meat to feed him, and for other useful by-products obtained from the horns, hides, and bones of this useful animal. Sheep are commonly dismissed as 'stupid creatures', but this does them less than justice. It is doubtful whether anybody used to working with sheep considers them silly, and the idea that they have no brains arises from the inborn characteristics of the animals. Highly sensitive and nervous, sheep are 'clannish' and have what in doggy circles would be described as pack instincts – but the correct word is not pack, but flock. Where one sheep leads another follows, and if a number of sheep are frightened they flee in panic. A man has little chance of stopping a flock on the move – unless he has a clever sheepdog.

Just any dog will not do, either. It must be fleet of foot, but sturdy. Substantial enough to stand up to a band-tempered ram or a defensive ewe with her lambs at foot, but not in any way heavy, cloddy or lumbering. A good dog can circumvent the swift-moving, heedless animals, can race ahead and dare them to pass, maybe turn them back and drive them through a gateway to a safe enclosure. If the sheep are driven up the hillside to graze, the dog may be needed to stay with them all day. They must be kept to one area, but the farmer has other urgent matters to attend to – so the Shepherd Dog takes charge. Hour after hour he trots, endlessly, tirelessly, round and round. The moment an animal strays his sharp eyes send him to the spot, and, as he approaches, the sheep scuttles back amongst its fellows. The Shepherd Dog goes about the work with the minimum of noise. An excitable, barking dog frightens the sheep and makes them scatter, harder than ever to control. And a sharp dog – one that nips and bites the legs and rears of sheep – can damage them as well as causing them to panic. Both types are rejected by the shepherd. His dog must be calm, placid, sensible, quick to learn, capable of thinking for itself and acting on its own initiative in emergencies. And such a dog must certainly have stamina and endurance. Picture the Shepherd Dog, stepping out with its smooth-reaching gait.

Consider the physical and mental qualities required. It at once becomes clear to all who know the German Shepherd Dog that here is a dog ideally fitted to do this work. And it is fortuitous that all these splendid qualities also equip it to do a multitude of other jobs as well.

It is not generally understood that working sheepdogs require enormous reserves of power, and that their endurance can be and often is, taxed to the limits. Some years ago a Scottish farmer used a pedometer for 28 days of the busiest lambing season, and he found that he himself was walking 30 miles each day. On this basis he estimated that his two sheepdogs covered at least three times this distance. One of them was fitter and more active than the other, and did most of the work. The farmer thought that she probably covered 100 miles day, on steep hill land and much of it very rough going. At times is was both cold and wet.

It is not disclosed if these dogs were collies, but it is supposed that they were. We tell the story to indicate that the German Shepherd Dog considered in its proper context as a working Shepherd's Dog, cannot be a fancy, over-elegant, or even over-large, animal, without losing much of its inherent usefulness.

Without doubt the sheep farmer, even in these days of mechanisation, cannot exist without a dog or dogs. The writer saw this admirably demonstrated on a visit to Australia, where, among many other interesting breeds, she judged German Shepherd Dogs at the Melbourne Royal Agricultural Show. An introduction was made to the indigenous sheep and cattle dogs of that great country, the kelpie and the mottled blue and brown native herding dogs. These have many of the German Shepherd Dog characteristics – the prick ears and sweeping tail, though both are smaller and lighter in build. The mottled dogs are mainly used for cattle, the slightly built kelpies often jumping on top of the closely huddled herds of sheep and running straight over their backs.

Presumably the various, often nondescript, types of dogs available for work with sheep in Germany at the back end of the last century left something to be desired. It must have been so, because two far-seeing breeders, Captain Rielchelmann-Dunau and Count von Hahn, were inspired to do something to improve the working ability and type of sheepdogs generally. To this end, they got together and founded a dog society known as the Phylax Club. This club, not unlike a good many of its ephemeral modern counterparts, came to grief after a short time, but the two founders, though probably sadder and wiser, were in no way discouraged. They carried on with their carefully planned breeding experiments, and in a very short time they were producing a recognisable type of dog. The results of their efforts had prick ears, thick but smooth coats, and were almost certainly very considerably smaller than the average German Shepherd Dog of today. They bore some resemblance to the dog we know, however.

In the year 1901, five years after the Phylax Club had collapsed, another breed society was born. This was Der Verein für Deutsche Schäferhunde (The Club for German Shepherd Dogs), ordinarily referred to as the S.V., a breed club that must rank amongst the oldest in the world, and one that is flourishing at the present time.

The S.V. began in Stuttgart, but its headquarters were later transferred to Munich, and, later still, to Berlin. From its inception the club has ruled breed affairs with an iron hand. British breeders say that they do not believe that the rules, which include the regimentation of breeders, dictating the number of puppies that may be reared upon a bitch when no foster-mother is available, and things of that kind, would be acceptable in Britain. There is a mistaken idea that the S.V. also dictates the sires that may be used on bitches, but this is not so.

Koerungs are held in Germany. These are breed surveys, conducted by specially appointed 'koermeisters', and there is no compulsion about entering dogs for these affairs. Dogs brought for survey are scored, on a regulation form, for every imaginable point, and graded accordingly. A dog with major faults is not 'angekoert' or passed for breeding purposes, and therefore not recommended. Breeding from it is not prohibited nor prevented, but clearly if there are plenty of approved stud dogs it is unlikely that the rejects will be of use to breeders. Faults and good points are equally pinpointed on the form, and if the dog comes out of the inspection well, it is described as 'angekoert for show and working breeding'. Frequently, remarks are added as to the suitability for certain bloodlines, and the inadvisability of mating with an animal carrying dangerous strains, or possessing faults that might be perpetuated.

In years gone by, efforts have been made to introduce the Koerung system to England, since it is clear that the high standard of the German dogs is in some measure due to the system. Indeed, two or three Koerungs have been held in this country, but in the main the idea did not meet with approval. British breeders wished to be free to make individual selections when it came to mating dogs and bitches, and scorned the advice of overseas experts, albeit from the cradle of the breed. The few who did take their dogs to be angekoert saw it in a different light and found the examination both interesting and helpful. Certainly the advice received did not need to be followed – there was no compulsion of any kind. The writer still has Koer certificates issued at a Koerung held at her home in 1933, the Koermeister being none other than Dr Werner Funk. A previous Koerung took place at the Seale kennels by courtesy of Mrs Howard, and those attending felt it very worth while. We breed very fine German Shepherd Dogs in Britain. But some think that the general quality could be, and should be, much higher than it is, and that while we have many outstanding specimens, we also have too many that are mediocre. It could be that the breed-survey system would help us to raise the standard. Most people in Germany think that it has been a great help to their breeders.

The S.V. Stud Book is the German Shepherd Dog 'Bible'. The volumes appear, year after year, with details of registered German Shepherd Dogs and their litter-mates, the colours, birth dates, parents and so on. British breeders have no comparable records.

If early breeders received much help from their club what material had they got to work with as they strove to produce better Shepherd Dogs?

Before we examine this important matter, it is necessary to consider the various types of Continental sheepdogs. One deliberately uses the word 'types' rather than 'breeds', because in the very early days, when there was as yet no S.V. and no registrations, no stud books, and no official pedigrees, the ancestry of the dogs was more likely to be recorded in the heads of the owners than on paper. Such 'pedigrees' would not be extensive, and would be confined to one or two generations. There would be very little incentive to found a pure strain, even if it were possible to do so. When recognisable types developed in various countries or in different areas of such countries it was probably for geographical reasons and not because any concerted effort had been made to produce dogs typical of a standard variety. After all, transport was primitive or non-existent. Community living was a necessary rule, and people often lived and died without ever travelling more than a few miles from their homes. Their dogs mated with local bitches, and doubtless a lot of close inbreeding took place. Close inbreeding is the quickest way to fix type, so obviously these haphazard relationships produced dogs that resembled one another, and could definitely be described as 'of the same type', though hardly spoken of as 'breeds'.

In their own little districts the dogs, as Nature took her course, may have become standardised, but in different areas there were many and varied types becoming fixed.

Britain, for instance, had rough and smooth collies, Old English Sheepdogs (the Bobtails) and the lesser-known Bearded Collies. Those close relations of the Collie, the Shetland Sheepdogs, and the varieties known as Welsh and Border Collies, were also recognisable types. There were, too, the cattle dogs. Wales had the Pembrokeshire and Cardiganshire Corgis, and Lancashire abounded with a variety now almost, if not quite, extinct, the Lancashire Heeler. Used mainly to drive cows, steers and wild ponies, these bright little dogs were sometimes called upon to help with the sheep, though in the main they were inclined to be both too noisy and too sharp.

The Continent of Europe had sheep and cattle dogs of every shape and size. They were large, small, long-haired, close-haired, prick-eared, drop-eared, shy, bold, friendly or fierce.

One is lost in admiration of the early pioneers whose remarkable foresight led us to gain our wonderful German Shepherd Dog breed, for the fact that we have it in its present form is due to their vision and to their earnest efforts. They knew, apparently, what they wanted and never wavered from their goal once they really got started. They wanted a tough working sheepdog with weather-resisting, dense but fairly short hair, of medium size and great intelligence. All these attributes were mainly utilitarian, but in addition they allowed themselves the luxury of adding the noble head and erect ears to complete the picture. It becomes clear, as we follow the progress of the early breeders, that while it may have been purely coincidental, most of the points selected as desirable were destined to produce an animal that often resembled, however superficially, a wolf.

This fact at once gave rise to the idea that captive wolves had been used to breed the foundation stock in the first formative years. Even today we find people ready to believe this, and it is difficult to convince them that such crosses were not only extremely improbable but probably impossible.

If wolf-dog matings ever took place at all the results were almost certainly sterile and never perpetuated. Certain zoological gardens have tried to cross wolves with dogs but have encountered all manner of obstacles, and there is no record of any strain of wolf-dog animals having been established. The idea that wolf blood was introduced into the German Shepherd Dog breed always seemed to assume that this happened in the very early days of the breed's formation.

But in those days the breeders planned to produce sheep-dogs. They had no ideas about breeding attractive dogs for the pet market, and at that time could not have foreseen that the German Shepherd Dog could possibly become so fashionable. Would serious breeders introduce wolf blood into a variety of dog destined to herd and protect sheep? Of course not. Such an idea would have been considered crazy. And quite apart from anything else, the wolf would have little to offer that might improve the German Shepherd Dog. If you do not believe this, go and have a look at the wolves at your nearest zoo. Compare them, point for point, with a picture of a Champion German Shepherd Dog. Just exercise your imagination and think of the wolf, on a collar and lead, being shown to a judge at a dog show. It would be last in any class!

Finally, if we are to kill the wolf-cross myth once and for

all, let us realise that even if wolf blood has ever been introduced into the German Shepherd Dog breed, such blood is by now so diluted, so far back, so utterly remote in any pedigrees, that it would be quite unlikely to exert any influences at all on modern stock.

This breed attracts more rumours and false information than any other; but it is certain that some experiments have been made to cross German Shepherd Dogs with wolves in order, it is said, to produce super guard and Police dogs. Recently it was reported that some trial matings had been made in South Africa, but as there has not been any sensational news of a development, we must conclude that the results were unsuccessful. Some wolf/shepherd dog crossing was done by Continental producers of animals for film work – for example, the classic shots of a wolf pack pursuing a sleigh over the snowy steppes – because the progeny were easier to train than the pure wolf. Here again, we have not heard of any follow-up with remarkable canine film stars. So it would appear it was a failure, as indeed we hope.

Once upon a time all dogs looked wolf-life, jackal-like, fox-like, and the oddest-looking fancy breeds today could trace back their ancestry to the same source. It so happens that a few breeds, of which the German Shepherd Dog is one, have been developed on natural and unexaggerated lines, and in some ways appear to resemble the wolf in type though not in finer points. Yet the German Shepherd Dog is no more a wolf than the gundog breeds with their soft expressions and pendant ears.

Although the old-established Phylax Club had such a brief existence, in so short a time it at least succeeded in interesting some highly influential people in its aims and objects, and some of them commenced trying to breed Shepherd Dogs with, as we already know, somewhat wolf-like heads and ears, and the enduring, slinky movement of the wild animals. As a means of producing dogs of this kind, sheepdogs from Thuringia were much sought after. The Shepherd Dogs from this district were predominantly wolf-grey in colour, and often had erect ears. They were small and stocky in build, but agile and energetic, and they tended to have rather curly tails. Herding dogs were also to be found in Württemberg, although these were not so much in demand because their ears were rarely up, but they were larger, well boned, yet active, and had better tail carriage.

The two types were in many ways ideally suited to each other, so in the natural course of events the dogs and bitches from Thuringia and Württemberg were interbred. Both types had some desirable points, but both had faults, and breeders tried to fix the best characteristics and to breed out the bad.

From the end of the nineteenth century, therefore, there were breeding kennels as such with standardised objectives, producing these dogs. To help them they had a stud book, and many of the dogs had brief pedigrees.

From all this activity there emerged two remarkable animals, Hektor Linksrein, also known as Horand v. Grafrath S.Z.1 and his litter brother Luchs (Sparwasser). Horand had many claims to fame, but not the least is the fact that he was the first Shepherd Dog registered in the Verein Stud Book. He was also, as his picture shows, a typical German Shepherd Dog at a time when they came in a multitude of shapes and sizes. He was born in January 1895, and is said to have measured 24 or 24½ inches at the shoulder. In this day and age, when the German Shepherd Dogs seem to be always increasing in size, with many being well over the 26-inch maximum, it is thought-provoking to learn that Horand, in his day, was considered to be 'large'.

The Adam of the breed was of Thuringian stock. He was considered to be outstandingly good-looking in his day, but was also of excellent temperament. From the description of his character and behaviour Horand must have been ideal in these respects. He appears to have been, like the majority of his fellows old and new, a very faithful one-man dog, marvellously obedient, a 'real gentleman', but in no sense a dull dog. Rather was he lively, always seeking and questing and curious, very amiable and extremely fond of children. And as if this were not enough he was said to have been a prepotent sire and to have handed down all or most of his mental and physical qualities to his children.

Horand's best son was considered to be Hektor v. Schwaben,

Sieger 1900–1, bred out of a qualified sheep-herding bitch of Württemberg strains called Madame v.d. Krone the Elder. Horand also sired Thekla I von der Krone, which was mated with her half-brother Hektor to produce the celebrated brothers Beowulf 10 and Pilot III. This pair were excellent dogs whose merits were attributed to their good fortune in having Horand as a double grandfather. Beowulf 10 and Pilot III were greatly admired and extensively used at stud. They may fairly be described as pillars of the breed, and were followed by such famous dogs as Roland v. Starkenburg, and the many noted dogs and bitches carrying the Kriminalpolizei kennel name. There were the Eislingens, the name Barbarossa, v.d. Krone again and again, Kalsmunt Wetzlar, v. Kohlwald, Berkemeyer, v. Boll, Uckermark, Eichenburg and many, many more.

Early breeders clearly appreciated the advantages of intelligent and well-advised inbreeding, which when understood is a marvellous short-cut to a standard type. One popular stud dog in particular was the result of a mother-to-son mating. Wolf v. Balingen was by Pilot III out of Nelly II Eislingen, and Nelly had a litter by Wolf containing Graf Eberhard von Hohen Esp. Graf sired, among other good Shepherds, a rugged, attractive dog that became the Sieger in the year 1908, Luchs v. Kalsmunt Wetzlar. Luchs in his turn sired the 1910 Sieger, Tell v.d. Kriminalpolizei. From his photograph Tell would hardly have pleased the present-day judges, but at the time he was described as the best dog of his day, and he was certainly heavily used at stud. It is probable that every German Shepherd Dog alive today can trace its pedigree back to Tell, and he may appear many times over, so widely disseminated are his bloodlines.

It is possibly of interest, too, that the Rozavel strain – and this is one of the real strains within the breed – was founded on a bitch born in 1921, herself a grand-daughter of an imported bitch named Crewkerne Louise, a full sister of Graf Eberhard v. Hohen Esp. Close line-breeding and inbreeding on this old working strain has given us what we want and has proved very rewarding.

Sieger 1911–12 was Norbert v. Kohlwald, very black with some tan markings, and with more than a touch of quality about him, something often lacking in the Siegers that had preceded him. Perhaps this elegance was, though unrecognised at that time, a warning that this might be carried to excess, for shortly after this the dogs and bitches became somewhat larger and certainly more streamlined.

The 1913 Sieger was a Tell son, Arno v.d. Eichenburg, but after this, owing to the First World War, no titles were awarded until peace was signed. The predominant post-war names that followed have a more familiar ring to modern Shepherdites – such prefixes and affixes as Grafenwerth, Glockenbrink, Blasienberg and Secretainerie were coming to the fore. Important, too, were the v. Haus Schutting and v. Bern kennels, destined to have a world-wide influence on the breed.

Most of the earliest Champions seem to have been rather square in build, with shorter bodies and longer legs than we see today, but they were also hard, dry, muscular and tough. A considerable number of the imports into Britain, commencing around 1918, were also this type of animal.

We can see by pictures in the early S.V. stud books that even as far back as 1910 and 1911 the dogs had started conforming to the standard. By 1922 and 1923 it is clear that the important winners were altering in type, and gradually evolving into something approaching the present-day conception of an ideal German Shepherd Dog. They still had a long way to go, however, and were predominantly higher off the ground.

One supposes that very few breeds of dogs have remained the same for 70 or 80 years. Indeed, certain breeds are reputed to bear very little resemblance to their original known forbears. Sometimes a breed tends to increase or decrease in size, sometimes it loses certain characteristics and often there is great improvement in general appearance.

The German Shepherd Dog has altered, for the first standard individuals were similar to Horand. The males stood about 24 inches at the withers or even less. They were very little longer in body than in height. Horand's contemporaries were not leggy, but in another generation or two the length of leg is markedly greater. The legs were straight, but without a superabundance of bone. Coats were short and dense.

Popular colours during the Horand era were hard dark greys and sables, though there were blacks with tan markings and blacks with brindled markings. The first hint of fading colour was attributed to Nores v.d. Kriminalpolizei. The dogs gradually became larger and more elegant, even if some still resembled their rugged ancestors and clung to the old original herding types.

During the 1920s breeders saw some very big, upstanding German Shepherd Dogs dominating the show rings and captivating the judges. Thinking breeders began to worry about the difference in appearance that was becoming so obvious. They wondered if the pendulum had swung too far in the other direction, and if these large dogs were still practical for working sheep. Why, they reasoned, if local farmers managed their flocks with agile little collies, need the Continental Shepherd Dogs be such a size?

It was not only the breeders in Britain who had seen the red light. Then Germany realised that subtle changes had crept into the Shepherd Dog breed, and that it was time to call a halt if the German Shepherd Dog was to remain unexaggerated working dog. Rittmeister von Stephanitz made his own views on the subject plain when he singled out some relatively small, low-to-ground dogs at shows and gave them high awards, thus encouraging breeders to make use of their services.

Size gradually began to level out, and to become more even and within the standard measurements.

Breeders were to see that king of Shepherd Dogs, the 1925 Sieger, Klodo v. Boxberg, followed by his sensational son, Sieger 1929 Utz v. Haus Schutting the dog that may fairly be said to have virtually re-made the entire breed. Colonel Baldwin, of Picardy fame, has said that in his opinion Utz was the first great dog with a really good body. Certainly he was quite different in type to most of the dogs that had gone before him, rather like the early herding dogs and sharing their strength and substance, but with proportions they never possessed – length, hind angulation, and shorter legs.

Utz was at stud in Germany before he was sold to the U.S.A. but fortunately for British breeders some of his stock came this way.

He sired the 1932 Sieger, Hussan v. Haus Schutting, which

resembled him in type, and with his rich colouring and aristo-cratic bearing was a fine-looking dog and every inch a Champion. Hussan was well patronised at stud, but unlike his sire and grandsire he was less successful. It takes time to assess the influence of a sire, but Germany does not consider Hussan a great producer.

We in Britain thank Utz for many things, not the least being the influence of his son, Voss von Bern. Zpr. H.G.H. P.D. T.D., imported by Mrs Barrington of Brittas fame.

Voss came at a time when the breed was settling down, thanks to Mrs and Miss Workman's Ch. Armin Ernaslieb who did so much to fix a good type and certainly improved tempera-ments. The happy marriage of Voss with an Armin daughter, Fee (Bell), led to Int. Ch. Gerolf of Brittas, the epitome of the Utz type and from whom so many Champions come down in direct line.

On a visit to the von Haus Schutting kennel in Hanover, Dr Funk offered the writer Voss's litter sister, Viper, but most unfortunately funds were low at the time and the sale never took place. This has been a matter of regret since, because Voss was such a splendid producer that we have often wondered what the outcome would have been had we had his sister. A third sister in Germany, Vicki, was a famous winner.

Because in some ways Utz's sire, Sieger Klodo von Boxberg, was not only a better dog but a better-balanced animal altogether, we have always thought it a pity that breeders were not importing a lot of stock about the time his immediate progeny might have been secured for this country. Klodo had many sons and daughters, and one of the best was the Reserve Sieger, Alf v.d. Webbelmanslust. We ourselves secured an Alf daughter, Sylvia von Schreckenstein of Rozavel Z.Pr., which we quickly made a Champion on her release from quarantine. Unfortunately – because she was so beautiful and had such a fabulous temperament – she was a most disappointing brood and spent most of her life as a pet.

Our other import about this time was Ch. Billo vom Gromberghaven Sch. H., who also attained his title in a short time. He was also a brilliant 'stunt' and demonstration dog, and excelled in gait, the like of which we have not seen since. Billo died shortly after he became a Champion but not before he had sired some winners, amongst them Rowena of Rozavel, which proved herself the mainstay of the Rozavel bitch line.

We have already referred to Ch. Armin Ernaslieb, but there were many other notable imports and home-bred stars in the Ceara kennels. Mrs and Miss Workman, in partnership with Miss Herta von Stephanitz, had spared no expense in building up a remarkably successful kennel on Hayling Island. Miss von Stephanitz is in fact the daughter of the founder of the breed, and lived with the Workmans' for some years before she returned to Germany. All the Ceara dogs had to work as well as win in beauty classes, and were outstanding for temperament. They did as well at Working Trials as at the Championship Shows, and Armin, together with his most famous son, Ch. Adalo of Ceara, were heavily used at stud. Adalo qualified PD. handled and trained by his owner. Other exciting imports included the Austrian Siegerin, Susi von Boll Sch. H.P.H. P.D. and the Siegerin Seffe von Blasienberg. Sch.H. Seffe came over in whelp to one of Mr Schwabacher's best dogs, Remo von der Secretainerie, and produced Ch. Ansa of Ceara.

Among others, Miss Workman also brought over Bero v.d. Deutchen Weken, a small, rich red-sable dog, sired by Utz and not dissimilar in type.

Bero was a controversial dog, as he was different from the majority of German Shepherd Dogs we had become used to seeing at the shows. His influence is difficult to assess but is probably most marked via his lovely daughter Ch. Biene of Dellside, because she was the dam of Ch. Dante of Charavigne.

Before Bero left Germany, Rittmeister von Stephanitz had created quite a sensation by awarding the Sieger title to a very large, drab-coloured sable dog (and to most people's thinking a very mediocre one), called Herold aus der Niederlausitz. Sch.H., and placing Bero second to him. It would be difficult to find two specimens of a breed less alike, and those who attended the Sieger show that year with the intention of sitting at the feet of the master to gain knowledge of the breed had something in the nature of a shaking-up.

Posterity records that Herold never sired anything of merit, but when one considers that Bero's daughter, mated to another import – the solid black, Ch. Dulo v. Minsweert, gave us Ch. Dante, one feels that in this respect at least *his* influence was vast. Dulo was probably not, in other respects, a sensational stock-getter, but from Dante came many winners, although, alas, he himself died young. Although his son Gottfried of Coulathorne was not a Champion, he was a marvellous sire, producing in one litter three bitch champions: Honey, Harmony and Herzig – all of Druidswood. He regularly transmitted his good medium-sized, rugged type, and although he had none of his sire's elegance and beauty his progeny were divorced from the leggy specimens of the 1920s. They approximated far more closely to the best dogs of the immortal Horand's day but without the cloddy build and lack of hind angulation that was a feature at that time.

Not one or two but virtually dozens of lines descend from Gottfried. Very few pedigrees are traced back without finding him in the background.

We cannot leave Utz and his son Hussan without remembering the puppies born in quarantine to a bitch imported in whelp to the latter. Colonel Baldwin was the breeder and in this litter were Ch. Dominant, and Distinguished, of Picardy. Dominant was a notable sire, and both brothers were of great interest to breeders, being, again, a more extreme type than had previously been commonplace, small, thickset but well made, with tremendous strength and substance in a modest frame. Utz, and consequently some or all of his children, are recurrently blamed for long coats and colour paling. Certainly both these faults, though not unknown, were rare before the Utz blood became widely established. Even so, Utz conferred so many benefits on his race that we should forgive him.

Mrs Barrington made very good use of Voss and his descendants, and from Int. Ch. Gerolf came Int. Ch. Vagabond of Brittas C.D., possibly Gerolf's most striking son. Vagabond was a rich dark sable of rugged type, excelling in bone and substance, and also in character – he was a 'great' Shepherd Dog – though not in size, for he was by no means a big one. We fell in love with one of Vagabond's sons, Galliard of Brittas, and used him to secure a fine litter which contained Ch. Sergeant of Rozavel C.D.

Closely allied with the Brittas line were the many excellent German Shepherd Dogs bearing the dual prefix/affix of Mr and

C. M. *Cooke*

Ch. Fenton of Kentwood

Ch. Ramacon Swashbuckler

Limestone sculpture estimated to date from 1400 B.C. found at Lycopolis, now in the Louvre

Sculpture by Fr. Diller based on modern German Shepherd Dog

Pilot III

Beowulf, 10

Sieger 1910. Tell v.d. Kriminalpolizei

Sieger 1908.
Luchs v.
Kalsmunt
Wetzlar

Nores v.d.
Kriminalpolizei

Sieger 1920.
Erich v.
Grafenwerth

Mrs Elliot-Vikkas and Hvitsand. Understandably many of the
Elliots' dogs resemble the Brittas type, which is strongly represented in their background by the best of the dogs and
bitches bearing that prefix. From time to time Mrs Barrington
has added imports to her kennel, and it was partly intelligent
selection and also, perhaps, a 'little bit of luck' that led to her
Arno v. Bibliserwald turning out a most suitable sire to tie in
with her established bloodlines.

All this time, winners were appearing from Mrs Howard's
Seale kennels, but her greatest was certainly Ch. Jet of Seale.
He was a son of Southdown Jeremy, owned by Mr Bertie
Dickerson who had become a German Shepherd Dog-world
personality in his own right, though the prefix was originally
founded by Mrs Leslie Thornton whose kennel Mr Dickerson
managed so ably for very many years. A great many Champions
bore the Southdown prefix.

Contemporary with Mrs Thornton was Mrs Lilian Leonard,
who under her previous name of Cecil-Wright ran the successful Louvencourt kennel. Following a second marriage she
ceased to breed and exhibit, living in a London flat, but her
home became the office of the German Shepherd Dog League
of Great Britain which for many years she ran with marvellous
enthusiasm and efficiency.

Mr Joseph Schwabacher's career as a breeder in Germany
came to a sudden close when the Hitler regime came into
power. He was imprisoned in Buchenwald, but was lucky
enough to emerge alive and to come as a refugee to Britain. He
had lost most of his possessions but not his interest in the
breed, and he eventually succeeded in getting together some
stock with his own bloodlines behind them, with which to
make a fresh start. As we have already mentioned in our
Introduction, Mr Schwabacher was lucky in finding Franze v.d.
Secretainerie's son Ingo and was instrumental, by advising
those concerned to effect certain matings, to help in the production of the celebrated Ch. Avon Prince of Alumvale, Ch.
Arno and Ch. Abbess, both of Saba etc.

If Utz revolutionised the breed at one time, Avon Prince certainly did it all over again some years later. Just as was the case
with Utz, too, breeders thanked Avon Prince for the improve-
ments he made, but reproached him for spreading some

undesirable faults, two of which are still causing some concern today – these being flat feet and weak pasterns, and colour paling. There are signs that the Cent z.d. Funf Geben son, Ch. Ludwig of Charavigne, already acclaimed as one of the truly great stud dogs of all time, has done and is doing a great deal to improve colour and pigmentation. Cent's sojourn in this country was a brief one, for he was resold to the U.S.A. when his owner, Mrs Dummett, found that breeders were slow to use him. His son, Ch. Ludwig of Charavigne, and another from the same litter, Lorenz, were widely used, Ludwig being a particularly prolific and successful sire. He did a great deal to promote the fame of the Hendrawen kennel from which so many outstanding winners keep emanating.

Reverting to the Schwabacher dogs, however, and their close relation, Avon Prince, we must pay tribute to this remarkable dog not only as a stud force but as a winner. He won 26 Challenge Certificates and sired a record number of Champions. Ch. Arno of Saba also sired a noteworthy bitch in Ch. Hella Secretainerie, a beautiful black and gold bitch which most people consider to be the best of the post-war German Shepherd Dogs bred by Mr Schwabacher. We ourselves owned, for a time, a Ch. Sparky of Aronbel son whose dam was inbred on Hella, and have successfully incorporated these bloodlines into our breeding programme.

Aronbel has for some time been a force to be reckoned with, Mr and Mrs Aaron producing a succession of fine dogs and bitches under this prefix. Sparky was a spectacular show dog, and a model of type and quality.

From Mrs Litton's Asoka kennel come many excellent top-class winners, one record-breaking C.C. winner and sire of Champions being Ch. Asoka Cherusker.

One could not leave a chapter on the development of the German Shepherd Dog without recalling the Kentwoods. Mrs M. Godden founded the kennel in the years before the last war, and, later joined by her daughter, they have kept one strain and gradually established an easily recognisable type. Several Champions have been crowned, but the most famous is their current star, Ch. Fenton of Kentwood, the first German Shepherd Dog to go Best in Show at Cruft's Dog Show, the greatest dog show in the world.

In recent years the number of German, and other Continental imports has increased greatly. Several kennels are engaged in obtaining these animals, some of which are here in quarantine before proceeding to Australia. Some excellent dogs have been produced from these imports, and some which are less good as well. Here we must mention the great producer, Ch. Cito v. Königsbrüch, who has sired some 20 champions and has made a great impression on the breed in type and particularly in movement.

This is a chapter that could have no end. Like the long, long trail in the song, the story of the progress of the breed and of the dogs and bitches and their owners has no end. We have mentioned many of the dogs which have influenced this progress, but have sadly had to leave out scores more, all of which have played a part. As one brick upon another grows into a mighty building, so a dog here, a bitch there, just a name dotted about in one pedigree or another, is responsible for the progress of this lovely breed of dog. There are hundreds of such names, and perhaps if just one of them had been missing we would not have had some of the great sires and great dams which we thank for helping us to breed true to type.

2

The Progress of the Breed

THE German Shepherd Dog has been well served by the keepers of the breed records. We have the German S.V. Stud Books, a mine of information, through which any modern pedigree containing German dogs exclusively can be traced. The first name is that of Horand v. Grafath, born in 1895.

We have, too, the British Kennel Club Stud Books, though these do not record every registered German Shepherd Dog as do the S.V. books. The dogs listed have won awards in the upper classes at Championship Shows or in Obedience and Working Trials, apart from a few which have qualified for entry by being sires or dams, sons or daughters, of winners eligible for entry.

The *Kennel Gazette* gives details of every registered dog, but it is not easy to make use of it when tracing ancestries owing to the lack of an index. Among the best sources of information about early pillars of the breed are the original copies – when obtainable, but alas, very rare – of the magazine *The Alsatian*, edited by Ernest Main and published in London in the year 1924. We are the fortunate owners of a bound set of these monthly publications up until February 1928, when it appears to have gone out of production. In the first year's editions we find Mrs Cecil Wright advertising Ch. Cuno of Louvencourt at stud. Many years later she became even more widely known under her second husband's name, Leonard, as the splendid organiser and guiding light of the German Shepherd Dog League. Mrs Howard, of Seale fame, was advertising a litter by Edu v.d. Secretainerie, and Mr Proctor Smith offered three dogs at stud at fees of 10 and 15 gns, one of them Gundo v. Simplon, a very successful sire. Mr F.N. Pickett's Ch. Caro of

Welham's stud fee was 15 gns. The Dundas kennel advertised nine dogs at stud, all but one imported from Germany, and also listed eight imported bitches.

There is a report of a show at Birmingham, held in the summer of 1924, by the judge Rittmeister von Stephanitz. The photograph of him makes it clear that even then this remarkable gentleman was quite old. He found that the major portion of the dogs he judged had correct elongated build, and that only a very few were oversized. But he thought a large number were over-fed, and adds: 'The number of weak backs was astonishing.' He criticised the handlers, deploring 'the habit of running too quickly, so that the distinctive trotting movement is lost and the dog is always on the verge of galloping. Some use too short a lead and therefore impede free movement.'

Dear me, I wonder what von Stephanitz would have said about the current fashion for stringing dogs up on tight leads, with collars under the chin and ears? I think I can guess.

Then follows the most damning condemnation from the founder of the Shepherd Dog breed: 'There were 15 shy dogs, and 25 shy bitches, out of a total of 143.' Shyness is a serious fault, because it can be transmitted from parent to offspring. Kennel life dulls the intellect of the Shepherd Dog.

The Open dog class was won by Ch. Caro of Welham, the Open bitch class by Mrs Leslie Thornton's Southdown Psyche. He thought Caro too big but otherwise excellent, and praised his movement. Ch. Allahson of If, in the same class and one of the 'greats' of all time, he graded 'Good'. He thought his legs too short and did not care for his 'panther-like' gait! Yet in his pictures Allahson looks, as few of the old dogs do, as though he could go into the ring today and hold his own. Psyche was too fat, but otherwise excellent and had a very good gait.

In 1930 Mrs and Miss Workman showed Ch. Donna vom Allerheiligentor P.H. This imported bitch is rarely found in pedigrees and would not qualify for special mention were it not for her extraordinarily unusual colouring. She was blue-brindle, with a black saddle. Mrs Hester (formerly Miss Akerman of 'Norn' note), had some dogs of this colouring, and so did Mrs Howard, otherwise it was extremely rare.

Int. Ch. Claus v.d. Furstenburg was at stud, owner Mr D.

Millington – and this dog's name is frequently found in pedigrees if they are followed sufficiently far back. The writer owned a bitch by him. He was very widely used, for his quality and elegance evoked great admiration.

Another Claus – v. Eulengarten – was featured in 1926. Owned by Mrs and Miss Workman, he acquires distinction not only because he was a fine upstanding dog but because he was the last import to enter Australia before the government down under put a ban on the importation of German Shepherd Dogs. The reason given was the fear that dogs of this breed would run wild and breed with the dingos – already a serious menace to sheep farmers. Shepherdites protested that dingos were likely to breed with any large dog, and a German Shepherd Dog cross was no more fearsome than any other. From time to time great efforts were made to get the ban removed, so far without success. In spite of the close intermingling of bloodlines and the fact that breeders have no access to outcross stock, German Shepherd Dogs are popular in Australia and under the circumstances breeders have made a fine job of maintaining the breed. The writer judged at the Melbourne Royal and was surprised at the entry in 1961 both in numbers and quality.

Back in Britain, Colonel Baldwin was showing his magnificent bitch, Ch. Cilla's Pinnacle of Picardy, together with other good ones. Cilla's sire, Ch. Cillahson of Picardy, was one of the great dogs of his day, and very many famous German Shepherd Dogs carried the Picardy name to glory over the years.

The gradual change of type is clearly seen in the illustrations in these books. Even within three years the dogs and bitches have acquired more shape, more substance, are less square, less high on the leg and shallow in brisket.

By 1927 such dogs as Ch. Armin Ernslieb P.H., and Ch. Boris of Rhalon – both much more nearly approaching modern type than many of their predecessors – were the vanguards, along with the Austrian Gd. Ch. Susi v. Boll and the two lovely Blasienberg Champions, Ulla and Seffe. So many of the modern show dogs can be traced back to these old stagers that one is inspired to try to do it – until it is realised that the pedigree, when worked out, would paper the wall of a good-sized room.

Because of the firm foundation they gave to the breed we are interested in the pre-1914 originals, but their influence has long been diluted to such an extent that the average Shepherd-ite is really only concerned with the later forbears of the modern dogs.

Particulars of the great post-1918 show and working stars, for instance, are welcomed, and some of these have been mentioned already. These were undoubtedly the dogs and bitches which exercised, and, possibly, are still exercising, some influence on current show-ring performers. Newcomers to the German Shepherd Dog breed never saw these past dogs, and if they have not had access to the hard-to-find photographs and pedigrees these famous animals are just names and numbers.

From even a cursory study of the foundation stock which became available to breeders in Britain we begin to see the way things were going from the time of the First World War. German breeders were already seeing the fruits of early efforts and producing the Shepherd Dogs to some sort of a standard, and in considerable numbers. The original material was such that early breeding must have been a chancy affair, and it seems they were fortunate in finding certain dogs and bitches which bred true to type, in spite of having a rather mixed ancestry not so very far back. They were quick to take advantage of this, and opportunity soon knocked.

The Shepherd Dog was already proving a very fine worker for farm use, but the war opened up an entirely fresh channel, and the ever-adaptable dogs demonstrated their extraordinary intelligence in other ways.

They excelled, for instance, as Red Cross dogs, searching for wounded, carrying first-aid equipment, as cable-layers, as messenger dogs, and of course as the unexcelled defenders of munition dumps and security posts. The breed's extraordinary capacity for serving mankind would hardly go unnoticed by those who came in contact with the dogs for the first time. In fact, Allied servicemen from the British Isles and elsewhere were profoundly excited by the discovery of this handsome and clever breed of dog, hitherto virtually unknown to them. Some dogs were actually 'taken prisoner' in the trenches and brought back to England. Other Army personnel bought dogs and bitches to bring home, and if they had insufficient funds to clinch the deal they often bartered for a dog or dogs.

Foremost amongst those who came under the spell of these wonderful dogs were three notable personalities – Major J.Y. Baldwin, Colonel the Hon. J. Moore-Brabazon (later Lord Brabazon of Tara) and Mr F.N. Pickett. These gentlemen were enthusiastic about the breed's possibilities, and between them imported a number of the best obtainable dogs and bitches of that time. They met with considerable success, Major (later Lieutenant-Colonel) Baldwin's kennel affix 'of Picardy' rapidly becoming known all over the world. Equally renowned was Mr Pickett's 'of Welham' kennel, and the prefix was attached to many famous dogs. Lord Brabazon owned some good dogs, and for a while exhibited them with success, but he did not continue to breed and exhibit, though his affection for the breed never diminished. Right up until his death in 1964 he was an official of the German Shepherd Dog League of Great Britain, and a regular attendant at its social functions. He was, in fact, President for 45 years. Both Colonel Baldwin and Mr Pickett took a prominent place in the show ring over a period of many years, and Mr and Mrs Pickett still had a sizable kennel of German Shepherd Dogs when Mr Pickett died.

When these early pioneers returned to a Britain decimated by the 1914–18 war their mounting interest in the breed they had discovered on the Continent led them to discuss amongst themselves a possible name for the breed. It already had a name, of course – it was the German Shepherd Dog. But the war had only just ended. Memories are said to be short, but certainly at the time there was an overall feeling of great bitterness and resentment throughout this country, and a loathing of anything German.

The individuals interested in promoting the new breed were worried – with reason – that its progress would be impeded if it was known to be a German dog. They thought it would probably be damned from the start. There were, they reasoned, dogs of the breed to be found in Alsace-Lorraine, which was surely not exactly German but more or less next door? Alsatian Shepherd Dogs? But wouldn't it help to cash in on the breed's distinctive appearance? What about putting some emphasis on the alert, wolf-like heads which everybody found so attractive? Alsatian Wolf Dog? The name stuck. Yet eventually, the choice was to be deplored, and blamed for all the allegations made against the breed. But this belonged to the future. At the time nobody realised that such a name would give birth to the 'wolf-cross' myth, and make it just that much harder for posterity to remove from a trustworthy and faithful breed the stigma of treachery.

It is so easy to be wise after an event, but it is at least likely that had the breed gone forth under its true name, the German Shepherd Dog, the wolf-image would never have arisen, and the impression would have been that of a good-natured sheep-dog and friend of man. A wolf dog. H'm. What sort of picture does that conjure up for you? Those who chose the original name did not forsee the consequences. They acted, as they thought, for the best, and at the time it must have seemed that they were right, for, whether glamorised by the name or not, the Alsatian Wolf Dog created a sensation.

The Kennel Club's breed figures are reliable indications of the rise and fall in the fortunes of a breed of dog. The German Shepherd Dog figures soared, then fell, then jogged along, then soared again. A rise and fall of such magnitude is unique in the history of pedigree dogs in this country, resulting as it did in such a magnificent comeback.

The Kennel Club's 'acceptance' of a new breed to this country follows a set pattern. Thus, when the first German Shepherd Dogs came over they were not listed as a separate breed, but under the heading 'Foreign Dogs'. In fact the very first specimens registered were called Foreign Sheepdogs. About this time, Captain Whitaker's 'Southwold' prefix was blazing the trail.

These were isolated registrations, but once the energetic efforts to pioneer the breed were in full swing, things changed. The Alsatian Wolf Dog Club was founded in August 1919, and in the same year the Kennel Club removed the 'Alsatians' from the Foreign Dogs group and elevated the breed to separate registration status, accepting the name 'Alsatian Wolf Dogs'. All those animals previously registered as Foreign Sheepdogs were required to be re-registered under the new official name.

In the year 1919 there were actually 54 Alsatians registered.

The following year there were 500! In 1923 the figure was 1,600, soaring in the brief space of two years to the astounding number of 5,000. And this was not even the limit because the 1926 total was 8,058, a figure that accounted for over a third of all the Non-Sporting breed registrations put together.

When this rate of progress is considered it is hardly surprising that the breed was suffering from excessive and indiscriminate breeding. It could hardly be otherwise. Inevitably this meteoric progress led to more clubs being formed, among them the Alsatian League of Great Britain which was founded in 1924.

There is always a certain amount of rivalry and competition about clubs within a breed, and at the time it was not always of the friendliest. It was a happy occasion, therefore, when differences were solved and the major societies decided to amalgamate. Thus the Alsatian Wolf Dog Club and the League pooled resources, laying the foundation of one of the most successful breed clubs of all time, and under its nomenclature of the German Shepherd Dog League of Great Britain it flourishes today with upwards of 700 members, including overseas Shepherdites in most parts of the world.

Another old-established club still going strong is the 'ASPADS', originally the Alsatian, Sheep, Police, and Army Dog Society which eventually opened its doors to owners of other breeds and changed the word 'Alsatian' to 'Associated'. The ASPADS remains the oldest club suporting Working Trials, and for many years it ran an annual Championship Show for German Shepherd Dogs. It has a long record of service to the breed, pioneering obedience classes and trials, and doing a very great deal to promote good public relations by encouraging the breeding of German Shepherd Dogs with sound temperaments and plenty of brains.

Another faithful and useful supporter of the breed is the British Association for German Shepherd Dogs, formerly the B.A.A. and always calling to mind the name of the late Frank Riego, whose close association with this club as President and Chairman and enthusiastic pioneer was largely responsible for its success today. It has an enormous membership roll, branches all over the country, and a long record of successful shows, not to mention obedience competitions, etc.

In spite of the fact that these breed clubs came into existence to help breeders to co-operate in producing good dogs, they could do nothing in the early days to stem the rising tide of prolific production.

Virtually any dog or bitch that could be described as a German Shepherd Dog – and there were some pretty poor specimens around – was seized for breeding purposes. Type and temperament were of little consequence; if it had erect ears and a bushy tail, its puppies sold like wildfire. A great deal of rubbishy stock was distributed to a gullible public, and the situation must have caused concern to the serious pioneer breeders. They had chosen their foundation stock with care, and because German and other Continental breeders were, not unnaturally, quick to take advantage of the boom period, had paid big prices.

It is only fair to say that by no means all the indifferent stock was being bred in Britain. People who were still only just beginning to learn how to judge the Shepherd Dogs and how to appraise the finer points were paying substantial sums for imported animals which were not worth buying at any price. Some fine specimens came over, but a lot of poor quality came too.

Fortunately for the German Shepherd Dog breed, its individuals have always succeeded in casting a spell over those who grow to love them. Because of this, while a lot of undesirable dealers and get-rich-quick-at-all-costs breeders were attracted by the demand, a great many worthwhile people came into the breed at the same time. These were the people who cared about the future of the breed, who appreciated its sterling worth, rapidly understood how easily its qualities could be lost or spoiled, and were determined to stay with it through fair weather or the stormy years that lay ahead.

If German Shepherd Dogs are the most faithful of dogs the years have shown that their owners have remained faithful to them, too, and worthy of their steadfast devotion. This devotion was put to the test as the registration figures reached their peak. It had become fashionable to own a German Shepherd Dog, which meant that about half the individuals who bought them were not really suitable owners for big, active dogs. When one thinks that half the dogs they bought were temperamentally unsuitable for companions and house dogs it does not tax the imagination to visualise the inevitable sequel.

Over 8,000 German Shepherd Dogs had been registered in one year alone, and many of the thousands registered during the preceding years would be still alive. Add to this the vast numbers that neither breeder nor owner bothered to register – and there are always quite a lot of these, especially when dogs are being bred especially for the pet market – and it is clear that enormous numbers of German Shepherd Dogs were being kept.

If one dog out of a hundred individuals of a particular breed bites somebody very possibly there is not a great deal of fuss about it and many never hear about the incident at all. Multiply this by 8,000, though. That means 80 people bitten – now that *is* something to shout about, isn't it? So by the law of averages it was quite inevitable that there would be cases of German Shepherd Dogs becoming involved in various unfortunate incidents.

Of course, there were plenty of nice-natured, well-behaved German Shepherd Dogs creating a good impression for the breed, but it is a sad fact that the public tend to forget the 99 good dogs and remember the odd man out which bites the postman.

The incidents became more numerous and appealed to the Press. Something of a witch hunt resulted – people got bitten by dogs of numerous breeds, and case after case was ignored – but when a German Shepherd Dog attacked it was headline news. It more or less culminated in a most unfortunate case when a German Shepherd Dog knocked down a small boy. It was never proved, so far as I know, that the dog bit the child, but a scratch on his knee went septic and he died from tetanus. It was a most tragic affair and one has the deepest sympathy for all concerned, but if the dog had eaten the child alive the case could not have been afforded more publicity. As so often happens, accounts of the court proceedings which followed were often very inaccurate and greatly distorted, and the whole thing was slanted to throw the most unfavourable light on the entire German Shepherd Dog breed. The tragedy occurred in January 1927, and it struck a blow from which the German Shepherd Dog took years to recover, for by this time is was being said that German Shepherd Dogs 'were treacherous', had 'wolf blood'. (After all, if they had not, why were they called wolf dogs?) People became very nervous of these reputedly savage creatures, and the sales dropped off. Puppy-factory breeders got out quick, counting their profits and cutting their losses. Only the breed's real friends stayed with it, those serious and devoted breeders who were ready to defend the German Shepherd Dog to the end. Even with their support a breed less worthy and without the marvellous qualities of the German Shepherd Dog might have slipped out of favour and into oblivion.

This could have happened, but it did not. The breed's fair-weather friends, the ephemeral newcomers who had so selfishly exploited it, were gone. It remained for the true supporters to try to repair the damage, pick up the pieces, and keep going. At the time they may not have realised how much their devotion would be put to the test, but remarkable though it may seem, perceptive new-comers actually strengthened their ranks!

The Shepherd Dog was bound to win through on its intrinsic merits, but the way ahead was rough and stony indeed. It would be many years before the 'wolf-cross' bogey began to die its lingering death, sales, even of good-quality stock, would be very much less brisk, and certainly the fancy prices that could be asked for German Shepherd Dogs had gone; it was often difficult to sell the dogs for anything like the cost of rearing.

The anti-German Shepherd Dog newspaper campaign eventually lost some of its velocity, but never completely died down. From time to time a German Shepherd Dog, usually as a result of mis-handling by the owner, got into trouble and the facts, greatly exaggerated, were invariably publicised. So concerned was the German Shepherd Dog League that on many occasions its council went to great pains to investigate alleged incidents involving German Shepherd Dogs. More than once the culprit turned out to be cross-bred with a vaguely German-Shepherd-Dog-like appearance, and sometimes, when indisputably a German Shepherd Dog was accused of misdemeanour, the prosecution's case was slender and it might well have been another dog that had committed the offence. The trouble was by no means confined to incidents involving humans, and spectacular cases of sheep-worrying were also highlighted. It was in such happenings that more than one dog was often involved, but the dogs of other breeds were seldom named in the newspapers – only the German Shepherd Dog.

The breeders who had the welfare of the German Shepherd Dog at heart continued to try to breed sound dogs with nice temperaments. As time went on, the dogs that were poor advertisements for the breed died, and the owners either bought better specimens or dogs of other breeds.

The better judges were ruthless in penalising shy or snappy dogs at shows. The breed clubs were encouraging obedience training, so very character-forming and desirable. The Guide Dogs for the Blind Association was going through a formative period and was finding German Shepherd Dogs most suitable for its purpose. Slowly – very slowly – people came to think of the German Shepherd Dog as a friend of man, the eyes for the blind, the nursemaid for the children, the family defender with the uncanny power of discriminating between friend or foe. From the point where the breed reached its lowest ebb it began to rise again, like a phoenix from the ashes of its own lost reputation.

The German Shepherd Dog's public image was gradually improving, though by no means good, when World War II came along. The breed's remarkable record of service with the Royal Air Force and the Army also became news, and brought it before the public in quite a new light. The registrations, as if a pendulum was swinging, began rising. The breed was on its way to the top again.

It does seem a pity that directly any breed of dog becomes popular, indiscriminate breeding and commercialism follow as night follows day. A certain amount of this inevitably took place during the war years and throughout the immediate post-war period, but on nothing approaching the scale during the 'boom' years. At least throughout this time many valuable and conscientious new breeders became interested and were welcomed to the ranks by the old supporters.

It is possible that even today there are not sufficient judges who are primarily temperament-conscious. The fact that the German Shepherd Dog had once earned for itself a largely undeserved reputation as an uncertain-tempered animal makes it doubly important to give primary consideration to character when awarding prizes. It is said that dog-show judges can make or break a breed and this is largely true. The dogs that win the top awards at the shows will be in demand for breeding. If they are fearless, good-natured, and reliable they are likely to pass on these pleasant characteristics to much of the stock they produce. If they are shy or shifty, nervous or snappy, they will spread these traits and untold harm can result.

The best type of breeder will never use for breeding an animal that is of weak temperament, no matter how beautiful it may be. But if judges give Championships to such exhibits there are always people dazzled by their beauty who will breed from them, hoping to get the looks and avoid the poor character. If their hopes were always, or even often, fulfilled, perhaps it would not matter quite so much, but the results are generally quite the opposite – the puppies are craven cowards, albeit handsome, and nervous dogs are always less reliable than those with sound nerves and a jolly, extrovert's approach to life.

It does sometimes happen that the most beautiful dog in the show ring is the one that backs away from the judge, and tucks its tail between its legs. Or perhaps it stands its ground, cleverly trained not to move when told to 'Stand, stay,' shivering with fear, shifty-eyed, and with that 'tell-tale tail' which the handler will hopefully pull from between the legs and tuck around a hock. The signs are all there – no competent judge should be hoodwinked. Such a poor advertisement for a noble breed has no place at the head of a class – it should be left out of the awards. Possibly the other competitors have not the same glamorous outline, the sweeping hind angulation, the crouching gait, but if they are typical of the breed, cheerful, tail-wagging, alert and free from nerves they are the real Shepherd Dogs. Give them the prizes they deserve. If none of the other dogs in the class are worthy of prizes – withhold the awards. But do not give them to the specimens that, through weakness of character, are not good Shepherd Dogs.

The German Shepherd Dog is right back in public favour. True, there will always be people who regard it with suspicion, but many of these, in some way or another, may gradually learn to appreciate the typical Shepherds – it is up to breeders to make sure that there are plenty of these important 'ambassadors' about to convert the heathen! At the present time the breed appears to be in a healthy state. The demand for good stock is steady – and, please note, it is for good stock. No one, nowadays, wants just 'a German Shepherd Dog' – regardless.

Crime is on the increase, people get coshed, houses get burgled, factories get robbed, nervous individuals dislike staying alone. These are the new German Shepherd Dog owners, and they want a sensible, bold type of dog, big enough to look formidable, not too big to knock the furniture about indoors or take up too much room in the car. A savage dog is a bore – and a menace in unskilled hands – so the new Shepherdite needs the type of dog that will play with the children or down an intruder on its own initiative if called upon to do so. The type of dog that can fit into the family is also the dog that quickly learns to work with the police or with security patrols. This dog is a typical German Shepherd Dog, with the character and intelligence the early German pioneers had in mind when they evolved the breed.

That it is wonderful to look at, as well as so exciting to train, is one of the things that we all love about German Shepherd Dogs. You cannot keep a good dog down – how clear this is from the German Shepherd Dog's see-saw history.

3

The Breed Standard

A DESCRIPTION of the breed ideal, known as the German Shepherd Dog Standard, has been drawn up and modified from time to time by groups of experts in both show and field. It is not to be expected that the novice, provided with the printed standard and confronted with a number of dogs in the judging ring, could hope to place them in order of merit. The correct interpretation of the standard demands a knowledge and skill at least the equal of that of the experts who drew up the original description. A study of the chapter on structural balance in this breed of dog will give the reader a broad conception of what to look for. It is proposed in the present chapter to make some comments in detail upon the interpretation of the standard. The German Shepherd Dog breed standard (below), as presented by the League and the B.A.G.S.D. to the Kennel Club, was approved by the W.U.S.V., the F.C.I. and the S.V. The Kennel Club Breed Standards Sub-Committee provisionally approved its acceptance for use by the specialist clubs on 9 November 1982. The Kennel Club Standard issued in 1986 and reproduced on page 191 by kind permission of the Kennel Club, is based on this and does not deviate from it, being merely a shortened version.

CHARACTERISTICS
The main characteristics of the G.S.D. are: steadiness of nerves, attentiveness, loyalty, calm self-assurance, alertness and tractability, as well as courage with physical resilience and scenting ability. These characteristics are necessary for a versatile working dog. Nervousness, over-aggressiveness and shyness are very serious faults.

GENERAL APPEARANCE
The immediate impression of the G.S.D. is of a dog slightly

long in comparison to its height, with a powerful and well-muscled body. The relation between height and length and the position and symmetry of the limbs (angulation) is so inter-related as to enable a far-reaching and enduring gait. The coat should be weather-proof. A beautiful appearance is desirable but this is secondary to his usefulness as a working dog. Sexual characteristics must be well defined – i.e. the masculinity of the male and the femininity of the female must be unmis-takable.

A true to type G.S.D. gives an impression of innate strength, intelligence and suppleness, with harmonious proportions and nothing either over done or lacking. His whole manner should make it perfectly clear that he is sound in mind and body, and has the physical and mental attributes to make him always ready for tireless action as a working dog.

With an abundance of vitality he must be tractable enough to adapt himself to each situation and to carry out his work willingly and with enthusiasm. He must possess the courage and determination to defend himself, his master or his master's possessions, should the need arise. He must be observant, obedient and a pleasant member of the household, quiet in his own environment, especially with children and other animals, and at ease with adults. Overall he should present an harmonious picture of innate nobility, alertness and self-confidence.

HEAD
The head should be proportionate in size to the body without being coarse, too fine or overlong. The overall appearance should be clean cut and fairly broad between the ears.

Forehead: should be only very slightly domed with little or no trace of centre furrow.

Cheeks:　should form a very softly rounded curve and should not protrude.

Skull:　the skull extends from the ears to the bridge of the nose tapering gradually and evenly, and blending without a too pronounced 'stop' into a wedge-shaped powerful muzzle. (The skull is approximately 50% of the whole length of the head.) Both top and bottom jaws should be strong and well developed. The width of the skull should correspond approximately to the length. In males the width could be slightly greater and in females slightly less than the length.

Muzzle: should be strong and the lips firm, clean and closing tightly without any flews. The top of the muzzle is straight and almost parallel to the forehead. A muzzle which is too short, blunt, weak, pointed, overlong or lacking in strength is undesirable.

EYES

The eyes are medium-sized, almond-shaped and not protruding. Dark brown eyes are preferred, but eyes of a lighter shade are acceptable provided that the expression is good and the general harmony of the head is not destroyed. The expression should be lively, intelligent and self-assured.

EARS

Of medium size, firm in texture, broad at the base, set high, they are carried erect (almost parallel and not pulled inwards), they taper to a point and open towards the front. Tipped ears are faulty. Hanging ears are a very serious fault. During movement the ears may be folded back.

MOUTH

The jaws must be strongly developed and the teeth healthy, strong and complete. There should be 42 teeth: 20 in the upper jaw, 6 incisors, 2 canines, 8 premolars, 4 molars, and 22 in the lower jaw, 6 incisors, 2 canines, 8 premolars and 6 molars.

The G.S.D. has a scissor bite – i.e. the incisors in the lower jaw are set behind the incisors in the upper jaw, and thus meet in a scissor grip in which part of the surface of the upper teeth meet and engage part of the surface of the lower teeth.

NECK

The neck should be fairly long, strong with well-developed muscles, free from throatiness (excessive folds of skin at the throat) and carried at an angle of 45° to the horizontal; it is raised when excited and lowered at a fast trot.

FOREQUARTERS

The shoulder blade should be long, set obliquely (45°) and laid flat to the body. The upper arm should be strong and well muscled and joined to the shoulder blade at a near right angle. The forelegs from the pasterns to the elbows, should be straight viewed from any angle and the bones should be oval rather than round. The pasterns should be firm and supple and angulated at approximately 20–35°. Elbows neither tucked in nor turned out. Length of the forelegs should exceed the depth of the chest at a ratio of approximately 55% to 45%.

BODY

The length of the body should exceed the height at the withers, the correct proportions being as 10 to 9 or 8½. The length is measured from the point of the breast bone to the rear edge of the pelvis.

Over or under-sized dogs, stunted growth, high-legged dogs and overloaded fronts, too short overall appearance, too light or too heavy in build, steep set limbs or any other feature which detracts from the reach or endurance of the gait, are faulty.

Chest: should be deep (45–48% of the height at the shoulder) but not too broad. The brisket is long and well developed.

Ribs: should be well formed and long, neither barrel-shaped nor too flat; correct rib cage allows free movement of the elbows when the dog is trotting. A too rounded rib cage will interfere and cause the elbows to be turned out. A too flat rib cage will lead to the drawing in of the elbows. The desired long ribbing gives a proportionately (relatively) short loin.

Belly: is firm and only slightly drawn up.

Back: the area between the withers and the croup, straight, strongly developed and not too long. The overall length is not derived from a long back, but is achieved by the correct angle of a well-laid shoulder, correct length of croup and hindquarters. The withers must be long, of good height and well-defined. They should join the back in a smooth line without disrupting the flowing top line which should be slightly sloping from the front to the back. Weak, soft and roach backs are undesirable.

Loins: broad, strong and well muscled.

Croup: should be long and gently curving down to the tail (approximately 23°) without disrupting the flowing top line. The illium and the sacrum form the skeletal basis of the croup. Short, steep or flat croups are undesirable.

HINDQUARTERS

The thighs should be broad and well muscled. The upper thigh bone viewed from the side, should slope to the slightly longer lower thigh bone. The angulations should correspond approximately with the front angulation without being overangulated. The hock bone is strong and, together with the stifle bone, should form a firm hock joint. The hindquarters overall must be strong and well muscled to enable the effortless forward propulsion of the whole body. Any tendency towards over-angulation of the hindquarters reduces firmness and endurance.

FEET

Should be rounded, toes well closed and arched. Pads should be well cushioned and durable. Nails short, strong and dark in colour. Dew claws are sometimes found on hind-legs: these should be removed 2–3 days after birth

GAIT

The G.S.D. is a trotting dog. His sequence of step therefore follows a diagonal pattern in that he always moves the foreleg and the opposite hindleg forward at the same time. To achieve this, his limbs must be in such balance to one another so that he can thrust the hind foot well forward to the midpoint of the body and have an equally long reach with the fore foot without any noticeable change in the back line.

The correct proportion of height to length and correspond-ing length of limbs will produce a ground-covering stride that travels flat over the ground, giving the impression of effortless movement. With his head thrust forward and a slightly raised tail, a balanced and even trotter displays a flowing line running from the tips of his ears over the neck and back down to the tip of the tail.

The gait should be supple, smooth and long reaching, carrying the body with the minimum of up and down movement, entirely free from stiltiness.

TAIL

Bushy haired, should reach at least to the hock joint, the ideal length being to the middle of the hock bones. The end is sometimes turned sideways with a slight hook; this is allowed but not desired. When at rest the tail should hang in a slight curve like a sabre. When moving it is raised and the curve is increased, but ideally it should not be higher than the level of the back. A tail that is too short, rolled or curled, or generally carried badly or which is stumpy from birth, is faulty.

COAT

a) The normal-coated G.S.D. should carry a thick undercoat and the outer coat should be as dense as possible, made up of straight hard close-lying hairs. The hair on the head and ears, front of the legs, paws and toes is short. On the neck it is longer and thicker, on some males forming a slight ruff. The hair grows longer on the back of the legs as far down as the pastern and the stifle, and forms fairly thick trousers on the hindquarters. There is no hard or fast rule for the length of the hair, but short mole-type coats are faulty.

b) In the long-haired G.S.D. the hairs are longer, not always straight and definitely not lying close and flat to the body. They are distinctly longer inside and behind the ears, and on the back of the forelegs and usually at the loins, and form moderate tufts in the ears and profuse feathering on the back of the legs. The trousers are long and thick. The tail is bushy with light feathering underneath. As this type of coat is not so weatherproof as the normal coat it is undesirable.

c) In the long open-coated G.S.D. the hair is appreciably longer than in the case of type (b) and tends to form a parting along the back, the texture being somewhat silky. If present at all, undercoat is found only at the loins. Dogs with this type of coat are usually narrow-chested, with narrow overlong muzzles. As the weather protection of the dog and his working ability are seriously diminished with this type of coat it is undesirable.

COLOUR

Black or black saddle with tan, or gold to light grey markings. All black, all grey or grey with lighter or brown markings (these are referred to as sables). Small white marks on the chest or very pale colour on inside of legs are permitted but not desirable. The nose in all cases must be black. Light markings on the chest and inside of legs, as well as whitish nails, red-tipped nails or wishy-washy faded colour are defined as lacking in pigmentation. Blues, livers, albinoes, whites (i.e. almost pure white dogs with black noses) and near whites are to be rejected.

The undercoat is, except in all-black dogs, usually grey or fawn in colour.

The colour of the G.S.D. is in itself not important and has no effect on the character of the dog or on its fitness for work and should be a secondary consideration for that reason. The final colour of a young dog can only be ascertained when the outer coat has developed.

HEIGHT

The ideal height (measured to the highest point of the withers is 57.5 cm for females and 62.5 for males. 2.5 cm either above or below the norm is allowed. Any increase in this deviation detracts from the workability and breeding value of the animal.

FAULTS

Any departure from the foregoing points should be considered a fault and the seriousness with which the fault should be regarded should be in exact proportion to its degree.

NOTE: Male animals must have two apparently normal testicles fully developed into the scrotum.

Only long experience and cultivation of 'an eye for a dog' can lend reality to the written standard. The novice must bear in mind the main qualities required in the German Shepherd Dog as fundamentally a working breed of dog. These are intelligence, boldness of character (which should not be confused with the aggressiveness which goes with fear), balanced conformation and perfect physical condition. Together these will give the tireless, working German Shepherd Dog. The reader desirous of becoming a good judge of the breed should cultivate the faculty of assessing the dog as a whole, not allowing the judgment to be unduly affected by details; for example, seeing in a specimen *only* a colour one personally dislikes, or *only* a gay tail or a soft ear. On the contrary, the good judge will cultivate the ability to give full weight to the ensemble of good points, seeing how far minor faults detract from the animal as a working individual and as a potential sire or dam of a future generation.

The first point of detail to be observed is whether the dog is correctly proportioned. The ratio of the length of the body to the height at the withers should be as is 10 to 9. Too long a back is a source of potential weakness. On the other hand, too short a back does not allow the long powerful propulsive stride of the hind leg to come into full play, for which the hind legs would have to pass outside the line of action of the front legs, a phenomenon typical of the galloping greyhound rather than the tireless trotting German Shepherd Dog.

The back should slope gently from withers to croup, being neither arched nor dipping. Young puppies sometimes show a high croup, but this often rights itself as the animal matures.

The next thing to look for is perfect alignment of the legs, viewed from front or back, and for 100 per cent angulation of both fore- and hindquarters and limbs. Good hind angulation gives good forward propulsion; good front angulation secures an even forward movement.

The tail helps to maintain balance. If the line of the back is correct, the tail will appear as a well-set brush, which is carried so that it scarcely rises above back level while trotting, but hangs loosely at rest in the shape of a sabre, with its tip swinging just clear of the hocks.

The head should be in proportion to the size of the body. It should be set on a neck of medium length, giving an impression of elegance and strength. The neck of the mature male should carry a heavy ruff, enhancing the masculine appearance of the head. The cranium should be capacious, and there should be good width at the bridge of the nose to give room for the sensitive olfactory mucous membrane.

There should be a full set of teeth, viz. 20 in the upper jaw and 22 in the lower. These consist on each side of 3 incisors, 1 canine, 4 premolars and 2 molars in the upper jaw, 3 in the lower. The first molar in the upper jaw is termed the carnassial tooth.

The incisors should meet in a 'scissors' bite, neither overshot, giving a snipy appearance, nor undershot, an unnatural state of affairs deliberately and mistakenly cultivated in a breed such as the bulldog. An even approximation of the incisors is equally incorrect. The upper incisors should close tightly over the lower ones, with no space whatever in between.

The canine and corner incisor teeth of the upper jaw are positioned somewhat behind those in the lower jaw. This ensures a traplike grip upon any object on which the jaws are closed.

The upper molar and premolar teeth are arranged so as to close outside the lower ones, giving a powerful shearing action to the bite.

The enamel of the permanent teeth is laid down during the early weeks of a puppy's life. Any serious illness at this time may result in an imperfect formation of the teeth, showing in the adult as a brown discolouration – the so-called 'distemper teeth'. This should not be adjudged a serious fault of conformation.

The ears should be erect, opening forwards and slightly out-wards. There should be no inward tilt.

The colour of the eyes should blend with the colour of the coat. There is no particular virtue in different colours of the iris, but complete lack of pigmentation (albinism) is a serious fault. Such eyes would appear pink or red. Light eyes are undesirable.

The Shepherd Dog should have a wind- and weather-proof coat. This consists of a short, soft and dense undercoat, overlaid by a harsh flat outer coat. The outer coat does not properly grow through the puppy wool until the Shepherd Dog is fully twelve months old. When fully grown it should be from 1½ to 2½ ins. long. Occasionally the outer coat is wavy, or longer than the standard. These are not serious faults if the coat is of correct harsh quality and accompanied by a good under-wool. The colour is not important, provided only that the animal is not albino and has good pigmentation of eyes, nose and claws. Whites are heavily penalised on this account, and on the Continent debarred from Shows. Most serious breeders would not allow a white puppy to live, as this fault reflects badly on the parents' potential as breeding animals, particularly as the majority of white puppies are albinos.

The diagrams illustrating disproportion, weakness of back and croup, badly shaped legs, badly set ears, and defective tail carriage are reproduced in the next chapter. Long-coated dogs are usually penalised by judges and severely handicapped in the show ring.

EXPLANATION OF TITLES AND ABBREVIATIONS OF TITLES OF GERMAN DOGS

Until 1937 the S.V. held an annual Championship Show, where the title of 'Sieger' went to the best dog and that of 'Siegerin' to the best bitch of the year.

These titles, however, were discontinued in 1938 because it was found that with only one Sieger there was too great a demand on his stud services, which meant that the field of breeding was narrowed down to too few strains. The S.V. therefore decided not to give one dog only the highest honour, but create a special selection class in which were included from the dogs awarded Excellent a certain number of dogs and bitches which, according to the judge officiating, were considered of outstanding or equal merit.

These specially selected dogs were called the winners of the Auslese Klasse (selection class), and on the first occasion on which it functioned (22–23 October 1938), 17 dogs qualified Excellent.

During the first years of this new system these winners were not placed first, second, third, etc., as they were supposed to be of equal merit. Later some judges placed them in order of first, second, third, etc., but other judges continued to follow the first method and merely placed them in Catalogue order, considering them to be 'equal in merit', or, to use the Latin term *acqualis*, meaning of 'equal quality'.

As a result of this new system, demands for services were less inclined to be concentrated on one particular dog as they were in the past, with the consequent danger of too much stock in the country from one animal, perhaps with an accumulation of any faults that sire might pass on. It meant that other dogs of virtually equal merit would receive more patronage from breeders. Mr Schwabacher said that when his dog Ferdl v.d. Secretainerie was being shown, it was one of the selection group at the first show where this system was introduced, and qualified 'Excellent'. In Ferdl's first year at stud, his owner received over 370 applications for his services, of which only 70 were accepted. How many more enquiries must have reached owners of the one and only Siegers!

However sound the new arrangement appeared to be, it apparently did not work out nearly as well as was intended. For one thing, the Germans found that the mounting excitement that preceded the judging when the Sieger was about to be chosen was greatly reduced, and far less glamour was attached to the shows. Possibly the owners who sold their selection-group dogs found also that outstanding specimens though they may have been, the buyers were less prepared to make spectacular offers than had been the case when there was competition to secure a Sieger.

At any rate, the Sieger – and of course, the Siegerin title in bitches – were re-introduced again in 1955, and the choice of one Sieger at an annual show continues as before. There are other dogs of merit classified Excellent at these shows, and probably there is the element of luck that we acknowledge when a Champion is made up at one of our own shows. Certainly with the high standard of quality predominating at the German shows and the enormous entries received for the Sieger show, there can be very little between the first half-dozen in the Open classes.

For those interested in the various classes at shows in Germany the following information may be of interest. There are three classes at the Sieger show. The GEBRAUCHSHUND class, similar to our Open class, is for dogs over the age of two years with a working qualification, and which have been graded V. (Excellent) or at least S.G. (Very Good) at one of the regional breed shows.

From the small number of V.-graded dogs a further selection is made of (usually) some 8 to 10 dogs of the highest quality, which are graded V.A. (Excellent Selected), and from this group the Sieger (Champion of the Breed) is chosen – the highest honour for dog and breeder alike. The bitch class is judged in like fashion.

Next in seniority is the JUNGHUND class, for dogs from 18 to 24 months, which is always interesting as one can see the potential of these youngsters and assess the bloodlines they represent.

Finally, the JUGEND class is open to dogs from 12 to 18 months, most of them raw and unready, as ours is a slowly maturing breed. Again this is a class of great interest, as one can see the early results from the use of top stud dogs, take notes and plan accordingly.

The following are a list of German training titles which are to be found in many pedigrees. Some have been changed in recent years as the vast scope of the work of our versatile breed increases, and in some of the old pedigrees they may be slightly different, but on the whole they should be similar enough not to cause confusion.

An X. before a dog's name in a show catalogue denotes that the animal is *Angekört*: it has been examined (and reported on) at a breed survey, and has been passed. The Sch.H. qualifications are the ones most frequently seen on imported dogs, so we will enlarge a little on these tests. Sch.H. I entrants are first gun-tested at the start of the heel-free exercise, and any which react badly are eliminated. These dogs are from 14 months old. Sch.H. II is a similar test for dogs from 16 months old. Sch.H.

A.D.	*Ausdauer*	Passed endurance test
B.P.D.H.	*Bahnpolizeidiensthund*	Railway Police Dog
Bl.H.	*Blindenfuhrhund*	Guide Dog for the Blind
D.H.	*Diensthund*	Working Dog (in a service)
D.P.H.	*Dienstpolizeihund*	Service Police Dog
F.H.	*Fahrtenhund*	Tracking Dog
H.G.H.	*Herdengebrauchshund*	Herding Dog
INT.PR.KL.	*Internationale Prüfungsklasse*	International Trials Class
M.H.(I & II)	*Meldenhund*	Messenger Dog
P.F.P.(I & II)	*Polizeifahrtenhundprüfung*	Police Tracking Dog Test
P.H.	*Polizeihund*	Police Dog
P.S.P.(I & II)	*Polizeischützhundprüfung*	Police Guard Dog Test
S.H.(I & II)	*Sanitatshund*	Red Cross Dog
Sch.H.(I, II & III)	*Schützhund*	Guard or Defence Dog
Z.H.(I & II)	*Zollhund*	Customs Dog
Z.F.H.	*Zollfahrtenhund*	Customs Tracker Dog
Z.Pr.	*Züchtprüfung Bestanden*	Passed temperament test for breeding

III is a very hard and comprehensive test for dogs from 20 months, and there is a compulsory six weeks' interval between entry for each stage. One can be sure that a dog with the qualification Sch.H. III has a fearless character and thorough training.

These are the qualifications awarded at breed shows.

V.A.	*Vorzüglich Und Auslese*	Excellent selected
V.	*Vorzüglich*	Excellent
S.G.	*Sehr Gut*	Very Good
G.	*Gut*	Good
B.	*Befriedigend*	Fair
M.	*Mangelhaft*	Faulty
U.	*Ungenügend (sometimes written O.)*	Unsatisfactory

4

Structural Balance in the German Shepherd Dog

THE study of the form of all mammals shows a striking similarity. Apart from freak and fancy breeds, their structural conformation is determined by function.

The horse is presumably of ideal size and construction for its way of life. In the wild state, its survival depends on high-speed evasion, not necessarily prolonged. It is anatomically arranged so as to apply a maximum output of muscular energy to the greatest advantage for a relatively short time. All four legs are used for propulsion, in the form of a gallop, with an abounding expenditure of energy. We see, therefore, a comparatively large shoulder-blade, taking the tension and leverage of the muscles which activate the fore limb (thus, incidentally, providing an ideal frame for draught purposes).

The wolf trails its prey at a steady trotting gait, eventually catching up with it by keeping on until it does so. It is anatomically arranged so as to apply a least possible output of muscular energy to greatest advantage for a relatively long time. The movement of progression which solves this problem of the conservation of muscular energy is one where the back legs propel and the front ones support and guide. This achieves the steady, tireless lope necessary to the preying animal which in the wild state hunts not singly but in packs.

The gait which enables the wolf to run down its prey through exhaustion is that which enables the wolf-life shepherding dog to conserve its energy in the course of its exacting work. In the German Shepherd Dog, the back legs propel, and the front ones support and guide. The front legs also eliminate all unnecessary movement of the body, the vertical acceleration and deceleration of which could absorb more energy than that

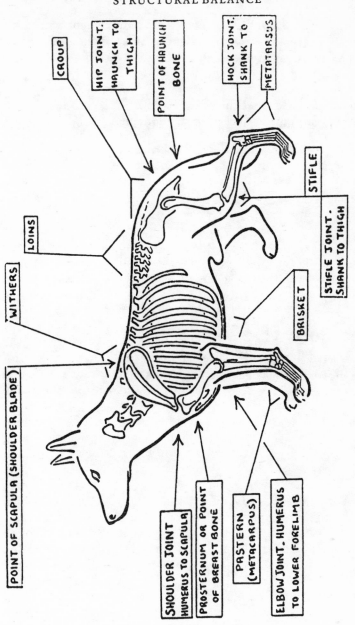

CROUP

HIP JOINT. HAUNCH TO THIGH

POINT OF HAUNCH BONE

HOCK JOINT. SHANK TO

METATARSUS

STIFLE

LOINS

WITHERS

STIFLE JOINT. SHANK TO THIGH

BRISKET

POINT OF SCAPULA (SHOULDER BLADE)

SHOULDER JOINT HUMERUS TO SCAPULA

PROSTERNUM OR POINT OF BREAST BONE

PASTERN (METACARPUS)

ELBOW JOINT. HUMERUS TO LOWER FORELIMB

1. DIAGRAM OF THE GERMAN SHEPHERD DOG

required for propulsion. This vertical movement would be occasioned by the movements of the limbs, if they were rigid, and by any unevenness of the ground traversed.

LIMBS

We will consider first the part played by the front legs in the trotting gait typical of the German Shepherd Dog. In essence

2. POORLY ANGULATED DOG

the movement may be described as a simple forward and backward swing of the fore limb and shoulder-blade, the range

3. WELL-ANGULATED DOG

Sieger 1926–1928. Erich v. Glockenbrink

Ch. Ingo v. Piastendamm

Sieger 1929. Utz v. Haus Schutting

Ch. Danko v. Menkenmoor of Hardwick

Ch. Gerolf of Brittas

Ch. Arno of Saba

Diane Pearce

Int. Ch. Druidswood Consort

Ch. Delridge Erhard

being controlled by the muscles of the shoulder, the only essential angular movement of the parts of the limb on themselves being at the pastern joint. However, angular movement at the other joints is required to eliminate the vertical body

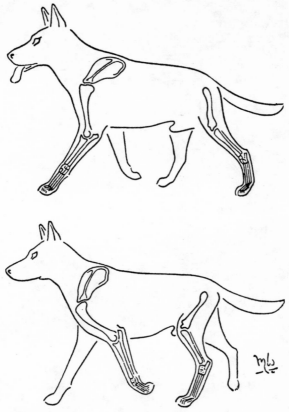

4. GAIT OF STRAIGHT-FRONTED DOG

movement which would occur, as explained above, if the animal had rigid legs. Part of this compensatory angular movement naturally occurs at the shoulder joint. If the relative effective lengths of the humerus and shoulder-blade were different, harmonious (i.e. proportionately equal) angular movements of these bones from their basic positions would result in an unsymmetrical displacement of the fore limb relative to the centre of gravity of the fore quarter of the body, which may be said roughly to coincide with the centre point of the shoulder-blade. This, of course, could not be tolerated, and

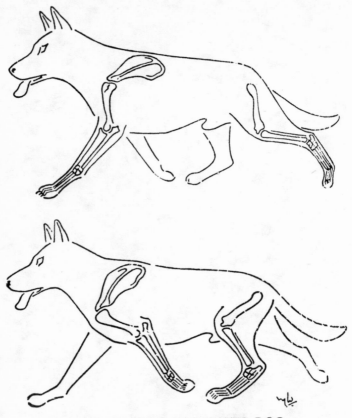

5. GAIT OF WELL-ANGULATED DOG

to prevent it there would have to be a contrary angular movement at the elbow. This in turn would involve a relatively greater displacement of the point of the shoulder and still further angular movement at the shoulder joint. These additional angular movements at the elbow and shoulder joints can only compensate for a slight disproportion in length between the humerus and the shoulder-blade. If the disproportion in length is excessive, awkward heaving movements of the shoulder-blades during progression will be inevitable. For compensatory movements of the component parts of the fore limb to be harmonious, therefore, equality in the effective lengths of the humerus and shoulder-blade is necessary. To

6. FAULTS IN THE HIND LEGS

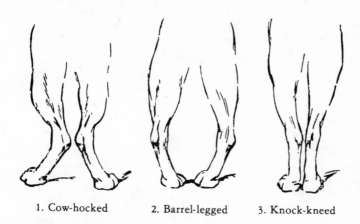

1. Cow-hocked   2. Barrel-legged   3. Knock-kneed

obtain the greatest range of angular movement between them, which is obviously functionally desirable, the humerus should rest at the mean between the two extremes of being parallel to the shoulder-blade, i.e. at 90°.

The shoulder-blade is controlled and positioned by muscles. Its axis of movement may be assumed to be roughly at its centre of area, this being the focal point of tension of the various muscles, and corresponding to the centre of gravity for the fore part of the body. At rest, therefore, this focal point should be above the point of support on the ground (i.e. the paw), in order to avoid dissipating muscular energy in counteracting leverage one way or the other – in fact to balance. In obtaining the desired angle of humerus and shoulder-blade, the elbow has to be brought behind the vertical line through the scapula centre. Therefore, to bring the paw into a position on this vertical line, the lower fore limb must either slope forwards as a whole,

7. CROUPS

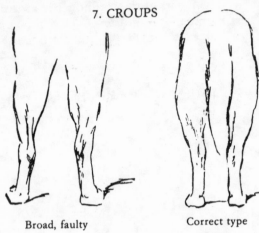

Broad, faulty   Correct type

which would be a sorry arrangement, or be brought into the desired position, as it actually is, by the admirable forward-

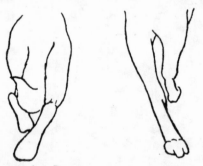

8. UNSOUND GOING AWAY   9. TOEING IN

sloping arrangement of the pastern, which also provides additional flexibility, agility and shock absorption, as well as providing for ground clearance on the forward swing of the leg.

The propulsive hind leg exhibits a simpler mechanism than the foreleg, on account of the thigh bone having a fixed point of application in the pelvis, through which the thrust is transmitted to the body as a whole, and also because it does not play an active part in maintaining balance. The farther the hind leg is able to push the paw from the hip, the greater the ground

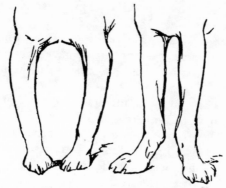

1. Barrel-legged   2. Knock-kneed

11. FRONT LEGS

3. Too narrow

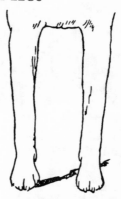

4. Correct type

covered in a stride. The limits of effectiveness of the length of this stride, however, lie in the ability of the front legs to maintain equilibrium and cover the ground in time with the back ones, thus avoiding consumption of any energy except that required for steady forward progression (the frog is an outstanding example of a creature lacking any arrangement to resolve into a uniform movement of progression the spasmodic propulsive thrusts of the hind legs).

The proportions of the component parts of the hind limb in relation to one another and to the rest of the body are such as to produce harmonious movements at the various joints. The thigh and shank bones are approximately equal in length, and the hind metatarsus is proportionate in length to the pastern in front, to which its function is similar.

The movement is a swing of the thigh bone from the pelvis, the shank bone thereby being thrust back. The shank bone rotates on the thigh bone as this rotates on the bone of the haunch, until the leg is fully extended. The hind metatarsus rotates on the shank bone to maintain the heel pad in contact with the ground, until at the end of the stride the paw lifts on to the toe pads. The thigh bone now reverses the direction of its swing from the pelvis and the foot is automatically lifted clear of the ground for the forward stride. Any kicking up of the foot at full extension of the leg, other than that due to actively decreasing angulation of the component parts of the leg as a whole, must be considered a waste of energy and potential stride.

BACK

The importance of the part played by the backbone is so well known that it forms the basis for several metaphors. In the Shepherd Dog it is strong, of balanced proportions and perfectly suited to all its functions. These in brief are to provide the basis of the skeleton and to take the ultimate strain of all muscular effort. This may be said to be its function in all vertebrates, but by reason of the active and energetic life of the Shepherd Dog, its backbone and the muscles activating it are expected to work overtime.

As the majority of readers will know the backbone is not one bone, but many. These are called vertebrae. They all lock together, and by themselves would form a very flexible chain. They run from the base of the skull to the tip of the tail. They differ considerably in their individual appearance and are named variously. As we are primarily concerned with the outward aspect and performance of the dog, we need only consider the dog as a whole and in the terms likely to be most familiar – in this instance, neck, withers, loins and tail.

It is logical to start with the main part of the back or withers, as by reason of its vertebrae carrying the ribs, with their muscles and cartilages, this is the strongest part of the back. The ribs give shape to the fore part of the body and form a protective cage for the heart and lungs, capacity for which is provided in our dog in depth. The ribs must not be curved like a barrel, for this would mean a loss in the lateral flexibility of this part of the back and would also make the chest more vulnerable to glancing blows. On the other hand, a flat-sided dog would have an excessively narrow body, with unnatural curves in the ribs. It is desirable that the curve of the ribs should give the maximum capacity in depth, with optimum strength for proportion. Such a shape of rib is not only most useful to the dog, but pleases aesthetically and mechanically.

The withers and ribs provide also a framework for an extensive and powerful muscular system, much of which is essential to the fore limb which has no other attachment to the body. Hence the range and deceptively complicated movements of the shoulder-blade.

Forward of the withers is the neck. This part of the backbone supports the skull, and its muscles control the movement of the head. The jaws being exceptionally powerful, while the whole dog is strong and of no light weight, a commensurately strong and well-developed neck is obviously necessary for the jaws to be used to their full potential for gripping, tearing, holding, levering and lifting.

The lumbar vertebrae, those of the loins, at the lower end of those of the thorax (withers), carry no ribs. Only a relatively small amount of weight is carried directly by this section of the back, but it has to take the thrust from the hind limbs via the pelvis and transmit it to the mass of the dog. It is also more flexible laterally than the thorax, and the muscles of the loins are the chief applicators of, and resisters to, turning movements.

The limits of flexibility of the back are displayed when the dog stretches his limbs, or is picked up by his hind legs; and when he is curled up asleep, or if he should have occasion to put a stop to the activities of a flea at the base of his tail.

The furthest bones of the back proper are the sacral vertebrae, to which are articulated the haunch bones supporting the hind limbs. It may be mentioned in passing that the length of the dog is measured from the rearmost point of the haunch bone to the foremost point of the breastbone (prosternum).

TAIL

The vertebrae are continued from the sacral region as the bony core of the tail, where they are known as the coccygeal vertebrae. The tail is most emphatically not an ornament, as so many people suppose; neither is it an agreeable foible that we should expect our dog's tail to hang relaxed when standing. The tail is essential to balance and agility, but there should be no waste of muscular energy when it is not required for movement. Its use may be likened to a balance weight and a focus of leverage. The tail does in fact wag the dog when required to do so. It will be obvious that a dog with a laterally curled or crooked tail must either waste effort in straightening it out for use, or obtain an unsymmetrical reaction from its movement. Carrying the tail raised uses energy which might be put to better use, and limits the balancing action of the organ by restricting its available range of movement. So when standing at rest, the tail should hang relaxed. When the dog starts to move, the muscles of the back and tail are tensed, and the tail is used as required in the ensuing movements. The tail has a further function, in acting as a convenient protection for the toothless end of the dog.

The actual number of coccygeal vertebrae varies in different individuals, and 18 to 23 may be considered as the normal range. This point is worth mentioning, as certain strains are alleged to have been short-tailed.

SIZE AND PROPORTION

It will be convenient at this point to comment on the desired proportions of the dog. There are several factors to be considered. As it is a working dog, the economic ones as well as the functional must be counted. Generally speaking, in the case of two dogs of equal working ability, the one which is cheaper to feed will best please the flockmaster or other user. We may thus be predisposed towards a small type of dog rather than a large one. However, a small dog may lack the physique

GOOD TAIL CARRIAGE

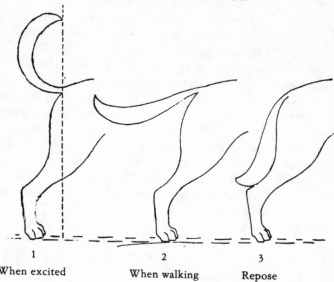

1   2   3

When excited   When walking   Repose

13. FAULTY TAIL CARRIAGE

4   5   6   7

Hook   Rool or Wheel

necessary for its work, either in point of actual strength or by reason of being continually extended to its limit of effort. If therefore we consider a dog of the desired type and conformation, it will almost certainly be of a size which results from a compromise in dimensions giving various advantages, and will be found to come within the limits of the standards which are based on working experience.

The simplest approach to considering this aspect of the dog is to indicate the disadvantages of variations from the desired ideal, as described in the standard, and some aspects of the work for which the dog was used. For instance, it was necessary that the dog should be of proportionate size to a sheep, much of its work consisting of containing sheep in a given area by turning the would-be strays physically, i.e. by brushing them aside towards the flock. A dog of small stature would not be able to accomplish this without excessive effort and undesired violence. Further a small dog would fare badly if faced with a recalcitrant ram, or a ewe with her lamb, even if it resorted to an attack – a situation which could never be tolerated. The dog must also be big and powerful enough to deal with marauders of any nature when with the flock.

On the other hand, the Shepherd Dog does not want a body so high that impact with a sheep would be taken on his legs. Such a dog would indeed be a giant. Size in excess of the desired optimum brings with it extra weight. This not only requires extra nutrition, as mentioned above, but means a less agile dog, a clumsier mover, and one sooner prone to fatigue. We are still considering the dog as being well proportioned, but it is rare to find an oversize specimen which does retain good proportions. The first concomitant of excessive height is almost certain to be poor angulation, accompanied by proportionate shortness of back. If, possibly, these defects were not present in a markedly oversize dog, what sort of animal should we have? Either a creature like a poor specimen of one of the gazehounds, or a monster of vast weight, with legs either too weak to support it or too clumsy for proper movement. Photographs of some dogs of the early 'twenties well illustrate these remarks.

The ideal height (measured to the highest point of the withers) is 57.1 cm. for bitches and 62.5 cm. for dogs.

2 to 5 cm. either above or below this norm is permitted. It is considered that any increase in this deviation detracts from the working ability and breeding value of the animal.

So much for the height. What then are the considerations governing length? Length is not a virtue in itself, for the greater the length of a structure, the greater the leverage applied by a given force. This means weakness in the back of a dog unless it is compensated by increased size of bone and muscle. This again leads to increased size and weight, bringing with it no advantage and the disadvantages already mentioned. On the other hand, shortness is not in itself desirable, for although it might save weight, flexibility is lost, and also the opportunity to apply the strength of the back. Further, the animal would lose what designers of automobiles and aircraft would call directional stability – there would be a greater tendency for it to move irregularly; or, conversely, greater effort would be required to keep it in steady movement. Again, shortness means greater proportionate height, which leads to a structure less easy to balance, particularly in motion.

To these considerations of mass and dimension must be added those of movement of the limbs. Any possibility of the dog tripping over its own feet is intolerable, as the ability for agile manoeuvre would no longer exist. Moreover, if the hind paws overtook the front ones in an animal with the typical wolf-like gait of the German Shepherd Dog, length of stride would be lost in the casting movement necessary to bring one paw outside the other.

We have already seen that the well-angulated dog possesses great length of stride by reason of its good angulation, and that this is obtained without excessive height. It follows, then, that in order to obviate the possibility of interference between hind and fore limbs, length must almost certainly exceed height. Improvement in angulation, however, enables the consequent increase in stride of the hind limb to become more effective in the range behind and away from the dog than at the forward limit of movement. Consequently the necessary excess of length to height is not as great as might be expected.

The standards obviously indicate the desired size and proportion of the dog, considered from all possible points of view; and the proportion of height to length stated represents that giving the best compromise of all desirable factors.

It might be added that of two similar dogs, the one which is better angulated is likely to be the lesser in height and to have greater stride, in which case good length is essential.

In view of the above considerations, two points of perennial interest may be mentioned. These are, first, that any suggestion that height brings with it some abstract desirable quality comes only from the realm of fancy; and second, that an undersized dog may well display a most attractive gait.

HEAD

The head carries the sensory organs, which in this dog are developed to the greatest extent possible in the canine race, and comprise a unique combination of powers. The head also carries the powerful jaw, which acts for the dog as mouth, tools and weapons. The head then must provide a suitable mobile

EAR CARRIAGE

Perfect   Faulty   Faulty

mounting to ensure the best use of so varied an equipment. The varied movements of the head when scenting, sighting and listening, inaugurate a succession of movements throughout the rest of the body, either of a compensatory or a complementary nature. A study of such movements is a matter quite beyond the scope of this book, but it is suggested that much interest may be derived by the reader from observation of his or her own dog in respect of such movements and others described.

PAWS

Thinking in terms of the Shepherd Dog, the feet are the point of contact with the ground. They have to withstand constant abrasion and a variety of shock loads. They are the points at which all the strength and weight of the dog are focused, and where most of its energy is eventually applied. They are the pivots of balance, and points of leverage for nearly all movement. They must therefore withstand wear and tear, grip the ground, be flexible and easily controlled, be not subject to or cause fatigue, and not absorb energy which might otherwise go to extending endurance The well-formed foot answers these varied calls with that perfection only found in Nature, and which the whole Shepherd Dog exemplifies.

The feet more nearly resemble the human hand than the human foot. In contact with the ground are five pads. The main pad corresponds to those callouses under the knuckles of the palm found in manual workers, and the four toe pads to those of the finger-tips. The main pad acts as a shock-absorber, and as a fulcrum for the toes. The four toe pads are used in applying force, for movement or balance. They are fitted snugly together and with the main pad, all five being arranged to distribute vertical loads over their area to maximum effect, since two or more pads are intersected by any vertical plane, thus sharing loads and providing mutual support. The foot being divided into pads gives flexibility without sacrificing essential toughness.

In movement on a smooth surface, flexing in the foot is confined to an angular movement between the metacarpus and the phalanges at the end of a stride, when the foot comes right up on the toes. In the course of a stride, contact of the whole foot diminishes from the rear, until contact only remains on the inner pads and part of the outside ones. The outside pads take the force of lateral strains in turning and balancing, with some support from the others.

From our previous discussion of the functions of the fore and hind limbs, it will be clear that the work of the fore and hind feet is not quite the same, and consequently there is also a difference in structure, the hind feet being more rigid, and more suitable for delivering thrust than the more flexible and versatile front ones. The flexibility and wider utility of the fore feet may be seen, for instance, when the dog is dealing with a bone, or endeavouring to perform some such feat as opening a box, or retrieving an object from some awkward place. The utility of the fore dew claws will also be apparent under these circumstances. Their true functional value, however, is not so easily appreciated, for the reaction obtained by tensioning its muscles is only likely to be fully understood by those who have recently lost a thumb. As the hind foot is used almost entirely for propulsion, the hind dew claw has no comparable function to perform and its muscles are to all intents and purposes atrophied. The thrusting function of the hind leg is well demonstrated in the canine habit of scattering grass and earth.

Faults of the foot may be divided into those of strength and formation. Assuming a harmonious proportion of foot, muscular weakness or degeneration will allow the pads to spread apart, giving the condition of splay foot. This fault is progressive, since as the pads spread apart they derive less support from each other, and have individually to support a leverage greater than that which originally proved too much. The condition is further aggravated by long nails, proper wear of which is prevented by the weakness of the digits. The root cause of the weakness which results in splay foot is usually a dog too heavy for its strength, or a dog allowed insufficient or unsuitable exercise.

Faults of formation may be divided into those due to excessive length and those due to excessive breadth of the paw. This issue is frequently confused by the use of the terms 'cat' foot and 'hare' foot. Besides overlooking the fact that the animal under consideration is a dog, individual interpretation of the terms varies. Further confusion arises from the use of the terms in connection with other breeds which have feet adapted to different needs. For example, the feet of a 'harefooted' Shepherd Dog might be considered excellently formed in a greyhound, whereas a 'harefooted' greyhound would provide astonishing feet for a Shepherd Dog.

However, the terms are retained in the accompanying sketches, which indicate:

1. The desirable pattern of pads, mutually supporting in all directions and sharing all but the smaller stresses. Sufficient

15. FEET

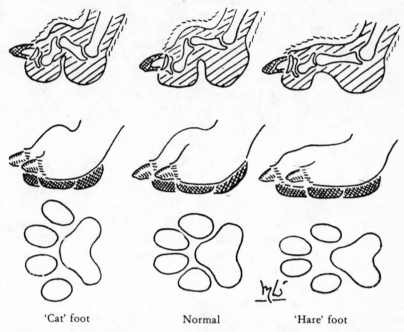

'Cat' foot   Normal   'Hare' foot

length of metacarpus and phalanges provides flexibility, without undue length leading to undue leverage.

2. The 'cat' foot, in which shortening of the middle digits tends to force the pads of the outer ones farther apart, giving a wide short foot, or a too small foot of normal width. The outer pads of the wider foot are subject to excessive leverage laterally, as they receive only small support from the rest of the foot. Besides this the two middle digits lack proper length as a lever through which motive power can be applied, while if their shortening is due to an exaggerated flexing of the phalanges on one another, rather than to an absolute shortening of the bones themselves, there will also be loss of flexibility in the paw. The rolling effect (in the 'heel-toe' sense, not gait generally) in the stride will be concentrated on a narrow band across the feet (the effect being similar to that of a small wheel, and actually as seen in the cat), giving concentrated wear and tear. In the case

16. 'CAT' FOOT

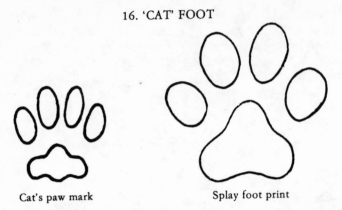

Cat's paw mark   Splay foot print

of the too small foot of normal width, there must of necessity be a reduction of area in contact with the ground, so that it will be less able to diffuse shock and will have to carry a more concentrated load.

3. The 'hare' foot. The theory that a long foot gives increased length of stride would be plausible if the dog could manage on its middle toes alone. For instance, as suggested above, if a foot of this conformation occurring in a dog of our breed could be transferred to a greyhound, the resulting animal might manage to run on it for a short time if it kept in a straight line; but on the heavier German Shepherd Dog, and indeed on the greyhound, the paw would soon develop the canine equivalent of the human 'dropped arch'. In essence the conformation is exactly the converse of that described as 'cat' foot. In 'hare' foot the lengthened phalanges result in a narrowing of the paw, in which the middle pads are displaced forwards relative to the outer ones. A glance at the sketch will show that a foot of this conformation is probably even less desirable than the foreshortened 'cat' foot. The pads are almost entirely lacking in mutual support. In the rolling of the foot ('heel-toe') the stress is first taken by the outer pads almost alone, and then by the middle ones, again almost alone. At the commencement of the movement the outer pads are in torsion from the carpus and subjected to lateral leverage, without support from the middle ones. As the movement progresses the middle pads, in their turn,

become subjected to a similar unsupported torsion and lateral leverage.

The desired essential for the paw can be summarised as compactness of a degree compatible with proper strength and flexibility.

5

The Art and Science of Eugenic Reproduction

THE ART of BREEDING

THE LAWS of heredity are the same for all living organisms. Experience shows that to achieve improvement in a breed of animals proper selection of mates is essential. The objective is to produce uniformity of the qualities that are present in the best animals. That is to say, we desire to breed animals not only perfect in themselves, but with hereditary tendencies to reproduce their own perfection, so that by careful selection of mates we may obtain universal excellence. This is more important to the breed than the individual excellence of any single animal. The two fundamental factors for success are a general knowledge of the laws of breeding and a particular knowledge of the hereditary tendencies of the animals one proposes to use.

An occasional good puppy in a litter does not establish the sire or dam as a valuable progenitor. The real value can be ascertained only by taking into account a considerable number of litters sired by this particular dog or whelped by that particular bitch. For instance, a litter containing five 'very good' specimens is of far more value to the breed than a litter with one 'excellent' specimen and the remaining four 'mediocre'. Of course one occasionally hears of a litter containing several qualifying 'excellent'. A study of their pedigree practically always shows that their breeder had a profound knowledge both of breeding laws and of the hereditary tendencies of the animals he was using.

We find that certain dogs are responsible for the transmission of faults such as the following: lack of character, unbalanced structure, cryptorchidism, imperfect dentition, soft ears, missing vertebrae at tip of tail, poor quality of coat, paling colour. Dogs known to transmit such tendencies should be avoided and substituted in a proposed pedigree by collaterals known to be free from the transmission of these particular faults. For example, it is generally thought better to use the Utz line through Gockel von Bern rather than through Hussan vom Haus Schütting to avoid paling colour.

The outward appearance of an ancestor (Phenotype) does not always correspond to the type transmitted by him (Genotype). Mendel showed that hereditary tendencies may be either dominant or recessive. If both a dominant and a recessive factor are present in the same animal the dominant factor will overshadow or mask the recessive factor. In the example given above Utz probably combined the factor for dark pigmentation and the factor for paling colour. The latter being recessive to the former, the dog in question would have shown quite good pigmentation, but in breeding back to him for his good qualities it is essential to choose a line not showing transmission of the factor for paling colour.

Owing to the large mixed population of the German Shepherd Dog breed, the hereditary tendencies of a pair of animals mated at random will be unpredictable, so that in a programme designed to improve the breed the animals we propose to mate should be as far as possible of known homozygosity. By this we mean animals which will breed true to type, having inherited similar characteristics from both sire and dam, and being fairly close blood relatives.

Relationship is customarily divided into degrees. Parents are said to be related to their offspring in the first degree; grandparents in the second degree; and so on. Every degree upwards doubles the number of ancestors shown in the previous generation, so that our usual pedigree chart shows thirty-two ancestors in the fifth degree. If these ancestors are not all different individuals, i.e. if some of them appear more than once in the pedigree, there is said to be loss of ancestors, but the loss is seen in obverse as a consolidation of the blood strain of those ancestors whose names are repeated. When the same ancestor appears once on the sire's side and once on the dam's within the last five generations it is called inbreeding, while if a valuable ancestor is repeated several times the pedigree is said to indicate a preponderance of his blood.

Inbreeding may be very intensive, as mating father to daughter, dam to her son, brother or half-brother to sister, and so on; but the most usual is to mate a dog with his dam's half-sister, so producing preponderance of his maternal grandsire's blood. Such a mating is an example of what is termed line-breeding, i.e. tracing our proposed pedigree back in a line both sides to an outstanding dog and consolidating his particular blood strain (*see* Table 1). Any inbreeding on relationships beyond the fifth or sixth degrees can be discounted in practice as of any value for a breeding programme.

TABLE I

	PARENTS (*related in the first degree*)	GRANDPARENTS (*related in the second degree*)	GREAT-GRANDPARENTS (*related in the third degree*)
SUPERBA XX	Roland	Beowulf	Utz
			Eola
		Thora	TELL X
			Cora
	Flora	TELL X	Odin
			Tunte
		Adora	Remo
			Erna

TABLE I.—SUPERBA XX is line-bred 2, 3 on TELL X. The chance of duplicating any given factor from TELL (X) in SUPERBA (XX) is 1 : 8; that is to say, the coefficient of inbreeding is 12.5 per cent (or 12.5 chances in 100).

It is well to remember that it is not of the slightest use to take the right dog, according to a paper pedigree, but with a straight front and a straight hind leg, expecting by mating him with your well-angulated bitch to produce a litter of puppies all having well-placed shoulders and a good turn of stifle. That is most unlikely to happen.

However, in artistic hands, the chance of producing a preponderance of animals true to type is definitely increased by careful line-breeding. We take a risk, at the same time, that in consolidating the good traits we may also secure an intensification of dormant faults. This is a very real danger. There is also ever present the possibility that in our efforts to select the more obvious perfections we may lose undisclosed good traits, mainly shown as vigour in our stock. One way to counteract this is by what is called intermate breeding. Two breeders agree to breed independently along the same blood line; but in case of loss of vigour in either stock, an exchange of animals may restore to the other the subtle factors that either has lost through too intensive inbreeding. If this fails, an outcross to unrelated stock may be the only salvation, with its resultant so-called hybrid vigour.

An outcross to unrelated (heterozygous) stock may also be necessary to introduce some desirable feature into our stock which it does not already possess. A good example is prick ears. This condition is due to a recessive factor and therefore easy to obtain pure. If a given pure breeding stock lacks good ear carriage, a single outcross, with a subsequent judicious inbreeding of the hybrids into the stock, can easily and quickly introduce the quality desired.

It will be seen that the art of breeding demands vast knowledge and long experience, while there is always a possibility of the perpetration of gross errors. As the old aphorism has it, experience is fallacious and judgment difficult. One experienced breeder confounded a novice with the explanation, 'If you keep on breeding with your own stock of dogs and get winners, there is no doubt about it that you are line-breeding scientifically; but if your luck is out, there is no doubt that you are inbreeding like a fool.' However, it is careful inbreeding and careful line breeding that has produced the German Shepherd Dog as we know it. If we relinquish these methods we shall soon lose what we have gained and revert to a primitive type.

THE SCIENCE OF GENETICS

Every living organism is made up on a cellular basis. The earliest form of animal life was probably an individual living cell, such as the minute single-celled animalculae living today. In the course of aeons groups of cells amalgamated to form multi-cellular animals; and as the animals became more complex the cells became differentiated into sub-groups forming the different tissues of the complex animal body. Throughout all these changes the ultimate control rested within the nucleus of each and every cell.

The nucleus of a cell is a specialised central structure which controls all cellular activity. The body as a whole can be compared dynamically to an electric grid system. The individual electrical (and chemical) transformers are contained in the nucleus of each and every individual cell.

Long study of individual cells in all phases of their activity has shown that the energy-transforming mechanism resides in a number of distinctively shaped structures which readily take up the dye stuffs used by microscopists to aid their observations. These structures have been given the name 'chromosomes' (Greek = coloured structures). They occur in pairs. In the dog the nucleus of every cell is estimated to contain 39 pairs of chromosomes.

The only exception to the above rule is the reproductive cells. After a reducing division each reproductive cell, male or female, contains only 39 single colour structures, not 39 pairs. When two animals mate, the fusion of two reproductive cells, the sperm and the ovum, into a fertilised egg-cell reconstitutes the 39 pairs necessary to the construction of a new individual. The physical and mental construction of every dog depends on the quality of the endowment he has inherited from sire and dam in respect of these chromosomes.

This, simply, is the story of genetics – the re-groupings of the chromosomes into their pairs with each new generation. It is called genetics because each chromosome pair determines so many characteristics that it is convenient to say that they are made up of so many 'genes'. Below genes one does not speculate. The gene is the ultimate indivisible of the science of genetics (reproductions) and the chromosome is the physical structure we can actually see and reasonably assume from the result of experiments to control a given number of inherited characteristics or genes.

GENETICS APPLIED TO BREEDING

In a previous section we discussed inbreeding and line-breeding in general terms as a method of consolidating the inborn qualities of certain animals as special blood strains within a breed. Our object was stated to be the raising of the standard of the breed as a whole to that of the best animals in it. We can now make a fresh approach to the problem in the light of our knowledge that the re-grouping of the chromosome pairs with each generation forms the basis of inheritance.

We can all picture in our mind's eye the dog of our ideal: well angulated fore and aft, with firm straight back, correct length of legs and forward-sloping pasterns, so that as he trots his whole movement is so smooth that were a glass of water balanced on his back not a drop would spill. Some of us know this dog, or believe we do. We call him our phenotype – our breed ideal. We want to breed his lineage into all our stock so that they are all him and he is all of them. To get some idea how this may be done we must first discuss the constitution of his genes.

While the exact arrangement of chromosomes (genetic groups) determining the characteristic of bodily form, intelligence and temperament is far too complex to be established in detail, there can be no doubt that the perfection of these qualities depends on the harmonious association of the chromosomes in their pairs severally determining the construction of the bodily parts. The dog we have chosen for our breed ideal (our phenotype) will naturally have such a harmonious pattern. The problem is how to hold on to the dominant genes in such a favourable combination? With every reproductive cycle the pattern changes. How can we retain a sufficient degree of constancy in the chromosome pattern to establish a true breeding strain, which is the aim of all scientific breeding? The answer is to breed back along ancestral lines to the animal we have chosen as our breed ideal.

To study this further let us consider the usual pedigree form. This goes back five generations, to the G.G.G. Grandparents,

32 ancestors at this stage. It will be obvious that the average chromosome contribution of any one of these will be no more than two or three out of the 78 (39 pairs) that make up each cell nucleus of the normal individual. The only way to get a greater number from any one ancestor will be to have that ancestor appear more than once in the pedigree. This is the method of breeding in line to the particular ancestor concerned.

A most instructive example is found in the breeding of Graf Eberhard von Hohen-Esp:

TABLE II

	PARENTS 50%	GRANDPARENTS 25%	GREAT-GRANDPARENTS 12.5%	GREAT-GREAT-GRANDPARENTS 6.25%
GRAF EBERHARD v. HOHEN-ESP	SIRE: Wolf v. Balingen	Pilot III	Hektor v. Schwaben	Horand v. Grafrath
				Mores Plieningen
			Thekla I v.d. Krone	Horand v. Grafrath
				Madame v.d. Krone
		Nelly II Eislingen	Hektor v. Schwaben	Horand v. Grafrath
				Mores Plieningen
			Nelly Eislingen, SZ11	Horand v. Grafrath
				Ella Gmünd
	DAM: Nelly II Eislingen	Hektor v. Schwaben	Horand v. Grafrath	
			Mores Plieningen	
		Nelly Eislingen, SZ11	Horand v. Grafrath	
			Ella Gmünd	

TABLE II.—Pedigree of Graf Eberhard von Hohen-Esp

I have indicated above in the pedigree the degree of genetic relationship between the dog Graf Eberhard von Hohen-Esp and his forbears. That is to say he takes 50 per cent of his chromosomes from his parents, 25 per cent from his grand-parents and so on. Of his 78 chromosomes we find by adding up that no less than 50 per cent come from Horand von Grafrath. This does not mean that Horand supplied one in every pair. With some pairs neither may have come from Horand; but for every pair where neither came from Horand, there must be another pair where both its members came from him. If the members of such a pair are identical they are termed homozygous, a Greek word indicating that the two yoke fellows are alike.

It is important that in selecting animals from each generation in the pedigree as parents for the next, the breeder who planned the combinations should have rejected all imperfections. It is worth noting that Graf Eberhard sired Luchs von Kalsmunt-Wetzlar, Grand-Champion 1908, who in his turn sired Grand-Champion Tell von der Kriminalpolizei, considered to be the best specimen of the breed in his day.

It is worth while to go more deeply into the reason for meticulous selection, for herein lies the whole art of breeding within the framework of genetics as a science. Horand v. Grafrath was an outstanding dog. It is easy to imagine that every one of his chromosome pairs was heterozygous (unequally yoked), i.e. that one member of each pair was a dominant and the other a recessive. We can picture that Horand, having a complete set of dominants, would appear perfect in all detail. But Horand would not stamp his type. In fact he could not, because his genetic groups (chromosomes) would split apart in the reproductive reducing divisions, so that sperms would carry dominant and recessive genes in an unpredictable manner from the various chromosome pairs. On the other hand, Graf Eberhard would stamp his type, as so many of his chromosome pairs would be homozygous, i.e. the equal yoke fellows go separately but equally surely into the sperm. The reader should note, however, that Graf Eberhard would only stamp Horand's type where he had inherited homozygous pairs of Horand's dominant genes, not where he had inherited pairs of Horand's recessive genes. Thus Graf Eberhard v. Hohen-Esp would have been a most pre-potent sire, but he would have transmitted his own obvious faults (recessives) as truly as his virtues (dominants), which alone were obvious in Horand, but which Horand could not be sure of transmitting.

We see above the evident distinction between phenotype (type that appears) and genotype (type that reproduces). Graf Eberhard was a more extreme instance of intensive line-breeding than any we shall find today. None the less the ultimate problem confronting the founder of a strain within the breed today is still the same, viz. the exhibition of a sire who will infallibly transmit his dominant genes to all his progeny. Every phenotype has in his chromosome pattern recessive genes. In breeding back to him we are obliged to use animals having other ancestors besides. This may bring in even worse recessives. Our problem is to breed them out, retaining in the genotype only the dominant genes that gave the phenotype his excellence.

Intensive line-breeding brings about a rapid duplication both of dominants and recessives in the chromosome pairs of the new generation. The reader has to reject animals showing duplication of recessives and retain for further breeding animals which may have duplication of the dominant genes. I say advisedly, animals which may have duplication of the dominant genes, for while it is easy to determine which animals have duplication of recessives (this is straightway obvious by outward appearance), animals having duplication of dominants are indistinguishable from hybrids with one dominant and one recessive in a chromosome pair except by further breeding experiments. With an example of what this involves I propose to bring this section to a close.

The writer has recently directed his attention to producing a dog which would be a genotype for a well-known strain, the phenotype of which we will call Blitz. It is desirable to use imaginary names for these actual dogs. The dam in this particular case will be called Golden Lady. Her breeding may be seen in the accompanying pedigree.

Golden Lady was mated to Greif, who was chosen for this mating as providing a perfect example of the pre-Mendelian Bruce-Lowe formula, viz. 'Return through the dam the best blood of the sire.' In this example the desired blood returns through Skyrocket and Moonstone.

The result of the mating was of great interest. The duplication of at least one factor was manifest from the moment the litter was whelped. This was a recessive which had not revealed its presence by outward appearance in any of the ancestors mentioned above. Two of the four puppies were white. This shows the power of intensive line-breeding to bring recessives to light.

It was quite easy to trace the origin of the whites. The bitch Moonstone had for grandsire on the dam's side a famous dog

TABLE III

	PARENTS	GRANDPARENTS	GREAT-GRANDPARENTS	GREAT-GREAT-GRANDPARENTS
BLANCO BLANCHE	SIRE: Greif	Geri	Skyrocket	Blitz
				Donna
			Snowshoes	Whitefoot
				Flora
		Adora	Apollo	Apache
				Coquette
			Moonstone	Blitz
				Pale Lady
BROWNEARS BROWNPAWS	DAM: Golden Lady	Skyrocket	Blitz	Pollux
				Gretel
			Donna	Hektor
				Liesel
		Moonstone	Blitz	Pollux
				Gretel
			Pale Lady	Whitelight
				Shadow

TABLE III.—Breeding a genotype (potential sire with homozygous dominants) for the phenotype Blitz.

well known to transmit a gene for paling colour. In similar relationship to Geri, a son of Skyrocket, stands another equally famous sire known to carry white. Once again, neither of these dogs was white himself.

The reader will think indeed that I had reaped the due reward of such intensive line-breeding. It is true that in the case of two puppies I had duplicated an undesirable factor; but the reader should also please note that no alternative blood lines to Blitz were available. Moreover, although two of the puppies are white, the other two have excellent pigmentation. It may be that in their case I have brought together only desirable factors. I shall be able to tell this for certain when the puppies are full grown, by mating the bitch with her sire and the dog with his dam. Either, or even both of them, will be rejected for any further breeding if this test mating proves them unsatisfactory. If, however, it becomes evident that there is no recessive factor in their make-up, I am one step further on the path to perfection, for I may consider that I have one or two animals, genetically, as well as to outward appearance, endowed with the desirable traits of this particular strain in the breed.

THE INHERITANCE OF DEFECTIVE GENES

It will now be apposite to consider some specific genetic defects which it should be the breeder's aim to eliminate. He will be aware from the foregoing discussion, as well as from his own previous knowledge of the breed, that defective genes are present in all strains unless by the greatest good fortune the bucket and bullet methods of the past have eliminated them. There are several good reasons for starting with a discussion of cryptorchidism. One is that it is the subject of much misconception and controversy; another that it is a matter vital to the survival of the breed; while yet a third reason is that it is so very much more widespread than is generally supposed.

Cryptorchidism
This is an abnormality which appears not only in dogs, but also in other species of animals. It is widespread among horses, sheep and pigs, so that its elimination presents a major problem in animal husbandry.

During embryonic life the reproductive glands (or gonads) are contained in the abdominal cavity of the foetus. After birth the gonads of the male (testes) migrate, under the influence of chemical substances known as hormones, outside the abdomen into the scrotal sac. Arrest of this descent may lead to the apparent absence of one or both of the testes.

Strictly speaking, the condition called cryptorchidism (Greek = concealed testes), is only the manifestation in the male of the dysfunction termed sexual hypoplasia, embracing also the female. Readers desiring fuller information may be referred to the paper by Van Lone on 'The Inheritance, Histology and Physiology of Sexual Hypogenesis in the Guinea Pig' (*J. Esp. Zool.*, 64, 1–31).

Bilateral cryptorchidism implies sterility, because the undescended testis is immature and produces no sperm. Unilateral cryptorchidism, i.e. monorchidism (Greek = one testis), does not imply sterility, because the single properly descended testis may function adequately and produce sperm. A monorchid, however, is necessarily an imperfect animal, whereas we seek perfection. It is illogical to countenance monorchidism while penalising faults less venal. One is reminded of the old saying about straining at a gnat and swallowing a camel.

There can be no doubt about cryptorchidism being entirely hereditary, since repeated investigations have shown that environmental changes do not influence the incidence of the condition, which does in fact follow the laws of inheritance for recessive genes.[1]

Monorchid males do not beget their like if mated to genetically sound bitches. In fact cryptorchids usually follow the service of an apparently normal male, but as in all cases of inheritance of recessives both the parents are responsible for transmitting the defect.

We must assume that there is one gene (or group of genes) for the normal development of the testes, and another (defective group) which determines the non-development of the testes, or what comes to the same thing – the absence of the natural hormone which brings about the normal descent of the

1. Modern thinking leans towards the idea that while certain forms of monorchidism are hereditary, others are not. – T.G.

testes. A dog gets his genes, or groups of genes (chromosomes), from his parents. Each parent contributes one group, whether it be normal or defective. It is the confluence of two defective groups, one derived from each parent, which bring to light the latent genetic defect, now made manifest in the unfortunate cryptorchid son.

To make this more plain, les us use symbols to illustrate the laws governing the inheritance of such a defective gene, or group of genes, as that producing cryptorchidism. The normal group we will mark ■ and the abnormal group ○. In a breed where cryptorchidism does not appear all the animals are free from ○. Their genetic construction, therefore, as regards these groups can be symbolised ■ ■. The mating of a pair of such animals can only give their progeny the normal inheritance.

In a breed where there are cryptorchids, these will be symbolised as regard the defective group of genes ○ ○. It may surprise the reader to learn that the bitch, as well as the dog, can carry a defective group of genes determining the maldevelopment or non-development of the male gonads, but it should be remembered that this group of genes controls not so much the specific development of the male (which is more obvious) as the production of the sex hormones in general. It would be very unusual to mate a monorchid dog ○ ○ with a sexually hypoplastic bitch ○ ○, but the result (if not sterility) would be the production of 100 per cent sexually hypoplastic progeny ○ ○.

We will now suppose a cryptorchid dog to be mated to a genetically normal bitch. All the progeny will get the defective gene ○ from their sire and the normal gene ■ from their dam. All the progeny will therefore be hybrid for these genes – symbolised ■ ○. Since the defective gene is recessive to the normal gene, all the hybrids will have a perfectly normal appearance. They will, however, all transmit the defective gene ○ to half their offspring, while half the offspring will receive the normal gene ■. It follows that a hybrid animal ■ ○ crossed with a normal animal ■ ■ will yield half normal progeny and half again hybrids. Similarly a hybrid ■ ○ crossed with a cryptorchid ○ ○ will yield half hybrids and half cryptorchids.

If hybrid animals are crossed we get the following combinations (*see* diagram), 25 per cent of the progeny normal, 25 per cent cryptorchids and 50 per cent again hybrids.

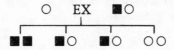

Diagram showing the mating of animals hybrid for sexual hypoplasia

Owing to the defective gene being recessive 75 per cent of the animals will be of normal appearance, but the chance of any one of these transmitting the defective gene will be an odds of two to one. In practice this is of great importance, as it means that in a strain where there are cryptorchid males there are very many more genetically unsound animals which appear normal. One should remember that this also applies to the bitches although with bitches the tendency to carry the defective gene is apt to be forgotten.

We must apply this knowledge to control the spread of cryptorchidism. It is clear that frank cryptorchids pass on a defective gene to 100 per cent of their progeny and so should be rejected for breeding purposes. Moreover, the occurrence of a cryptorchid tells us at once that the defective gene is present in the strain. Both its parents have transmitted the defect and will do so again however normal they may be to outward appearance. We must therefore put them also on a black list as regards breeding stock.

Now the parents in their turn inherited a defective gene from at least one of their own parents. This means that two of the grandparents at least may be expected to transmit the defect. It is not easy to find out which of the grandparents were the culprits, so that all of them come under suspicion for breeding purposes.

Next we have to consider the siblings (brothers and sisters) of the defective mating pair. Some of these also may have inherited a defective gene and will transmit the defect. In practice it is not advisable to use for breeding purposes either the apparently normal siblings of cryptorchids or the siblings of their parents.

With nearly all breeds cryptorchidism, although to outward appearance rare, is really so widespread that it is impossible to eliminate all carriers of the defect at once. This is true of all recessive genes that we want to get rid of. It is possible, however, to confine the defect strictly to a minimum, by applying the practical rule given above.

Paling Colour
The German Shepherd Dog standard demands deep pigmentation in animals belonging to this breed. There are doubtless many genes involved, but we may say roughly that a group of genes for dark pigmentation is dominant over another group which shows depigmentation. In some animals genes of both groups are present. As the genes for dark pigmentations are dominant over those for depigmentation we cannot detect from outward appearance all animals which may carry the recessive genes, but in the reducing divisions of the reproductive cells these genes will pass into half the sperms or ova of these animals. The general rule is that if a given mating pair produce any offspring in a litter paler than themselves (usually an albino), then both carry genes for depigmentation. If the sire throws puppies paler than the dam, then he transmits the defective genes, and vice versa. One should avoid so far as possible using a line through a dog or bitch known to have thrown an albino whelp. Such animals are said to carry genes for paling colour.

The White German Shepherd Dog
The true white, as distinct from the depigmented albino, is very rare. It can be distinguished by its dark eyes, nose and toenails. Any depigmentation of nose or nails with a light-coloured eye must be regarded as due to recessive genes.

The genuine white would have a dominant gene for coat colour, while the spurious white would have a recessive. Theoretically it should be possible to establish a strain of pure whites with black points, but owing to confusion with the albino white was not accepted as a legitimate colour by those responsible for drawing up the official standard of points for the German Shepherd Dog.

J. Y. Baldwin

Ch. Avon Prince of Alumvale

Voss v. Bern z pr., H.G.H., P.D., T.D.

Int. Ch. Vagabond of Brittas

Thomas Fall

Ch. Sergeant of Rozavel C.D.

Diane Pearce

Ch. Archduke of Rozavel

Diane Pearce

Aus. Ch. Rozavel Wyatt

Ch. Ludwig of Charavigne

C. M. Cooke

Int. Ch. Asoka Cherusker

Shaggy Coats

It was the opinion of the late Captain v. Stephanitz that neither long nor wavy hair should be penalised so long as it was hard and harsh and accompanied by good underwool. On the other hand, he did not believe that we should endeavour to breed it purposely. For the exacting service of the sheep-tending dog short smooth hair with a good waterproof undercoating is much preferable to the long shaggy hair of the so-called Old German Sheepdog, which tends to be sadly lacking in the waterproof underwool. A wavy coat is attributed to a crossing between shaggy-haired and smooth-haired dogs. Shaggy and wavy-coated dogs from North Germany were introduced in the early days of the breed. The condition is now carried as a recessive in certain strains, in the crossing of which duplication of the recessive may occur, with the consequent production of occasional long-haired puppies.

Defective Dentition

Once again, certain strains of dogs, as of other animals, carry recessive genes, a duplication of which results in lack of a complete second dentition. This can be avoided by a knowledge of sires or dams known to transmit the defective gene.

Missing Terminal Vertebrae of Tail

This condition was first seen in Nores v.d. Kriminalpolizei. Nores sired some excellent stock although, to the author's personal knowledge, out of several hundreds of litters sired by Nores, three showed puppies with the same tail defect.

Bitchy Appearance of the Male

This condition is not due specifically to any particular defective gene or group of genes, but, like straight front, short back and unharmonious body build is a matter of general configuration which can be corrected by proper selection on the part of the breeder.

TRANSMISSION OF HEREDITARY DEFECTS

The reader will be aware from the foregoing discussions that recessive genes will be transmitted to 50 per cent of the offspring of parents carrying a single recessive factor, but will

reveal themselves to outward appearance only when two such
factors are brought together in one and the same animal. It
goes without saying that in such a case recessives have been
transmitted by both the sire and the dam.

When a given ancestor is heavily represented in the pedigree,
the transmission of the recessive gene is often attributed to
him, although it is not always certain in the case of remote
ancestors that the transmission of the defect may not have been
due to some of the bitches coupled with him in the pedigree (see
the example of line-breeding to Blitz, where Moonstone and
Geri transmitted the defect). The transmission of a defective
gene can be attributed with certainty to a given dog only if any
of his immediate progeny definitely manifested the defect.

The author appends a list of some well-known dogs in the
past history of the breed which are thought to have transmitted
hereditary defects:

Cryptorchidism
There is practically no strain free from this defective gene. It
used to be claimed that dogs descended from the famous brood
bitch Flora Berkemeyer transmitted this defect.

Paling Colour
The lines from Horst von Boll, which include Falko v.
Scharenstetten, Nores v.d. Kriminalpolizei, Dobber v.d.
Peterstirn, Greif v.d. Peterstirn and Junker v. Nassau trans-
mitted this defect. Some authorities claim that Utz vom Haus
Schütting carried genes for paling colour through his dam
Donna sum Reurer, but it is possible that these genes may have
come from bitches coupled to Utz, as he has probably been
more extensively used for line-breeding than any other sire in
the history of the breed.

Shaggy Coats
Among others with long coats we find the following well-
known dogs mentioned in the early stud books: Carex
Plieningen, Prinz v.d. Krone, Luchs v. Eulau and Gr. Ch.
Roland v. Park. We find the latter away back in the pedigree of
most of the dogs having long hair.

Missing Dentition

Luchs Uckermark, Nores v.d. Kriminalpolizei, Erich v. Grunen Eck, Falko v. Indetal, Edo v.d. Buchheide, Dobber v.d. Peterstirn, Claus v.d. Fürstenburg, Erich & Harras v. Glockenbrink and Bodo v. Inselberg.

Missing Terminal Vertebrae of Tail

Nores v.d. Kriminalpolizei.

The list given above of dogs thought to transmit hereditary defects was compiled from information obtained from the S.V. Breed Surveys. Since, however, the first Breed Survey (1922) was not carried out during the life-time of many of these dogs, it cannot be definitely proved in every case whether a given dog did actually transmit the defective gene, except in the case of Nores and the shortened tails. The impression is rather that heavy line-breeding on these dogs did produce puppies with the defects.

The position would be quite different with modern dogs, where certain sires are known definitely to transmit hereditary defects, although in the absence of a voluntary Breed Survey in this country it would be invidious to mention any by name. Indeed the required information is extremely difficult to obtain, because there is no organised system of progeny survey. There is no doubt that for one or another reason much progeny is silently suppressed. Disposal of defective stock is widespread among breeders of perfect honesty and the greatest repute, who give no thought, or are even not aware of the possibility, that these methods may not in fact be furthering the true interests of the breed.

So long as these methods prevail we shall not improve the biological standard of our dogs and their wide variation in type. The occasional outstanding dog will be seen in our show rings, while in our kennels and on the streets we shall have a motley collection. An intelligent application of the principles of eugenic reproduction would leave no room for doubt as to which country possessed the best specimens of the breed, while the cry for the importation of fresh blood from abroad would be silenced forever.

6

General Management

THE GERMAN Shepherd Dog bitch may come into season at from seven to twelve months of age. After this, a normal bitch will come into season about every six months. The German Shepherd Dog is a large dog, and unlike many smaller breeds, develops slowly. It may not reach full maturity, or come to its best, until it is about three or even four years old. It is therefore inadvisable to mate the bitches too early in life. A well-grown bitch in good condition may be mated when she is 18 months of age, but many breeders wait for the third heat which is likely to occur when the animal is about two.

The first sign of a 'season' is a swelling of the vulva, and a noticeably bright red discharge. The latter gradually fades in colour, until by about the 12th to 14th day it has altered its appearance and has become clear and pinkish. This should be a good time to introduce the bitch to the chosen sire, always remembering that bitches vary in their heat cycles: we have known a productive mating to take place as early as 11 days and another at 19 days. A few German Shepherd bitches are not really ready until the 15th or 16th day.

This makes things rather difficult for the novice owner, and indeed for anybody planning to breed from a bitch for the first time, though her habits will probably remain constant throughout her life and the subsequent stud services will be more easily anticipated. On the whole, if the right day for a mating is in doubt, it is best to try the bitch early rather than late. Bitches mated rather earlier than they should be are, nevertheless, often pregnant, but if mated on the late side they generally 'miss' to the dog.

German Shepherd Dogs are strong, heavy animals and it is essential that two persons be present when a stud service is to be effected, and at least one should be an experienced handler. The bitch may show all the signs of flirting with her kennel mates at home, but fight like a tiger when introduced to a strange dog. Here the value of the training class shows itself, for the bitch will usually have manifested an interest in other dogs for some days before she shows 'colour' and will have become flirtatious with them, which makes the introduction to her chosen mate much easier. One individual, preferably the owner of the bitch, should hold her collar firmly with both hands, while the other helper supports her tummy and holds her tail aside to make things easier for the male. Once a 'tie' is finalised, the helper will gently lift the dog's hind leg and enable him to turn and relax comfortably till the pair are released. The tie may last for anything from two or three minutes to over half an hour.

A stud service without a tie is less likely to be productive than one that results in at least a short coupling, although bitches are known to produce puppies after some very unpromising services. It is most satisfactory when there is a tie of ten minutes or more, though then no guarantee can be given that puppies will result, since numerous factors can cause a disappointment.

A Veterinary Surgeon can sometimes detect the early signs of pregnancy, but it is usually four and a half to five and a half weeks before the layman can be sure that the union is to be fruitful. This may be forecast with hopeful accuracy by some-one very familiar with the habits of the bitch. A poor feeder suddenly becomes greedy, a bitch fond of her food becomes finicky and hard to tempt. A placid one seems consistently rest-less. There may be signs of a coming litter if the bitch vomits froth while otherwise seemingly in perfect health. But the surest sign is a swelling of the flanks, and this is always most marked after a meal. At this stage it is not unusual for the teats to be pinker than usual, and a little larger.

Many well-meaning owners begin to feed a bitch with extra quantities of food immediately after mating, and this is a mistake. Her requirements in this respect do not become pressing until the sixth week. We do not recommend giving calcium tablets or bone meal during the period of gestation, as this makes for solid bone in the puppies, and difficulties can result at the time of parturition. Surplus flesh is not an asset, but by stepping up the protein in the diet by increasing the meat ration, we are giving sufficient nourishment. For the last week, raw egg beaten in milk may be offered as an extra, and perhaps a little extra biscuit meal if the mother-to-be is particularly ravenous. She should not be allowed to get fat and podgy. Throughout the period the bitch should have normal and sufficient exercise. She may run and play if she wishes, though rough games with other heavy dogs are to be discouraged, and jumping is taboo.

A week before the whelping date, the bitch should be introduced to her bed and kennel, which should be warm and free from draughts. The ideal arrangement is a kennel not less than eight feet square, and ideally larger, which has a pop-hole door always open, the whole surrounded with a sizable run so that bitch, or puppies when they start to toddle, can go in and out at will. Provided with a cosy sleeping bench bitches whelp comfortably and in the cleanest conditions on any of the advertised 'furry' types of bedding mats, such as Vetbed. These can be cut to the size of the sleeping bench, and changed and washed daily to preserve hygiene.

The sleeping bench will need to be about three feet wide and four feet long. It should be raised on legs a few inches high, and have a rim about eight inches deep, one side of which is hinged to drop down. This will be necessary when the puppies begin to walk. German Shepherd Dogs rarely undergo complicated parturition. The majority have their puppies easily and seldom require veterinary attention. The breed as a whole produces good mothers, and few bitches fail to sever the cord, release the puppy from the membraneous bag, and lick it dry. There is always an exception to any rule, however, and if a young bitch seems tardy in performing her duties it is wise for the attendant to take matters in hand. The cord should be severed a couple of inches from the body, preferably with a sharp fingernail, and the puppy should be rubbed well with a clean towel before being put back with the dam. The less one interferes with a whelping bitch the better, so if all goes well, and the puppies appear at intervals of half an hour to an hour and are receiving the mother's attention, it is best to leave her alone. Just look in occasionally to make sure that things are in order, and offer a drink of milk from time to time.

German Shepherd Dogs may produce quite small litters, but frequently have 10 or 12 puppies. Even larger litters have been recorded. Opinions differ as to the number that a bitch can be expected to rear well. Experienced breeders, prepared to feed with lavish disregard of cost, and to spend unlimited time on the litter, can be relied upon to rear a litter of 10 or 12 puppies of above average size and weight and excelling in bone and substance.

Many beginners try to do this and fail lamentably. Sometimes they have only themselves to blame – maybe the bitch was not in good condition when mated, or was not pre-natally fed in the desired way. More often than not the novice owners are worried about the cost of buying so much food, all of which is very expensive in these inflationary times. They embark on breeding German Shepherd Dogs without any real idea of the substantial cost of the undertaking. They pinch and save, and the results – poorly developed puppies and a debilitated dam.

It is because of this that advice is often given to leave no more than six puppies with the mother. It is definitely easier for her – and the breeder – to 'do' a few really well, and it is such a waste of time and money if the puppies are undersized, slight boned, slab-sided and the owner unlikely to recover the cost of bringing them up at all. It must also be remembered that the quality of the dam's milk is affected if she has too large a litter, the minerals being dissipated by the demands of many greedy mouths. In Germany, the breed clubs do not allow more than 6 puppies to be reared on a bitch. All over this number must either be fostered or destroyed at birth.

It is sometimes possible to obtain a foster mother for a large litter, and this is much better than attempting to rear puppies by hand. The two-hourly feeds become very exhausting, the preparing of bottles, sterilising, cleaning the puppies and encouraging their little insides to function after every feed, takes a lot of time. Add to all this the fact that it is rare indeed for bottle-fed puppies to have the robust constitutions of those left with the dam, except in grave emergency the task scarcely seems worth the time and effort it involves.

If a foster mother is unobtainable and very often advertisements in the dog Press, telephone calls to other breeders and to Veterinary Surgeons and dogs' homes, all draw a blank – then it is best to have surplus puppies put to sleep. One feels wretchedly hard-hearted at the time, but it is no kindness to breed dogs with poor constitutions, and much better to produce a few that are robust and sturdy and likely to enjoy good health and long lives.

Once the puppies are born, the bitch will start needing considerable nourishment, and all sorts of supplements may be given. At Druidswood kennels, the first meal given is white fish, cooked in milk and carefully boned, with a raw egg beaten into the mixture and a slice of rusked wholemeal bread crumbled in at the last minute so that it does not become sloppy. Ample calcium is a 'must' now, and three tablets crushed into both breakfast and the last milk feed should be given. Meat is given on the second day after whelping, and the amount of rusked wholemeal bread increased as the appetite returns with the demands of the hungry litter.

The bitch may have a breakfast of milk with a teaspoonful of honey and three calcium tablets stirred into half a pint of boiled semolina porridge, which is made by sprinkling a large tablespoonful of semolina into half a pint of cold water and boiling well stirred for eight to ten minutes. Double quantities can be made at night, putting half in a Thermos ready for breakfast, as the supper meal is the same. Take care it is not fed too hot. Ample raw meat is a basic necessity, and up to three pounds a day is not too much if the increase is gradual.

Her first main meal is taken at 11 a.m. and the second at 4.30 p.m. Each of these consists of half the total ration of meat, plus some wholemeal rusk (according to appetite) with two seaweed tablets and two vitamin C tablets crushed and mixed in with a little bone stock to moisten (no rich gravies or made-up sauces, but weak Marmite is good if stock is not available). A milk and water drink (half and half) sweetened with a teaspoonful of honey can be given at 2 p.m. to ensure a good supply of nourishment for the litter. Ideal or Carnation milk is suitable, diluted as directed, since cow's milk varies in quality and seems to cause scouring.

The German Shepherd Dog needs great substance and strong bones, and it is advisable to commence weaning at a relatively early age. Some puppies are sufficiently precocious to show interest in tiny morsels of finely scraped raw meat as early as two to three weeks. At this point they should also be given the chance to learn to lap some half-and-half milk and water sweetened with a little honey and with half a calcium tablet per puppy crushed up finely; it is easier and safer to measure the supplements in tablets, as spoons vary so much in size and correct dosage is important. At four weeks give the puppies a bowl of semolina porridge, as made for the mother, allowing half a pint of porridge and half a pint of diluted evaporated milk to each four puppies or pro rata. The calcium should be increased to one tablet per puppy at each milk feed, plus one 100mg vitamin C tablet.

Milk and meat feeds are gradually increased, and their dam will only be with them for short spells now, always returning to keep them warm at night; but see that she has a bench, so that she can jump up and keep away from the demanding brood or be able to jump in and out over a low partition.

By the time the puppies are five or six weeks old the mother may tire of them, and it is then time to remove her, except for an occasional friendly visit of a few minutes, as most bitches enjoy playing with their puppies and fret if taken away altogether.

From now on the puppies require four meals a day, plus a warm drink of diluted evaporated milk midway between the two main meals. The semolina breakfast, which can be increased as their hearty appetites grow, should be followed by minced or finely chopped raw meat at 11 a.m.; then meat again, or carefully boned white fish, mixed with rusked wholemeal bread crumbled and moistened with stock or weak Marmite at 4 p.m. One seaweed tablet per puppy should be crushed and added to each main meal. At six weeks, three to four oz. of meat or fish should be allowed for each meal per puppy, increasing gradually to six oz. by eight weeks, making a total of ¾ lb. per puppy per day. Supper, which should be the same as breakfast, can be given around 10 p.m., thus ensuring the puppies will be well-fed and comfortable for the night, so that everyone can sleep peacefully. The quantity of meat will increase to 8 oz. by nine weeks, and 12 oz. by twelve weeks – a total of 1½ lb. per day. If the dish is not cleared at mealtimes, feed a little less next time, as puppies' appetites vary a little when they are teething. All left-over food should be removed from the pen after a reasonable time and thrown away.

Puppies should always be fed at regular times, and the meat should be at room temperature, never straight from the refrigerator, and always properly de-frosted well in advance if frozen meat is used.

An initial worm dose should be given at five weeks. Consult your Veterinary Surgeon for the dosage, as modern worming methods change with the times. The dose is usually repeated in eight to ten days for complete clearance, which is vital for healthy growth.

The puppies' weight can vary in a large litter. An average dog puppy should weigh 12 to 15 pounds at eight weeks, and the bitches one to two pounds less. Smaller puppies in the litter often make rapid gains in weight at weaning time, and catch up with their bigger litter mates. Watch carefully at feeding times to see that each puppy gets a fair share, and feed a slow or backward one separately until he can establish his rights. When a German Shepherd puppy has a gastric attack all food should be stopped and veterinary advice sought. A visit at the onset can save a long period of illness, or worse.

Remember that fresh air and freedom for exercise, through play, are essentials. No amount of good food will produce fine puppies if they are confined in a small run. Puppies develop rickets through malnutrition, but even well-fed litters will become rickety through lack of exercise.

Keep kennel and run scrupulously clean. If the puppies are shut in at night, the kennel will almost certainly be very dirty and smelly in the morning. When this has to be done, it is best to have two houses. The puppies can be transferred from one to the other, while the soiled floor is thoroughly cleaned, scrubbed with hot water and soda or pine disinfectant, and allowed to get completely dry before the dogs go back. If, however, it is possible to leave an exit open to enable the puppies to go in and out at will, it will be found that their naturally clean instincts predominate and they will seldom mess indoors, but will trot out to a chosen spot to relieve themselves. Alternatively, the floor can be sprinkled with sawdust and then covered with newspapers, enabling the soiled parts to be easily removed and replaced when the weather does not allow the puppies to go outside.

Some breeders part with puppies at six or seven weeks of age. Others feel that by keeping them a further fortnight they are giving them a better start in life. Most puppies find new homes between the ages of two and three months.

Considering the expense, time and energy a growing litter demand, it is better to dispose of surplus puppies and concentrate on feeding and training one or two selected show or breeding prospects to enhance the reputation of the breeder. It is a common mistake, but many beginners run on too many of their young 'hopefuls'. No breed thrives better on individual attention than the German Shepherd Dog.

7

Choosing a German Shepherd Dog

THE GERMAN Shepherd Dog, as we have already learned, is a dog of many parts. Consequently, if we want to choose one for ourselves, our requirements are not necessarily exactly the same as the next man's, and there are all manner of things to be considered. When we buy a dog, whatever the breed, whatever the purpose for which we will use it, we are agreed that it must be healthy, it must be sound, and it must be of good disposition.

It is after these basic but important requirements have been met that we delve deeper into the problems that confront us. Are we after foundation stock for breeding? And if so, do we plan to join the rank and file who breed primarily for the show ring? Or are we interested in the working side of things, and prepared to leave showing in the beauty rings to others? Does the idea of breeding stock for the police force, or to offer to the society which trains dogs for the blind, appeal to us? Is it possible that we number ourselves among that very small minority – those farmers who use dogs for what is indubitably the German Shepherd Dog's real forte – the herding of sheep?

Maybe we have no great aspirations. We cannot be bothered with the fuss and the hard work that breeding and showing entails. All we ask for is a handsome, reliable dog as friend, companion and guard for the home, and indeed if this is our heart's desire – well, nothing can give it to us better than a good German Shepherd Dog. Perhaps we can examine the various requirements in detail, to find out what we must have if our dog is to be the right one, and what things we can regard as less important when the final choice is made.

First, what does the novice breeder need? He needs to be

absolutely certain that a German Shepherd Dog is, in every way, the suitable dog for him, his household, his home. We ourselves think it would be dreadful to long for a German Shepherd Dog and never own one, but we have to admit that, as is the case with any large, active breed, they are not everybody's dog. Plenty of people can offer suitable homes for small dogs, but are either incapable of managing, or unable to properly accommodate, an animal weighing 80 lb. or so.

If we consider breeding, and we have plenty of time to devote to our dog, if we have a reasonable amount of room, and last but certainly not least, if we are prepared to face the expensive outlay incurred in raising a litter of puppies, then we can go straight ahead.

What about the owner who wants a family friend? or a worker? or a guard? Whatever the destiny, do nothing in haste. It is easy to pick up local newspapers, to glance down the 'Dogs for Sale' or 'Livestock' columns, and more often than not there are advertisements offering 'Pedigree German Shepherd Dogs for Sale'. The announcement may have been inserted by a reputable breeder with sound stock to offer, but it is just as likely to have been worded by someone with a mediocre litter dragged up without proper feeding or care, and bred from poor quality parents. We have to confess that one does see a great many German Shepherd Dogs around which are of poor type, light-boned and greyhoundy, often light of eye and nervous, and it is from such litters that most of them have originated. Similar advertisements have often been put in by dealers or pet shops, as a means of re-selling stock, perhaps the throw-outs bought from other kennels, and puppies from such sources are frequently not even healthy.

The beginner should really have amassed at least some knowledge of what is required in the German Shepherd Dog breed before spending good money on a puppy. Failing that, or if such knowledge gained is scanty, go to a long-established, well-known kennel with a good reputation. Do not try to hoodwink the owners into thinking you know more than you do – they are used to meeting people who do just that and they are very perceptive. Be quite candid. Just say: 'I am a beginner. I do not know a great deal about German Shepherd Dogs and that is why I have come to you. I have been told that you will give a novice a square deal. I will explain to you just what I want, and I hope you can help me.'

The difficulty, of course, is to discover which are the best kennels to patronise and which are not. The Kennel Club, 1–4 Clarges Street, Piccadilly, London W1, are very helpful, and will supply names and addresses of breeders, but even so it is up to the individual to choose the right one. Advertisements in *Our Dogs* and *Dog World* are very informative, and so are the reports on the shows held in various parts of the country, and the lists of successes in obedience tests and at Working Trials. References to achievements are sometimes made in the breed notes in these papers, and it is quite possible to build up a picture of some of the more prominent kennels after studying all these items for a few weeks or months. Choose one or two likely addresses, make appointments and visit them. If you make an appointment to call to see dogs, keep it – or advise by telephone or letter if you are unable to turn up after all. You would be surprised how often people fix a day and time to inspect a kennel and then do not arrive; the poor owner has had to wait around wasting time when much work is needed to be done.

Kennel owners, almost without exception, are exceedingly busy people. They work extremely hard and they work very long hours. Visitors are welcome, but they disturb the kennel routine and whilst this upset can be minimised when callers are expected, it turns the work programme completely upside down if people come unannounced at particularly inconvenient times.

If kennel owners specify that their establishment may be inspected 'by appointment', it does not mean that they have a lot of unhealthy dogs they want to shut in the bathroom before you arrive. It simply means that they want to be able to plan their day and get ahead with the work in order to be in a position to spare some time to show you the dogs and discuss your requirements.

Get a rough idea of current prices before you start 'doing the rounds'. You will waste your own time and other people's as well if you set out expecting to buy a top-class puppy for a few pounds. Because your Auntie May bought one for £25 ten years ago it does not mean that you can get a dog worth buying for that figure, since prices always tend to rise. The costs of keeping dogs go up so consistently that the surprising thing is that prices and stud fees remain as low as they do. Almost anyone who sells a German Shepherd Dog puppy at less than £150–200 does so at a loss. There are some philanthropists around for whom dog breeding is a hobby purely and simply and who are in the happy position of being able to subsidise the pastime. They may wish to move the puppies at an early age for a variety of reasons, and to do this will accept prices well below the practical figure quoted above. Such puppies may be sturdy and good, but all too often the cheap puppy is the badly reared specimen, and by the time the buyer has paid a string of Veterinary Surgeon's accounts for its ailments, it proves by far the most expensive in the end.

If the idea is to obtain a bitch for breeding, then the pros and cons of a young puppy, a half-grown youngster or an adult must be most carefully considered. German Shepherd Dogs are not one of the easiest breeds when it comes to evaluating the potentials of a puppy at an early age. It may be that a well-bred puppy from really typical and good-tempered parents will turn out very well, but to some extent it is a lottery no matter how promising it looks at a few weeks old. It may mature into a Champion – or turn into a 'Chump'! Puppies alter all the time as they grow up, and breeders themselves often run on what appear to be the best puppies from their current litters only to reject all or most of them at a few months old as faults appear.

The problem of assessing the worth of a puppy works both ways, however. While the promising puppy may break hearts when it turns out to be just another nice dog of pet standard, many a breeder has kept what seems at the time to be the certain Champion in an even litter and sold off another, only to find that they have parted with the best after all.

When one buys an older animal, then of course it is the finished article. You see what you are buying, and any time after about a year old it will not alter very much. But naturally if a breeder has reared and trained a puppy to adult age, and it promises to be good, it will command a very much higher price than it would have cost straight out of the nest.

So it all depends upon how much you feel able to pay, how much you prefer to bring up your puppy from the earliest possible stage yourself, and what stock is available when a purchase is about to be made. It is rarely easy to persuade a breeder to part with a really outstanding adult bitch.

We keep using the word 'bitch' because we do not think that the beginner should start with a male dog. It is a better policy to spend what money is available on the best obtainable bitch or bitches, and for the first few years mate them to the best and most suitable stud dogs. Such dogs are available in various parts of the country at most reasonable fees, some have been carefully bred from the cream of British stock, others have been imported at great expense. To import, or to campaign a dog through a spectacular show career, costs hundreds of pounds. Yet other breeders can usually use such dogs to sire a litter for a fraction of the cost of keeping such a dog. Take advantage of the wide choice of good sires and, looking to the future, try to breed your own Champion stud dog.

Naturally if you are primarily interested in working dogs you will not pay so much attention to finer show points but will look out for character. Many working Champions have not been very much to look at, but at the same time past records show that there have been talented breeders who have succeeded in producing dual purpose animals. An outstanding example was the late Mr G. Crook, who bred the famous Champion and Obedience Champion Danki of Glenvoca. It is of interest that Danki was out of one of Mr Schwabacher's bitches, Ch. Sabre Secretainerie, by yet another double 'star' – Champion and Obedience Champion Terrie of Glenvoca; so Mr Crook bred two generations of dual Champions, an achievement that may never be surpassed.

It must surely be more satisfactory to own a good-looking working dog than one that looks all wrong everywhere, so the wise ones consider beauty when seeking brains even if they pay greater attention to the latter. It never pays *anybody* to breed for the pet market. The truth is that however carefully a mating is planned, even if the litter contains some outstandingly good dogs, there are nearly always some others that are not up to show standard and definitely nowhere near Championship Show quality. These are the dogs, well-bred and – we hope – well-reared, that make ideal pets and there are always plenty of them for sale at reasonable prices.

As we have seen from the above paragraph, if we try to breed Champions we will still breed some pets. If we are silly enough to just mate any dog to any bitch just to get companion-class puppies we are most likely to get rubbish.

The 'man in the street' who wants a house dog and family friend at what is referred to as 'pet price' is obviously not in any position to be too fussy about the quality of the dog he is getting. But he is entitled to expect it to be well boned, average size, and erect-eared. Especially it should be healthy and of firm temperament. It may lack some hind angulation, it might be short in body or square over the croup. It could be straight in shoulder, but even wih such faults there is no reason why it should not look like a German Shepherd Dog. Generally speaking the average person who asks for a pet wants an upstanding dog with prick ears, and bothers little if at all about other points. In fact this type of buyer is not nearly particular enough about making sure that the puppy is bred from stock noted for temperaments, temperaments being of paramount importance in any German Sehpherd Dog and absolutely essential in a dog for the home.

Because there is a useful demand for pet puppies, breeders are able to breed their litters knowing that they can be sold even if they are unlikely to grow up beautiful. Dog breeding is always a lottery – in fact, so is livestock breeding of any kind. If it were not so, every colt foaled would be a possible Derby winner. Everything easy becomes a bore eventually, but dog breeding is difficult and consequently is never dull. Each new litter is a fresh thrill, a new challenge. Will it be better than the last? As good as some famous litter born to another fortunate breeder who used the same sire? Or even more wonderful? Or does disappointment lie ahead? Will it become clear that the dog and bitch, in spite of careful planning, careful studying of pedigrees, are not well suited after all? Only time will tell us what is in store for the precious puppies as they are born into this world.

We know too well that their destiny cannot be worked out with mathematical precison. We must plan, and hope, and accept the fact that Nature almost always has the last word.

The breed standard was originally drawn up as a guide to enable breeders to produce a dog ideally suited to perform especially exacting work. If such a dog conforms to the standard, it will also be beautiful, which is an encouraging fact.

When we want a puppy, we try to choose one that fits the standard insofar as this is possible, although we know it is not easy to find perfection. Whereas a great many other breeds, as puppies, look like miniatures of the dog they represent, the average baby German Shepherd Dog looks more like a cuddly Teddy Bear than anything else. Little Cocker Spaniels, little Beagles, in fact all sorts of dogs are easily recognisable at a few weeks old – but not the German Shepherd Dog. We know that this floppy, heavy, woolly animal which grunts like a little pig when we lift it up, has a coat like a thick Turkey carpet and a blunt little head with – often – pendant ears, will one day grow into a big, shapely dog combining elegance and substance. But its appearance up until it reaches the age of three or three and a half months is such that it adds to the difficulties of determining its potential merits. One or both ears are probably down, but even if they are both erect one day they may flop the next, especially if the puppy is cutting teeth. We have noticed that the best show dogs carry their tails down, in a graceful sweep, but the baby German Shepherd Dogs have theirs waving in the air! This is quite usual, we are told – but oh, dear! how can one judge tail-set or know if the tail will be well carried as the dog gets older?

The puppies look very black, too, though we know they are almost certain to get much lighter as they change coats. Puppies that look dark all over with just a little colour on legs, cheeks, inside of ears and on the chest may finish gold or silver or fawn with just the backs black and shiny. The eyes of young puppies have a bluish look but gradually darken. Only very pale, almost silver, eyes can with certainty be expected to finish yellow – an unattractive fault.

The first or 'milk' teeth will fall out and be replaced by permanent teeth, and dentition is usually complete or almost complete by the time the puppy reaches the age of six months. The bite – that is the two rows of teeth that meet in front – should be level at all times. The word level is common dog show parlance for a scissor bite, the upper set fitting closely over the bottom row. Level does not mean edge to edge with the top teeth resting on the edge of the lower set. An overshot mouth is when the upper teeth project beyond the lower, conversely an undershot jaw means that the lower teeth stick out like a bull-dog's. Any deviation from a scissor bite is a fault, and the absence of any premolars (the small, crag-like teeth each side) is also serious. Missing teeth are most severely penalised on the Continent. In Britain many judges view them more leniently though others regard them as bad and strongly hereditary faults. Missing teeth can only be noted when the puppy has finished teething, but bad 'bites' are easily seen at any time.

What about gait? The German Shepherd Dog movement is distinctive and totally different to any other breed's action. It has been said that it should be possible to imagine that a glass of water could be carried on a German Shepherd Dog's back without a drop being spilled. This pre-supposes a very smooth, even gait brought about by reaching straight forward with the front legs (without waving or flapping the limbs) and at the same time thrusting and propelling with the hind legs. A short, choppy hind movement will never give the desired transmission. German Shepherd Dogs moving well seem to travel with the minimum of effort. If a puppy is fat and wobbly it can hardly gait well, but if it is a well-made youngster and sound (no loose elbows, bowed front legs, weak hindquarters) there is no reason why it should not progress normally, developing muscle and tightening up until it moves properly. The front legs should be thick and straight, with firm bone, nothing spongy about the limbs, and set on tough, tight, round feet. Puppies lollop around, tumbling and playing and it is most difficult to even try to judge the movement. If a second person can coax the puppy away and let it run to and fro it helps, and it should be possible to make sure that it is, though naturally babyish, perfectly sound.

Choose a puppy that looks longer than its height, and see if it has a thick, substantial body and well-sprung ribs. The opposite to this is slab-sides, and if you look down on the animal it looks narrow. Feel the shoulders. Mr Schwabacher always maintained that this was by far the most important point in a puppy's conformation, and if shoulders were well-placed, the correct amount of hind angulation would be sure to follow. Certainly most puppies do not look well angulated at eight or nine weeks old, but gradually the hindquarters take on an appearance of elegance and by the time the puppy is past the 12 weeks' stage one can usually say that it will or will not be well let-down in hocks.

The angle of the croup is also most difficult to assess, for almost all puppies appear to have high-set tails, and many are discarded for this fault, yet later they grow up enhanced by nice sloping croups.

Ear carriage is another problem. It might be thought that erect ears in a six or seven weeks' old puppy was a very great advantage, but curiously enough this is not so. Very heavy, lavishly reared German Shepherd Dog puppies invariably put their ears up late. Undersized, badly fed puppies frequently have their ears up from four or five weeks old onwards. In fact, very young, prick-eared puppies are quite likely to be suffering from worms or malnutrition and should be carefully examined.

German Shepherd Dog puppies do odd things with their ears at all stages, and may hold them at one angle in the morning and another at night. Both ears can tilt inwards, one may go up and the other hang down, ears can be half up and tipped over – the permutations are endless. In particular the ear carriage is almost always erratic during the teething processes. By the time the puppies are four or five months old, however, their ears should go up and stay up for much of the time, just dropping occasionally for a day or two before moving again. If ears are not permanently erect, or almost erect, by the time the dog is six months old, one is justified in feeling a little uneasy even though many dogs have ears that do not stand up permanently until they are 10 or 11 months of age. A few rare instances of ears going up even later have been recorded, but these are isolated cases and in general floppy ears at a year old stay down.

Ear carriage can be helped by treatment with adhesive tape, with or without the additional use of spoon-shaped pieces of thick chiropodist's felt pressed inside the ear. There is quite an art to taping ears, as if done badly it does more harm than good so it is best to ask an experienced Shepherdite to demonstrate the best method. Mr Schwabacher used to suggest shaped pieces of camera film, or balsa wood, stuck into the ear with seccotine but we never had any luck with either. The secret of success lies in keeping the ears supported for as long as possible – preferably at least three weeks – before removing the tape. Sometimes the ears stand up for a few days, everybody concerned shouts, 'Hooray! it works!' and great disappointment is felt when the ears go down once more. Perseverance is required and so long as the ears do not get sore, keep on trying.

We have spent a lot of time going over the important physical qualities of a puppy, but what about the temperament, the most important consideration of them all? Temperament can only be evaluated up to a point in a young puppy. First, ask to see the dam, and if possible, the sire. If either is shy or snappy, do not bother looking at the puppies – look elsewhere.

Ordinarily, German Shepherd Dog puppies run to strangers, so a puppy that bolts or hides is to be avoided. The normal puppy is bright, busy, interested in what goes on around it, and craves human company. In the first formative months the German Shepherd Dog has not developed the suspiciousness of strangers, a trait that comes later. Normally a puppy may jump or start at sudden noises but should not run away. Rather, once the initial shock or surprise is over, it should show curiosity and tentatively explore the source of the sound. People do stupid things, like clapping hands, throwing down books, banging doors and the like, believing that they can test temperaments by making loud noises. But any normal puppy will be scared and startled, and if it did not react it would probably be deaf. Sudden apprehension is understandable but the puppy should never run away or cringe.

Finally, having considered show points and character, we must make certain the dog is healthy. It appears lively and well –otherwise we would not have given it a second glance – but if there is the slightest doubt, do not buy it until it has been seen by a Vet. Healthy puppies romp and play, unless they have just had a meal when they become very somnolent and reluctant to wake. If disturbed they take a few minutes to get going, and may move slowly, yawning occasionally. A puppy in good condition has a thick, well-covered body. Pick it up, and it feels solid, heavy and its exterior might well be upholstered with foam rubber! If the puppy feels hard and bony, if the fur and skin feels thin and dry, it is not in good health. There may be nothing seriously wrong – perhaps the little dog has worms – but it has been neglected if it has got into such a state. Do not buy trouble of that kind.

The conditions in which the dogs are kept will almost certainly be reflected in their state of health. Clean kennels do not smell unpleasant, and strong odours invariably mean that the rules have been neglected. Kennels have to be scrubbed, sawdust and bedding must be constantly renewed. Lavish sprinklings of strong disinfectant do not deceive experienced noses; they are no substitute for hot water, household soda – and hard work with the deck scrubber and mop.

Soggy, discoloured sawdust, flattened-down, broken straw or shavings, soiled floors and runs – these are indications of poor animal husbandry and sloppy kennel management. Please yourself – but *we* like to buy our dogs from kennels where scrupulous attention to cleanliness is beyond doubt. Such horrors as lice, fleas, mange, and germs of all kinds breed in dirty kennels and neglected runs, not to mention worms which flourish and re-infect dogs of all ages under such conditions.

We have accepted the obvious fact that, while a young puppy constitutes a gamble, an older dog, virtually the finished article, is a safer though usually far more expensive investment. We need hardly speculate as to whether the adult dog has good ear carriage, dark eyes, sloping croup and correct tail, etc. If we have studied the standard and the conformation desired in the ideal German Shepherd Dog it should be clear that when we inspect a dog, the desirable points are either present, or missing. But to obtain a fair picture of the dog we ought to ask the handler to show it to us on a loose lead. We should be able to approach it, stroke it, and feel its legs, back, and quarters. It need not fawn on us or greet us enthusiastically, because we know that the German Shepherd Dog is not interested in strangers, but it should stand its ground, alert and attentive to the handler, and should certainly show no aggressiveness or nervousness.

The breed standard (1982) describes the characteristics of the German Shepherd Dog thus: 'steadiness of nerves, attentiveness, loyalty, calm self-assurance, alertness and tractability, as well as courage with physical resilience and scenting ability. These characteristics are necessary for a versatile working dog. Nervousness, over-aggressiveness and shyness are very serious faults.' This description gives a very complete picture of our dog's wide range of talents and his fantastic ability as a working dog. He *needs* all these characteristics to become a typical specimen of his breed, and those who breed them, and those who keep them as companions, *must*, with patience and understanding, give the German Shepherd Dog the care and attention it requires to develop these great qualities. Gentle handling and a gradual introduction to the outside world, lots of affection (to which a puppy will respond 100 per cent) and constant human companionship will reveal his full potential. He is, after all, a sheepdog, born and bred to live close to man; and it is only by living thus that he will give his owner the full benefit of his unique nature.

When we come to choose our foundation bitch, if we decide to look for an adult, we are bound to be restricted by the price we are able to pay. Adult German Shepherd Dogs are often advertised at prices ranging from one hundred to several hundreds of pounds, the higher prices being governed by show successes, or sometimes by the fact that the bitch has already produced winning stock, or is of exceptional breeding with a reputation for good reproduction.

In one respect we must be firm with ourselves. We will not be biased by colour. German Shepherd Dogs come in such a variety of colours and combinations of colours that it is difficult not to like one more than another. It is easy to say, 'I know that bitch is just what I am looking for, but I really wanted a black and gold,' or, 'I do realise that this one is the better of the two, but I do not care for sables.' Colour, providing it is rich, with good pigmentation, is of negligible importance in a

working Shepherd Dog. It is probably the least important consideration, yet some foolish people allow it to blind them to
many other breed characteristics.

If the 'best buy' bitch is not the colour that attracts you most,
you can always try to find a dog to mate with her, which will give
you the colouring you admire. While we would never, for a
moment, allow the colour of a stud dog to influence us, the fact
is there are so many well-bred dogs available that it is often
possible to indulge one's fancies even within a strain. Few
families of German Shepherd Dogs adhere rigidly to one particular colour or marking.

We beseech the beginner, therefore, to pay attention to
temperament and type – for the most glamorous-looking
German Shepherd Dog is a worthless creature if it is shy or
uncertain-tempered. Satisfy yourself that the character of the
animal is beyond reproach, and then, only then, begin to look
for the various show points that go towards making an ideal
Shepherd Dog. Do not buy any animal which you do not feel
attracted to and like as a specimen, or one that does not like
you: a mutual warmth of feeling is the best basis for a future
happy relationship between dog and owner.

8

Bringing Up a Puppy and Keeping an Adult

WE INTEND to start this chapter by assuming that you have acquired a sturdy puppy. For if you have been unwise enough to saddle yourself with one that has not been given a good start in life, we can only offer sympathy and the suggestion that, while our advice will help, probably nothing can undo the harm already done to the puppy in the first few weeks of its life.

It is usual, with each puppy purchased, to receive a pedigree, a Kennel Club registration card and transfer – if it has been registered – and a diet chart.

Breeders do not all think alike when it comes to feeding puppies. Some give as many as five or six meals daily, others think that three or four suffice. Milk and cereal meals may take many forms but on one point everyone who understands the rearing of good dogs agrees – German Shepherd Dogs, from an early age, require plenty of meat.

The aim should be to get as much nourishment into the puppy as it will take without being overfed, and it must have plenty of food to keep it growing. A check in growth and development may make a great deal of difference to the dog, and can turn it into a companion-quality specimen instead of a winner.

We give the simple feeding plan used in the Druidswood kennels. The diet chart received with the new puppy you buy elsewhere may be much more complicated, but we think that it cannot give better results. We advise, however, the buyer to adhere as closely as possible to the breeder's suggested diet. A change of homes, atmosphere, and a journey are all calculated to upset a young puppy and to add a change of food as well is adding to the stress. Any alteration that seems necessary should be introduced gradually, and when the puppy has started to settle down. The quantity of food given needs to be slowly increased as the dog grows, but otherwise, if it looks well, it seems a pity to chop and change.

Be sure to ask the breeder the number of meals the puppy has been having, and the times, and try to keep to this programme for the first few days, at least. Then if you wish to give the meals earlier or later, do so gradually. For instance it does not matter much if the puppy has its breakfast at 7 a.m. or 8 a.m., so long as the regular time is punctually adhered to, and providing the next meal is spaced out properly.

Our own programme covers four meals daily, and our feeding times are 7.30 a.m., 11 a.m., 4.30 p.m. and 9.30 p.m. The only meal that varies occasionally is the late supper, which is light, and it does not seem to matter if it is given later. As a basic rule, milk is best fortified with one cereal or another. Meat must be minced or cut very fine when the puppies are less than ten weeks old, after that it may be given in half-inch cubes, gradually increasing in size until the dog will enjoy chewing and tearing at quite large chunks. Biscuit meal should be puppy grade, and this is kibbled into small crumbs. It must be soaked to a crumbly-moist consistency – the dogs do not like it dry and it upsets their tummies if it is sloppy. Pet-food stores and grocers shops can usually offer a variety of dog biscuits, but generally the light brown, wholemeal type are best, and the white or highly coloured meals the least desirable.

Some breeders think that home-made rusks and biscuits are superior to any bought meals, and feed their dogs on ordinary brown bread, cut into slices about three-quarters of an inch thick, or into cubes, and dried in a slow oven over a long period. Home-made dog biscuits may be concocted in a great many ways – indeed the permutations are almost endless. A useful biscuit is made from oatmeal, mixed to a very thick, gooey paste with some melted dripping and water or milk. A little sugar, grated cheese or meat extract can be added, and the mass turned into a large baking tin, flattened with a knife and marked in squares. Long, slow baking in a cool oven produces biscuits that taste and smell delicious. Whether they are, in fact, better and more nutritious than good-quality proprietary brands is hard to say, but certainly if one keeps a lot of dogs it is hardly practicable to bake their biscuits, and far easier to buy 56 lb. or 112 lb. in sacks.

Broth is made by boiling some of the meat, which should not be fat, and pouring it on to the biscuit when it is hot but off the boil. For some reason, boiling stock makes biscuit meal pasty and unappetising. If, by accident, you pour too much broth into the bowl, pour the surplus away, or strain it off and squeeze the excess out of the meal which thus becomes crumbly. When cool, it is ready to feed – hot food gives dogs diarrhoea.

We are always hesitant about suggesting the quantities of food required, for even within a breed, individual animals vary greatly in their requirements, and of course puppies also vary in size. A litter of nine or ten puppies however well-reared will start off smaller than the puppies on a dam that has whelped a mere two or three. Clearly, the larger puppies will eat more.

We have given a rough idea of the amount of food likely to be needed with our diet sheet, but an intelligent approach is needed. If the puppy looks blown out and distended, if the tummy feels taut and hard, and if it grunts, sits down looking uncomfortable and uneasy, it has had too much to eat. Give less next time. The puppy should look full, nicely rounded out, and should still be licking the dish or sniffing around for crumbs, if it has had sufficient, but not too much.

Clever puppy rearers are sometimes thought to possess a special gift, just as people with 'green fingers' are those whose gardens flourish with apparent ease when others struggle with theirs unsuccessfully. In fact, beautifully reared puppies are the product of plain commonsense, of feeding ample and good quality foods, and of devoting a lot of time and attention to their well-being. You cannot make a good job of puppy-rearing if you count the cost every time you buy a sack of meat and try to economise. Nor will you succeed if you need to go out and about and leave the puppy or puppies at home for hours unattended. Do not say, 'It won't hurt him to miss a meal or two now and again,' because it will. Do not say, 'I had to leave the puppy shut up today but I don't suppose it will matter' – if it misses its exercise and fresh air, it will suffer. If you plan to bring up a puppy or a litter, be prepared to stay at home and make some sacrifices. The results will be rewarding.

After all, a puppy is only a puppy for 12 months, and towards the end of that period it is fast becoming grown up. At the end of that period it will only require one or at the most two meals per day, and although it will need more exercising it should be able to fit in better with the household routine and become far less demanding.

Careful feeding should keep the puppy free from stomach troubles, but admittedly it does not take much to upset a young German Shepherd Dog. Very warm food, as we have said, is bad, but even worse is food taken straight from a refrigerator – this should always be kept in a warm place to remove the chill before feeding. Irregular feeding times may cause an upset, a change of biscuit meal, too much food at one time, etc. Loose stools caused by something of this nature can be fairly easily corrected and as long as the puppy is lively and has no temperature there is no need to worry. Sometimes the matter can be put right by just letting the puppy miss a meal and go eight hours between meals with just a drink of water. If this does not do the trick, stop meat and biscuits and put the puppy on carefully boned boiled white fish. Cod or haddock fillet are suitable, and not ruinously expensive. Boiled rice, made palatable by a *very* little gravy or sugared milk, is splendid, too, but it must be well strained and fed stodgy and not sloppy.

If the disorder persists for more than a couple of days it is best to call the Veterinary Surgeon, who should be summoned immediately if the puppy appears dull, disinclined to eat or is vomiting.

When the puppy is about five months old, three meals are sufficient. Breakfast should consist of milky cereal, the main meal of raw or lightly cooked meal, and the other of terrier-grade (this is larger than the puppy meal) biscuit soaked with stock.

As an adult, the quantity of food depends not only on the size of the dog, but on the kind of life it leads. A pet German Shepherd Dog, living in a suburb, taking most of its walks on a leash with perhaps a short, sharp gallop in a park, will not need nearly so much food as a working police- or sheepdog, ranging over open country and probably covering as much as 20 miles each day.

The domesticated dog will do well on 1½ lb. of meat daily, plus biscuits to appetite, the working dog can take double, and the in-whelp bitch will eat up to 6 lb. meat when she is showing heavy.

A wide variety of 'extras' are on the market, and new preparations are constantly being advertised. These include yeast tablets, calcium in various forms, bone meal, seaweed powder, and compound vitamin powders. Also tonics such as Parrish's chemical food, Minadex, and cod-liver oil, with or without malt. Virol and Roboleine, though not cheap, are excellent and dogs love the toffee-like flavour. Most puppies will lick these, and also cod-liver oil and malt, off the back of the spoon.

In our own kennel we use yeast tablets, sterilised bone flour, seaweed powder, and Minadex; we buy the latter in huge bottles known to the pharmaceutical profession as 'Winchester's', a saving on the small bottles more in demand for human youngsters.

Throughout all this well-planned feeding programme, care must be taken to make sure that the dog is free from worms. All the good food, all the extras, will be wasted if the puppy is infested with these parasites. Very few puppies are naturally free from worms, and it is now thought that they are often born with them. Consequently we worm our puppies twice before we sell them – at five or six weeks, and at seven or eight weeks, and most breeders do likewise. Check this when you take delivery of a new puppy, but if you suspect worms, ask the Veterinary Surgeon to prescribe something. There are several relatively new preparations that are most effective, only obtainable through the Veterinary profession and not sold over the counter at the chemist or the pet shop.

We have come a long way since the dog book, published at the end of the last century, advised a mixture of turpentine and powdered glass to kill worms. We are quite prepared to believe it killed them – also that it often killed the dog as well. Most of the older but far less alarming 'cures' were safe and effective but involved fasting the dog for twelve hours or so, and produced distressing colic and vomiting. Some were tiresome to give, two doses at hourly intervals, followed with castor oil an hour later, being required. The modern preparations may be given immediately following a light meal, do not distress the dog unduly and effectively clear the worms. What are the signs of worms? A worm or worms may be passed in the stools. The dog's coat may lack lustre, and it may look unthrifty in spite of having a voracious appetite. A pot-bellied appearance after meals is another indication. Round worms are common in puppies, tape worms more usual in adults. Both types require different medicines to clear them, and the latter are by far the most obstinate and difficult to eradicate. If in doubt as to whether a dog has or has not got worms, if the type of worm is uncertain, take a sample of a stool to the Veterinary Surgeon. He will examine it, and if it contains the larvae of the pests, prescribe the right cure.

Once a dog has been cleared of worms, scrupulous cleanliness will help to prevent re-infestation. Concrete runs are easily disinfected, but grass enclosures are difficult to keep hygienic and are considered to be a fruitful source of worms in dogs. Probably the ideal is to have two runs, keeping the dogs in one while the other is rested for a period and if necessary dug or ploughed up and limed, or treated with a flame-thrower. Farmers sometimes use the latter to destroy weeds, and though they need to be used with care by experienced people, they are marvellously effective at their job.

Kennels should be kept clean all the time, but extra swabbing with hot water and domestic soda, with or without some disinfectant, is the answer. Cracks in a floor are easily treated with a blow-lamp. The new Calor gas blow-lamps are much easier to work than the old-fashioned petrol or paraffin types, and much safer. Apart from destroying worms, all the above treatments are recommended for fleas, lice, and germs that may be left after a dog has been suffering from an infectious disease or a skin complaint such as sarcoptic mange.

A puppy kept indoors will run on carpets, and these should be well washed with a cloth wrung out in hot soda water and detergent. It is really unwise to bring up more than one young puppy at a time indoors. It makes house training very difficult, to say the least of it, if there is doubt as to which culprit has 'spent a penny', and although German Shepherd Dogs are a naturally clean and fastidious breed (we have one which will not walk across a dirty floor) they do need some teaching when they are living in the house.

A puppy should be taken out whenever it wakes up from a sleep, and whenever it has had a meal – these are the real 'danger' times, though accidents can and do happen at most unexpected moments. Stay with the puppy until it does what is expected of it, praise it, fuss it, congratulate it, but scold it severely if it makes a mess inside. Training is seldom much of a problem if there is a garden, but brave people who go about it in a town house or flat have special problems. The flat dweller is probably wise to start putting the puppy on newspapers after meals, and whenever it is possible to take it downstairs and outside, to place a square of paper on the spot where it is invited to perform. The piece of paper can be gradually reduced in size by which time, with ordinary luck, the puppy will have got the hang of things and will be using that corner of the yard.

The ideal place for a German Shepherd Dog is in the home, with the family. Not only does this environment develop his character, but it also puts him in the very best position as a watch dog and guard. The silliest idea is the old one, with the watch dog chained to a kennel outside. He can bark a warning but is otherwise useless. Loose around the house he is a real defender.

If there are a number of dogs, then it is scarcely practicable to keep them all indoors. Kennels and runs must be provided, but every effort made to give them companionship in turns. Kennels can be sectional, of wood, or made of asbestos; or built from breeze or concrete blocks, or of brick. Floors can also be of wood, of concrete, or tiles. Wooden kennels must never be set directly on the ground, but raised up to allow a free circulation of air.

Roomy wooden sleeping benches should be provided, also raised on short legs and with a board at least six or eight inches high, to keep the bedding from becoming scattered about. Young puppies need an opening at one side, and if the bench is fairly well raised, a duck board to act as a little gang-plank.

Two benches for puppies are perfect – one clean and dry and

in use, the other scrubbed and left to air in the sun and wind. A puppy run does not call for very high fencing, but it is always best to design a kennel which is suitable for dogs of all ages, and it is as easy to put up six-foot-high chain link or weldmesh as the shorter wire. A suggestion would be to plan a kennel not less than six feet square and preferably larger, with a run as large as possible.

Gates must be sturdy and made of mesh on a strong angle-iron frame. Strong bolts are essential, because a German Shepherd Dog will soon learn to lift a latch or turn a door handle.

Fresh, clean water should be available at all times for dogs of all ages beyond the very baby puppy stage (up until eight weeks or so they seldom drink water but paddle in it and slop it all over themselves and their kennels) so provide a heavy bucket or trough.

Given a nice big run, and released for play periods in house and/or garden at intervals throughout the day, the puppies do not need to be taken out for walks on streets or in public parks. Until their inoculations against hard-pad and distemper become effective, it is unwise to take them anywhere where other dogs may have been carrying infection.

Resistance against disease gradually builds up after the injection, and should be complete at the end of four weeks. During that period, however, the dog is receiving some degree of protection but is not immune. Promising experiments have been made with a measles vaccine, said to produce immunity against virus diseases in dogs and suitable for administration at a very early age.

Once it is thought safe to take the puppy out, it will benefit from trips into the great wide world. Lead training should take place in the home, and by the time it goes on the street the puppy should be used to collar and leash. It seldom takes long to get the puppy going well, German Shepherd Dogs are so anxious to please and so happy to follow at heel.

The German Shepherd Dog is a large, active dog. If you enjoy walking, or if you live near open spaces where the dog can gambol, fetch sticks and exercise himself with the minimum of effort on your part, he is your dog. But if you live far from parks or commonland, if you do not have the time or the inclination

Ch. Athena of Hatherton

Voss v. Bern 'holding up' a flock of sheep

Sally Anne Thompson

Six months dog preparing to go on the arm for manwork

A guide dog shows its skill

Guide dog and owner off-duty

Sally Anne Thompson

Druidswood Octavia

Sally Anne Thompson

Actionnaire of Druidswood, six months puppy in show stance

to take a dog for good long daily walks – please get a much smaller breed.

Plenty of people keep German Shepherd Dogs in London and yet manage to do them justice. It is a question of how much time one is able and willing to spare, since most people can get to parks if they are not in too much of a hurry and do not have too many other things to do. It is not always town dogs that suffer from lack of exercise and freedom, either. Lots of dogs are kept in country districts by people who are too lazy or too thoughtless to take them for proper walks, and it is very unfair to the dogs.

Be firm with the puppy – it is laughable if it is disobedient and naughty when it is three months old, but a serious matter if it keeps its bad habits until it is fully grown. Scold the little creature when it does wrong, but be sure to praise and pet it when it behaves well. We will deal more fully with actual training in Chapter 10, for the subject is all-important. A young dog is much easier to train than one that is older, and a well-disciplined, obedient dog is a joy to own. Time and trouble spent on the puppy's education is an investment that pays off handsomely as it grows older.

Druidswood puppies are fed four times daily from two months onwards. The early breakfast is important, as the little ones are hungry after the long night. Milk is not really a dog's food and can cause diarrhoea if fed undiluted. Also, it varies in quality and freshness, so tinned evaporated milk (Ideal or Carnation) tends to give better results. It is also more convenient and a little cheaper than dairy milk. These comments do not apply to those fortunate enough to keep cows or goats; but the milk should be diluted half-and-half with warm water, or poured onto the porridge and mixed well.

Breakfast
7.30 a.m.
¼ pint of semolina porridge or lightly cooked barley flakes (obtainable loose from health shops)
One teaspoonful honey, glucose or brown sugar
2 calcium tablets with Vitamin D crushed up
½ pint diluted evaporated milk, or dairy or goat's milk.

For the porridge, sprinkle a dessertspoonful of semolina into water, bring to boil and cook for 10 minutes, stirring well. When cool, add the honey, calcium and milk, taking care the mixture is not too warm when feeding. The barley flakes need only a few minutes' cooking. Make a double quantity at night, and keep the breakfast portion in a thermos.

Lunch
11 a.m.
8 oz. fresh chopped meat, either raw if fit for human consumption, otherwise lightly cooked. One handful wholemeal rusk.
2 seaweed tablets crushed up. One dessertspoonful finely grated carrot. Mix with a little bone broth.

Tea
4.30 p.m.
Repeat the 11 a.m. meal.

Supper
9.30-10.30 p.m., or even later
Same as breakfast, after which the puppy should be taken outside to relieve himself and have a run in the fresh air. Give him a large cooked marrow bone (raw ones are liable to contain maggots, and small ones splinter and can cause damage to throat and stomach). Alternatively give a large wholemeal biscuit to chew, so that he is less likely to be noisy when left alone for the night.

We always feel that sending a puppy to its new home is rather like sending a child away to school: the things which are most missed are familiar foods and routine and, for puppies, familiar smells, too. So we do our best to ease the transitional period by giving full instructions to the new owners, also promising them any necessary help or advice if required at any time. When a puppy is booked, we ask the clients if they will send a small piece of old blanket or a small sweater to put in the puppy's play kennel. There it is dragged around, sometimes torn a little or wet upon, all of which gives it a lovely comforting scent when the lonely one is given it to sleep upon.

9

Showing the German Shepherd Dog

BEFORE we contemplate taking our German Shepherd Dog to
a show we need to know something of the complexities
involved. To begin with, there are various types of dog shows,
though all must be held under Kennel Club rules.

At the bottom of the scale come the Exemption Shows and
the Matches. The former are frequently held in conjunction
with horse shows, agricultural shows, or charity fêtes. They
may have four classes confined to thoroughbred dogs, and any
number of 'fun' classes in which any dog, mongrel or otherwise,
may compete. Dogs entered for any of the classes at Exemption
Shows do not have to be registered at the Kennel Club in order
to compete, though in fact many of the competitors at this type
of show probably are registered.

Matches are organised by dog clubs, and entrants are judged
in pairs, rather the same system used at a knock-out tennis
tournament with semi-finals and finals and an ultimate single
winner. Sometimes these matches are for any variety of dog,
sometimes they are one particular breed against another breed,
or a breed against 'the rest' which may be any kind of dog.
Shows of this type have a leisurely atmosphere and are regarded
as social gatherings rather than serious competitions. They are
very useful 'nurseries' for puppies destined for greater things,
and many a budding Champion has been introduced to the big
wide world at an Exemption Show or Match. It cannot be said
that wins at either are of very great consequence, but for
schooling inexperienced and partly trained dogs they have
much to offer, and are generally enjoyed by experienced
exhibitor and raw beginner alike.

The next step up the ladder is the Sanction Show. This
usually consists of around 20 classes, sometimes subdivided

into classes confined to breeds popular in the neighbourhood with a few, any variety, classes, sometimes with variety classes only. Then there are Limited Shows, so called because they are restricted to members of the organising clubs, some provide benches for dogs, others do not. Open shows are not very far removed from Limited, but generally put on more classes and are sometimes benched – the other types of show mentioned seldom are.

Open Shows, as the name suggests, are open to all and not confined to members of a club or society. Challenge Certificate winners may be shown, but they would not be eligible for the other types, excepting in the case of Exemption Shows. The fact that they can be shown at these, the most humble of them all, seems odd until we realise that if the Kennel Club does not require competitors to be registered it cannot control the amount of winning the entrants may have done since it has no way of checking up on the prize-winners. Very occasionally one hears of a Champion being shown at an Exemption Show, but this is rare indeed, and, in general, owners consider it beneath their dignity to parade their star exhibits at these little shows, and regard the practice as 'pot-hunting'.

A great many carry the sporting spirit still further and do not show Champions at Open Shows though this is permissible. Opinions differ as to the rights and wrongs of this custom, many holding that as there are plenty of Championship Shows for the best dogs to go to, it is showing a grasping mentality to collect prizes at the smaller shows. Better to leave them for the up and coming winners, they say.

Championship Shows are the 'Ascots' of the world of dogs. At the present time, there are twenty-three all-breed Championship Shows at which Challenge Certificates are offered for German Shepherd Dogs, and about half a dozen Championship Shows put on by breed societies and/or training clubs. At first it sounds like a great number of chances to make a dog a Champion, until one considers the enormous entries and our system of making Champions, which we will deal with later in this chapter.

A one-breed show, run by a senior breed club, is rated immensely important by the exhibitors and the public, but without question the greatest of all dog shows is Cruft's. Held in February each year, always in London, this is the world's largest dog show and draws fantastic numbers of dogs under one roof for three consecutive days. The German Shepherd Dogs are so numerous that two judges are appointed, one for dogs and the other for bitches. In 1958, when the writer judged German Shepherd Dog bitches, there were 6,916 dogs entered, of which 305 were German Shepherd Dogs. Since then the total entry continues to rise at speed, and it is becoming a problem to know how to accommodate so many animals and people.

At the end of this remarkable show there is the exciting competition for the dog adjudged Best in Show. Although all the best German Shepherd Dogs, down the years, have been exhibited at Cruft's, and although some have come very close to the top, it was not until 1965 that a German Shepherd Dog was selected as Supreme Champion. This great honour went to Ch. Fenton of Kentwood, owned and bred by Miss Sonnica Godden, and we have a picture of this magnificent dog on the first page of the first photographic section.

A prize of any kind at Cruft's is greatly coveted, but so are the awards at all the other Championship shows. Especially valuable, and always hard to win, are the Challenge Certificates. The Kennel Club has a carefully worked-out system of allocating these certificates annually, the number offered for various breeds depending on the respective registration totals. Registrations effected in, say, 1974, determined the number of 'C.C.s', as exhibitors call them, which any breed received in 1976.

Rare breeds may not qualify for certificates at all. Other scarce breeds may manage sufficient registrations to gain them four or six sets of certificates in a year. German Shepherd Dogs, at the present time and enjoying as they do such continued popularity, tot up very high registration figures year after year, and consequently they are able to compete for certificates at all the general Championship Shows as well as their various breed-club events.

The Challenge Certificates are always offered in pairs, one for the best dog, the other for the best bitch, and the judge must be able to sign a declaration stating that the animal is 'of such outstanding merit as to be worthy of the title of Champion' – otherwise the C.C. should not be awarded.

Three certificates won under three different judges, and the dog or bitch is a Champion. Reserve Best of Sex awards are also made to the deserving runners-up in each sex, and these are referred to as 'Reserve C.C.s'. In the event of a Challenge Certificate winner being disqualified after a show, through some contravention of the rules, the judge is asked if the Reserve Best of Sex winner is worthy of the C.C. and if the answer is 'Yes,' it is thus awarded. It might be thought that to win a Reserve C.C. implies that the animal has had to play 'second fiddle' to a more successful dog, but in fact such awards are highly valued by exhibitors even though they do not help a dog to gain a title. An exhibit that wins Reserve C.C is usually a very good specimen, and probably little divides it from the one above. Under different judges they may well change places, thus it is generally conceded that a Reserve C.C. winner has a good chance of becoming a Champion.

Under our system in Britain, it is much more difficult to make dogs Champions than in most other countries. In the first place, competition is tremendous with great numbers of dogs being shown. Secondly, once a dog becomes a Champion he need not be retired from winning certificates. True, collecting them does not make him a Champion over again, but every C.C. won emphasises his superiority and has tremendous prestige value. Among the most successful 'collectors' of C.C.s in this connection were Ch. Caro of Welham, Ch. Roland of Coulmony, Ch. Avon Prince of Alumvale, Ch. Asoka Cherusker, and Ch. Athena of Hatherton; and latterly, Ch. Hendrawens Spartacist, Ch. Royvon's Red Rum (record holder with 48 C.C.s), Ch. Delridge Erhard and Ch. Muscava's Rocky, all of which won impressive numbers of the essential and highly valued big green certificates.

The system which allows famous dogs to continue to win Challenge Certificates after gaining the first three has always come in for some criticism, since each C.C. won deprives another dog of a step towards its title. On the other hand, the argument put forward is that if Champions retire, the next best

dog moves up and wins, that dog retires when it has three certificates leaving the field open for the next. It is easy to see that
this must eventually lead to inferior dogs becoming Champions if the best retires in favour of the second-best, and then
the third-best moves up to make way for the fourth in order of
merit. Certain other countries do in fact work their Championships on very much these lines, and they do, as one would
expect, make large numbers of Champions, the best very good
but the majority somewhat inferior.

In our own country, however, there have been many instances
in which a dog (or bitch) has won two Challenge Certificates,
and then, in spite of it being widely exhibited and given every
chance to get the all-important third, it has met defeat from
reigning Champions. Perhaps such Champions are just adding
to their collection – a perfectly legitimate pastime and accepted procedure at dog shows – and it does seem hard that the
other, probably deserving, dog is recurrently pegged back. It is
very discouraging to be awarded, say, eleven or more Reserve
C.C.s while the longed-for certificate is just one more 'scalp' for
the Champion's score. Under this system it cannot be denied
that very many worthy dogs have narrowly missed becoming
Champions, and it is sadly disappointing for their owners. At
the same time it is an insurance against 'cheap' 'two-a-penny'
Champions, and until somebody thinks up a better system we
have to accept it as it is now.

The German Shepherd Dog breed has had recurrent periods
during which certain outstanding dogs and bitches have
dominated the big shows, and many a good dog or bitch has
been retired without ever gaining its deserts. Today, however,
the quality throughout the German Shepherd Dog breed in
Britain is such that there are normally half a dozen or more
dogs of such equal merit that they change places under different judges whose opinions vary from show to show.

At the present time no one animal is having things all its own
way, and competititon is very strong indeed. There appears to
be no reason why an outstanding German Shepherd Dog,
faultlessly conditioned and shown, and consistently cam-
paigned, should not go right to the top, and to reach this pinnacle is the aim of every exhibitor. There is a saying that

success, if easily attained, is not worth having. Very true – but success rarely comes easily to the dog breeder.

Many beginners plunge straight into the deep end, metaphorically speaking, by starting as they mean to go on and entering their dog or dogs at a Championship Show. There is nothing wrong about this, but in general it is wiser to give a dog a trial run at a smaller type of show. Entry fees for these little shows cost less, and it means that the dog can get some practice and the handler can judge how he behaves before embarking on an expensive showing venture for which each class may cost £7 or more. If we watch the expert handlers showing their dogs, it all looks too easy. The dog stands in the correct position, one hind leg extended, both front legs true, elegant neck extended, ears erect, a picture of nobility and poise. The cleverer the handler, the less he or she seems to do – the dog appears to do it all. One wonders who is showing whom! Then the gaiting commences, the dog flows over the ground, striding out with the front legs, thrusting forward with powerful hindquarters – there is nothing to it, we think. How wrong can we be!

Weeks of patient training have produced this picture. Years of perseverence have taught the handler the skills required to get the best out of a dog. We should not expect to compete with them on equal terms, at least until we have had more practice.

The remarkable interest in training, which continues to expand at such an astounding rate, means that classes are held in most parts of the country, and only a few unlucky people live very far away from such valuable means of instruction. The ambitious dog-show exhibitor should join a club, seek out classes and persevere until the dog is obedient. It should, when possible, start attending classes any time after its inoculations against distemper are deemed effective – and this is usually about four or five months of age. It is important to make sure that the puppy enjoys his outings, and that lessons are gradual: 'Cramming' is undesirable.

Study the pictures of Champion German Shepherd Dogs. See how they are posed to show off their good points. Standing four-square, not leaning back on the front legs but perfectly balanced, with one hindleg extended backwards. Tail hangs down, ears are erect and the general expression is keen and alert. These dogs have also learned to trot on a loose lead, never pulling or lunging forward, never hanging back. And never, but never, leaping in the air or galloping. These dogs have also been trained to stand quietly while strangers examine their teeth, feel their muscles, press their backs, and they must not flinch or draw back. Certainly they must not show any resentment.

This is dog-show procedure for the German Shepherd Dog breed, and until a puppy knows the ropes it is a waste of time and money taking it to an important show. As soon as it becomes obedient and attentive, however, the puppy may be taken to a show – and preferably a small one, as we have already suggested.

Dog shows are advertised in the weekly dog Press, *Our Dogs* and *Dog World*. These can sometimes be bought off station bookstalls and newsagent's counters, but commonly have to be ordered in advance. Choose a show conveniently located, and write for a schedule.

When this arrives it will contain details of the classes, the names of the judges, other information such as the time the show will commence and finish, and an entry form. There will also be definitions of classes and regulations, all of which should be carefully studied. This is plain sailing to any experienced exhibitor but can appear complicated at first glance, so if in doubt as to the best classes in which to enter, or with any other queries, telephone the secretary or ask another exhibitor friend for advice. Help can usually be sought from the person from whom the puppy was purchased, or if it is home-bred, from the owner of the sire.

Never send entry fees in cash – always by cheque or postal order or money order. Note particularly the date when entries close – if yours arrive late they will probably be returned. By the time the entries are made the dog should be in show condition, for if it is over fat, on the lean side, or shedding its coat, there will not be sufficient time left to get it into show trim by the great day.

There can be no relaxation, though. Regular daily exercise and brisk grooming are both essential, and very careful feeding to keep the puppy in peak condition is advisable. Loose hair should be removed with a metal comb with teeth about ⅛ in. apart (the type with a wooden handle is most suitable) and two brushes will be needed. One should be an ordinary dandy brush, the fibre type such as are used for horses, the other should be oval in shape and made with short, stiff bristles. It may have a webbing or leather strap across the back, making it easier to hold. After combing, brush well all over with the dandy, then with the bristle brush, and finally polish the coat well – especially on the body – with a square of corduroy velvet, a soft yellow duster or a silk handkerchief. Brushes should be frequently washed, rinsed well in cold water and dried in the fresh air.

If a dog gets muddy or wet during exercise, it can be cleaned and dried very easily by the following method. Get a bucket of hot water and a fair-sized chamois leather. Wring out the leather in the water and wipe the dog well paying great attention to the thick ruff, the hair on chest and under the brisket, and to the fluffy trousers and under part of tail. Keep dousing the leather in the bucket, wringing it dry, and rubbing. The dog can be spotlessly cleaned by this method and if properly carried out, it renders it almost bone dry, far more efficiently than drying with a bath towel – and who wants to launder muddy towels, anyway?

A dog groomed daily, dried as described above, and healthy, very rarely needs a bath. In rural districts many German Shepherd Dogs go for years without being washed, but in industrial or sooty areas it may be necessary to dip them to brighten up the coats, especially the light-coloured portions.

If a bath is thought necessary, be sure to do it well ahead of the show date – otherwise the water will make the coat loose and woolly, it may fluff up and spoil the appearance. Coats take a day or two to settle after thorough wetting, so bath four or five days before the show.

Any good make of dog shampoo, or the best makes used for human hair, are suitable, but beware of household detergents of the powdered type which are not good for dogs. Always rinse the dog well, any soap left behind makes the hair sticky and dull, and wipe him dry with a clean chamois leather and fresh, warm water. Finish with a clean terry towel if thought necessary and give him a sharp gallop in the fresh air. Never bath a dog and put it in the garden or a run until it is bone dry, for if allowed to sit about on a chilly day it can get a cold.

A day or two before the dog show, pack a canvas 'zip' bag with the various items likely to be needed. It will say on the schedule if the show is unbenched; if benched take a chain and a well-fitting leather collar. Bench chains are made in various weights, with swivels either end and rings at intervals so that the dog can be safely secured. It must be able to lie down comfortably but not be able to lean right out or fall over the edge. The collar should never be tight, but if loose the dog might wriggle out of it. If two or three fingers can be slipped between collar and neck it is about right.

Most handlers like to show German Shepherd Dogs on a fine link chain collar and a light bridle leather leash. There is a right and a wrong way of putting a chain collar over a dog's head, and any experienced show-goer or training enthusiast will demonstrate this to a beginner.

Chain collars give the handler more control over the dog than is possible with a round or flat leather collar. Pack a brush and comb, polishing cloth, and a small rug or square of blanket to make the bench more comfortable and less bare-looking. If you feel that all this amounts to more than you can conveniently carry, take a roll of newspapers instead of a rug. They do not look very nice but are quite warm for the dog to lie on. Pack a plastic drinking bowl, two if you plan to feed the dog at the show. Order a half-pound of liver from the butcher, boil it, drain it, and cut into small squares. Put it in a plastic bag in a cold place, tie a knot in your hanky in case you forget it. Pack a tin of meat or the dog's usual meal in another plastic bag, unless you expect to arrive home in time to feed him when you get back. The liver is needed in any case to keep him alert in the ring and to reward good behaviour.

Take a small towel, in case the puppy gets wet or muddy between railway station or car park, and the show. It might be needed if he is travel-sick, and if possible he should be used to motor cars before a show day, as chronic vomiting takes a lot out of an animal and almost always upsets it. Some German Shepherd Dogs love travelling and never feel sick, others begin to dribble at the sight of a car and even before it is backed out of a garage. This type needs sedatives and the Veterinary Surgeon should be consulted. Unfortunately the tablets prescribed do tend to make the dog rather dull and dopy, but probably less so than when it is ill throughout a long drive.

Allow plenty of time, in any event, so that the dog gets a chance to look around and become adjusted to the strange surroundings before judging commences. Rushing the dog straight out of the car and into the ring is not fair, and prejudices chances of success. On arrival, finish grooming and let the puppy rest quietly on his bench. Stay with him if he does not like being left, but keep an eye on the ring. Stewards sometimes walk round the benches herding up exhibitors, and sometimes classes are called by loudspeaker, but this is not compulsory and the onus is on the exhibitor to be in the right place at the right time.

The steward will hand out numbers. Pin yours firmly to the left-hand side of the chest so that it is clearly visible to the officials in the ring as you walk round with the dog led on your left-hand side. Judges get very irritable with people who tuck their ring cards into breast pockets or wear them inside jackets and coats.

Hold the loop end of the lead in the right hand, steady the dog with the left, and follow the other exhibitors as they circle the ring at a brisk pace. Don't let the dog pull or gallop, and do not allow it to sniff the dog in front. One by one the exhibitors will take their dogs to the judge, who will examine it, ask the age, and wish to see the teeth. It is here that many a novice falls down for want of practice, for the dog should stand or sit quietly while the lips are gently lifted, first in front to show the 'bite', then one side, then the other. Busy judges with a long list of classes to judge by a certain time have neither the time nor inclination to participate in a wrestling match in which they, the dog, the handler, and perhaps the stewards all struggle to hold the dog still long enough to see if its dentition is correct.

On request, the dog must be walked up the ring and down again, and then trotted round in a circle. Wait quietly in line until each dog has been seen, and then when judge or steward indicates that the class should play follow-my-leader again, get ready to walk round once more.

The judge may start placing the dogs in the chosen order as they circle the ring, or may halt the class and ask the selected four or five to come into the centre of the ring to be placed. The steward hands out prize cards, the judge marks the judging book, makes notes if necessary and the exhibitors leave the ring. If you are lucky enough to receive a card, you are well and truly launched, and are clearly off to a very good start. If your dog has not been placed, however, do not be too despondent. In spite of the fact that there is a breed standard, it is a fact that different judges put different interpretations on it, and it is not only possible for a dog to win a first prize at one show and be ignored at another – but it frequently happens.

If the dog has won a pize, it will be criticised and reported on in the subsequent edition of the dog Press, and the judge's opinion will be publicly proclaimed. The losers do not come in for comment, however, and very often their owners are most anxious to know why they have not appealed to the judge.

Judges are much too busy to talk to exhibitors until all the classes are completed, and even then some of them have to rush away to catch trains or planes, or to try to beat fog and bad weather by road. There is no harm in approaching a judge, however, and asking an opinion on a dog. If there is no time for this, just drop a line after the show, giving the dog's name, number and the first class in which it appeared, and enclosing a stamped addressed envelope and a short note saying that a critique would be appreciated. Most judges will co-operate whenever possible.

Failing the opinion of the judge, it is well worth while asking some of the successful exhibitors what they think about the loser's future chances. True, opinions may vary and the puzzled owner may feel he knows more and more about less and less – but it is more likely he will get some concrete information and be told, bluntly, if it is worth while showing the dog at other shows under other judges, or if it is really not good enough to justify the expenditure of time and money.

For instance the dog may be promising but simply too immature to reach the heights. The remedy for this is obvious – wait a while, then enter for another show. Maybe it could be improved with more weight, less weight, more exercise, better ring deportment – a little advice on such matters and things may work out better next time.

In German Shepherd Dogs, the splendid thing is that if a favourite dog turns out disappointing from the beauty angle, if the temperament is all right it can still become an obedience class star or even a working Champion, for brains and not looks are called for here. Of course, it is wonderful to combine both, and the most commendable thing in the world is to own a dog that is of Champion class in construction, type, movement and character, and which can go to the top at Obedience Shows and Working Trials. But there have been plenty of magnificent workers, not only homely to behold but often downright ugly. Yet they have made names for themselves, given their owners pleasure and been splendid ambassadors for the breed.

If a dog wins well, it is an encouraging start and there is an excuse to travel farther afield in search of fresh triumphs. Many beginners, wisely starting off at one or two small local shows, find themselves caught up in the whirlpool of dog shows, and whenever possible dash off to all kinds of distant places in the hopes of attaining honours at important shows all over England, Scotland, Ireland, and Wales.

This becomes, alas, expensive, but the more widely a dog can be exhibited the greater a reputation it can build for itself. Once a dog rises to really great heights and is considered to be in the running for Challenge Certificates, it is almost certainly necessary to travel the country if it is to have a show career to match its merits.

Is such an outlay justified? Is there any hope of recovering expenses? This is hard to say, for too many factors are involved. In general a Champion will be in demand at stud, and if much patronised by breeders can be a very acceptable source of income to its owner. Bitches are less likely to repay the cost of a campaign, since even if they become Champions their litters seldom fetch very much more than the current price for good-quality puppies.

A Champion can usually be sold for a substantial sum, though comparatively few go to new homes. One likes to think that it is not only the possibility of profitable stud fees or puppy sales coming in that decides owners to turn down large offers for their best animals, but the fact that the bond between man and German Shepherd Dog cannot be severed. Making a dog a Champion involves much travelling about together, the sharing of disappointments and triumphs, and success invariably calls for close understanding between dog and owner. During this period of sunshine and shadow, thrills and disappointments, it is scarcely possible to avoid an attachment. A dog may be the most magnificent Champion in its breed, the finest specimen in the world, but if it is also the beloved companion and friend of its owner, it simply has no price; and this is something that many people, especially some overseas buyers prepared to pay large sums, cannot understand.

Most people, if they are honest, admit that the most enjoyable dog shows are those at which they win well. After all, they show to win and it is hardly worth the cost and the trouble to keep on turning up without some rewards. Quite a number of people, however, seem to be satisfied with very occasional, often very modest, successes, and enjoy the shows as much for the social atmosphere as for anything more. Meeting other dog enthusiasts, watching beautiful dogs being shown, win or lose, it is a day out, and worth the effort anyway.

Why, then, do we place so much emphasis on showing? As we have seen, it is an expensive business, success is seldom certain and often elusive, it is always time-absorbing, usually exhausting. Yet it has an indescribable fascination for the majority of people who become interested, and it is easy to become almost fanatically keen on dog shows.

There is no doubt whatever that the value of a dog is enormously increased if it becomes a well-known prize-winner. In general, it needs to be a consistently well-known winner if it is to build up a lasting reputation. While any prize won is an asset, isolated wins tend to be soon forgotten and to make a great name for itself, a good dog should be kept in the public eye.

Show-goers who are constantly in the news are usually able to sell any puppies they breed easily and well, apart from benefits in the shape of stud fees.

The routine involved in conditioning a dog for show is basic the world over, though, of course, the amount of exercise, the required bathing, and the type of food and the quantity must vary a little in different climates.

The methods of actually presenting dogs in the ring to best advantage are also universally accepted, but the shows may be quite different where the arrangements of the classes are concerned, and methods of making Champions are many and various.

When we plan to show dogs in Britain, we need only familiarise ourselves with the Kennel Club rules and show regulations. The law of the land, which requires all dogs brought into the British Isles to be detained for six months in licensed quarantine kennels, makes it almost impossible for breeders to show their dogs outside the country. Such dogs would have to undergo quarantine after the international shows, and the expense, coupled with the loss of half a year's breeding and showing potential, hardly makes such an enterprise economical or practical.

Far-thinking breeders appreciate, however, that it is a mistake to become insular, and that there is often something we can learn from overseas dog breeders; consequently we like to read about shows abroad, even occasionally visit them. To appreciate the results it is important to know something about their methods of making Champions, and the way in which they arrange their shows.

In Germany, for instance, they never have the plethora of classes for German Shepherd Dogs which we have come to expect at our big shows. German shows schedule three main classes for each sex. There is the Jugend, or Youth, class, for dogs from 12 to 18 months of age; the Junghund or Young Dog class, for dogs of 18 months to 24 months old, and the Gebrauchshund class for dogs over the age of two years owning working qualifications. There are no 'certificates' such as we have here, no 'points' like they have in the U.S.A. – just one title at one show each year. This is awarded at the breed Championship or speciality Show, and the best dog is crowned as 'Sieger' with the best female as the 'Siegerin', and these titles imply that the animals are Grand Champions, for that particular year. Another year if they beat off all opposition again they can repeat their triumph, or some other outstanding animal may defeat them. The other animals are graded, the best being rated 'Excellent', the next 'Very Good', followed by those that can only receive 'Good', and then, 'Satisfactory' and 'Faulty', just as the judge assesses them. The creation of only one Champion of each sex per annum adds tremendous excitement and glamour to the German shows. When one considers that the Open Dog class in 1989 had an entry of nearly 300 animals, and that it took the judge three days to assess and grade each exhibit and then to choose the ultimate winner – the Sieger – one can easily imagine the tension and excitement as the class finished.

There is a disadvantage in having such a supreme winner, namely the ensuing rush to breed from the one male – the Sieger. No one dog can suit all bitches, and there is a limit to the amount he can be used. Some of the Siegers have turned out to be valuable and prepotent sires. Others have proved grave disappointments and obviously if such a widely used animal is a poor sire, a great deal of harm can be done to a breed. Because of this, the S.V. restricts the number of bitches which may be accepted to the Sieger – or to any dog, come to that – to 60 per annum. Not unnaturally, there has been a constant heavy drain on the Siegers over the years. While a number have remained in Germany, many have been sold overseas at astronomical prices, the U.S.A. having taken quite a large proportion over the years, and others have gone to Japan, etc. Very few German Siegers have ever come to Britain.

Mindful of the manner in which so many of what had been adjudged to be the best male German Shepherd Dogs were leaving the Fatherland, the Germans tried a new plan. In 1938 they abolished the Sieger titles altogether and instituted what they called the 'Vorzuglich Auslese' group. This comprised the animals graded 'Excellent' at the Sieger show, placed in order of merit. Thus the best dog (he would have been the Sieger under the old method) was rated Excellent I, his closest competitor, Excellent II, and so on down the line. On average something like a half-dozen dogs received Excellent and were thus graded at the principal show of the year.

Either this arrangement did not work out as hoped, or the Germans decided that spreading the major awards took most of the thrill and glamour from their major show, but at any rate in 1955 they reintroduced the Sieger titles once more. Yet another method of awards has been found workable in the United States of America, that enormous country where so many fine German Shepherd Dogs have been bred. They are used to their method and to them it seems simple but to us it is complicated.

They have, rather like the Germans, fewer classes than we do. Such classes as Puppy, Novice, Bred by Exhibitor, American-bred and Open classes are usually scheduled for each sex. Apart from a few Match Shows which resemble our Sanction Shows, virtually all the American shows are of Championship status. To win the title of Champion, a dog must win 15 points. The number of points a dog wins at a show depends upon the number of dogs entered and shown in the breed classes, and to make things even more difficult, upon the location of the show. North America has been divided into groups for the purpose of allocating points, and the American Kennel Club has the knotty problem of deciding how strong the competition will be in the various areas.

The maximum number of points that can be won at any show, irrespective of the strength of the entry, is five. Therefore no dog can win its title at less than three shows, and in this respect alone it is rather like our own system. Many minor regulations are involved, for at least two of the shows counted towards the 15 points must have entries to the value of at least three points each, and wins under the same judge do not count.

The 1st. class prize-winners compete for the designation 'Winners' and the best of the bunch – the 'Winners' dog and 'Winners' bitch – take what points are available. Then the pair compete for Best of Winners. If, for example, the entry of males earned only one point because there were few dogs shown, but the large entry of bitches rated three or five points, the dog – if he beat the bitch – would take the points due to her. The complications do not even stop here, though. Suppose the 'Best of Winners' is compared with the 'Specials' class winner. 'Specials' are the Champions, entered only in this class and able to win Best of Breed but not to collect further points nor able to prevent a non-Champion gaining points. Suppose the 'Winners' exhibit goes Best of Breed. It then goes into the Working Group, and in our hypothetical case, wins it. In this group there are dogs of other breeds which have topped large entries which entitle the winner to more points than were available in the German Shepherd classes. But the Shepherd has beaten these dogs in the group – so he gets their augmented points, better than his own.

Does this sound complicated? Well, it is! While our own system is far from perfect, it does at least react harshly on the making-up of Champions which remains difficult in almost every breed. It is hard indeed on the owners of good dogs which never quite make the grade, never quite manage to displace the reigning Champions, but it is a method whereby the making of an inferior Champion is very rare indeed.

The American system, by moving the Champions from out of the way of their next competitors, means that the best are always leaving the coast clear for second-best animals to win. The second-best move on to the upper house, and there is then nothing to stop the third-best becoming champions. Of course it does not work exactly like this all the time and in all breeds, for new exhibitors keep making appearances. But on the whole enormous numbers of pedigree dogs do become Champions in the U.S.A. and inevitably some are very much less worthy of the title than others.

The system adopted in Eire by the Irish Kennel Club is similar to the American system whereby points are offered and allocated. It does differ, however, in one important respect and that is that Irish Champions do not make way for the up and coming winners. The best dog and best bitch at I.K.C. shows win 'green stars', and these green stars may be worth one point or more according to the rating and to the number of exhibitors at that particular show. But a Champion may win one green star after another, and often does, thus making it harder for the others and keeping the standard high.

Green stars only count towards Irish Championships, and not towards English titles. Northern Ireland comes under Kennel Club rules and has one Championship show, at Belfast, each year. Challenge Certificates are offered, and these count towards the English title. A dog that has won a Championship in Eire and in England is usually referred to as an International Champion.

There is no quarantine between Britain and Northern or Southern Ireland. Nor, may we say, is there any means of importing dogs through Ireland or the Channel Islands or in any other way that obviates quarantine. We mention this because many people believe that it is possible to 'wangle' a dog into the country in some such way, but in fact dogs entering Ireland, Jersey or Guernsey from any countries other than those islands or the British mainland must go into quarantine.

10

The German Shepherd Dog at Work

EVERYBODY interested in dogs knows that there are some breeds of dogs known to be more intelligent than others. A few breeds are said to be stupid or brainless or stubborn, but even within such breeds there are found, from time to time, clever, trainable dogs that are the exception to the rule. And in a great many breeds there are a lot of very trainable dogs. But the German Shepherd Dog is unique, we believe, in being (a) the breed in which lack of trainability and intelligence is rare, and (b) the breed that not only learns to do as it is told but yearns to serve and please.

Lots of other breeds can learn to do the same sort of things one teaches a German Shepherd Dog. But they have to be *trained* to do it. The word 'trained' is used to describe the equipping of a German Shepherd Dog to do some useful work, but it is really not descriptive of what does, in fact, take place. Bluntly, one *shows* a German Shepherd Dog what to do – and it does it. True, it may be necessary to demonstrate several times, perhaps over and over again, but all the time the dog is trying to understand, is anxious to please, and is not, as is the case with many other breeds, being subjected into doing something. Until one has tried to teach a German Shepherd Dog obedience tests or other useful 'tricks' or 'stunts', and also pursued a similar course with dogs of other breeds, it is hard to understand the point we are trying to make. Regular attendants at training classes will understand because every week they see this comparison made, even if they have not, themselves, been in a position to make it by handling dogs of different breeds.

In every walk of life we meet versatile people who can 'turn a hand to anything'. Of all the varieties of dogs known to man, surely none can 'turn a paw' as does the German Shepherd Dog, achieving as it does, in varied circumstances and over and over again, tasks and deeds of valour and skill exceeding almost anything that can reasonably be expected of a member of the canine race.

It is unfortunate that the breed has never been accepted as a sheepdog in Britain. In various parts of Europe, but of course particularly in its native Germany, Shepherd Dogs can often be seen tending the flocks, and the specialised manner in which farming is managed in some areas provides the dogs with strenuous and tiring work. In our own country, sheep are normally kept in either of two ways – given free range over moorland or hill country, or fenced into meadows, enclosed by sheep-wire netting of hurdles. Our sheepdogs are expected to gather the sheep and drive them from one field to another, also to single out individual animals.

For instance, the farmer might notice that a ewe was lame, or about to start lambing. He would whistle up the dog to round up the animal and drive it into a small pen where it could be given individual attention.

With large flocks of sheep, farmers often work two or three dogs at once. Continental sheepdogs may be expected to perform these and similar tasks, but they also have to act as a 'living fence', and in the following manner. Farm land in many parts of the Continent is not enclosed into small or large paddocks as is the case in England.

Often large areas are differently cropped – grass on one section, alfalfa on another, roots or kale on the adjacent plot, and so on, with no wire or other divider between the sections. The farmer may wish to keep the sheep grazing on the strip of grassland, or perhaps, if keep is short, will let them feed on the roots for a few hours. How can he stop them straying, perhaps trampling and spoiling the other crops? If the area is not enormous he might, in this day and age, run an electric fence round the perimeter. But in the old days, and in our own time if a big piece of land is being utilised, the sheep can only be controlled by a dog. And as a matter of fact, a dog is likely to be more effective than the most modern invention, since the thick fleece renders the sheep impervious to the mild electric shock obtained by touching the wire, and unless they receive the shock via nose or horns they quickly learn that they can push through.

It is quite possible that the traveller in Germany, and in other lands, may see a Shepherd Dog running up and down a dividing line between two plots of land. On the one side the sheep will be grazing, on the other will be some other crops growing, or perhaps the same crops being preserved for later when the flock has eaten the first field bare. It can be understood that a dog capable of great endurance is required to do this. With slow, loping gait – breaking into a gallop if it sees a sheep attempting to cross the line – the dog trots to and fro, up and down for hours on end. We have watched German Shepherd Dogs at work under these conditions, and apparently showing no signs of fatigue.

There is no reason why the German Shepherd Dog should not work sheep in Britain; the breed is good at the job and quite capable of doing it anywhere, and certainly adaptable enough to be able to work well under the slightly different conditions under which sheep are normally kept here. In fact, various Shepherdites – amongst them Mrs Barrington and Mrs Beck, respectively owners of the famous Brittas and Letton kennels – have owned German Shepherd Dogs trained to herd sheep and cattle.

But the breed has never been taken up by farmers as a whole. This is because, in the first instance, when the German Shepherd Dog came to our island, we already had native breeds of sheepdogs. These were splendid workers and indeed left nothing to be desired, therefore there was no reason for farmers to try another, new, breed of dog. Shepherds were satisfied with the Shetland Sheepdogs and Scotch, Welsh and Border Collies, and their fathers and grandfathers before them had kept these dogs on their farms, together with dogs of the bob-tail type.

As we already know, it was not long before the German Shepherd Dog was getting itself a bad name through a few thoroughbreds, and cross-breds of German Shepherd Dog type, getting themselves accused of chasing and worrying sheep, and thus farmers tended to be anti-German Shepherd

Dog rather than pro-German Shepherd Dog. In any case a good deal of emphasis was put on the breed's capabilities as guard and police dogs and far less publicity given to the fact that it had been bred to be a shepherd's dog, and this all tended to discourage use in its original sphere. This situation has not greatly changed, and even today it is not uncommon to meet people who have no idea that a German Shepherd Dog is, in fact, basically just as much a sheepdog as a collie.

But whereas not all the other sheepdog breeds can be readily trained for man-work and tracking, the German Shepherd Dog shines as a star performer of the many exacting tests such work entails. The breed has had every opportunity, throughout the years, to demonstrate its aptitude for work of this nature, and is universally recognised as being an outstanding working dog.

Until the German Shepherd Dog made its presence felt, the Airedale Terrier was widely used and a number were quite successfully trained as Army and guard dogs, but once the German Shepherd Dog had been tried extensively its superiority led to it being almost exclusively kept for these important services.

Many of the imported dogs were already trained when they came over. Leading breeders made prolonged trips to Germany to study the methods there, and as one thing led to another, working trials were held and amateurs were encouraged to work their dogs.

The rules and exercises for these tests are changed from time to time, and latterly the number of entries and strength of competition have led to their being made rather more complicated. But basically the major exercises are the same as they were at the original Police Dog and Tracking Dog Trials.

The important requirements call for a dog that is able to use its nose. It must be capable of following a track, scenting any article or articles dropped by the 'escaping criminal', and retrieving same, or at least indicating the spot to the handler. For instance, a man on the run might toss away a gun or a knife, something that has been stolen or some other all-important piece of evidence. A detective searching for the criminal or chasing him would never find a small object dropped in long grass or among heather or undergrowth; but the tracker dog can find anything – even a key. The police dog has to be able to quarter the ground where, it is thought, a suspect might hide. The dog ranges over the area, using his eyes and his nose, peering into bushes, running up to sheds or outbuildings and looking into corners and crannies. If he finds a person he never attacks. He stays there, giving tongue, until the handler arrives and gives further commands. One such command might be 'Watch him,' and the dog would stand eyes fixed on the suspect, ready to spring if an attempt to escape or to attack the handler be made. If it was a perfectly innocent bystander, the dog would be called off and told to continue to 'Seek him' elsewhere.

At working trials the 'criminal' is protected against indiscriminate biting, and dogs that bite unnecessarily or are in any way badly controlled are heavily penalised and lose marks. The protection may take the form of a completely padded suit, or just a padded arm. When the 'criminal' tries to escape, he fires a gun loaded with blank cartridges as the dog runs after him, and a good police dog will ignore the explosions and seize the arm, bringing the runaway to a halt. As long as the man stands still, the dog releases him and remains there, watchful and alert but never biting or nipping. The handler arrives, disarms the man, arrests him and marches him off to the 'police station'. If he makes a run for it, or pretends to hit the handler, the dog has hold of him again immediately. Otherwise, the dog keeps close to heel, walking at the left side of the handler.

Other important tests include guarding an object – perhaps a haversack or a handbag or pocket-book – while the handler is out of sight, staying alone in sitting and lying positions until told to move, long and high jumps, and scent discrimination. Not forgetting, of course, the many important obedience tests which are the basis of all advanced training. Dogs must never be taught attack and defence work until they have learned obedience tests and are under complete control.

In any case by no means everybody is equipped to own a police-trained dog. Obedience-trained, yes – such a dog is a joy to one and all. But only very experienced handlers should attempt to do man-work.

Training, therefore, is done in carefully graded stages. Rock-firm obedience, with emphasis on a swift and unfailing recall,

154   THE GERMAN SHEPHERD DOG

are essentials. Only when these are perfected does the trainer progress towards guard and defence exercises, for a big dog in careless or unskilled hands is a dangerous weapon if it is likely to be disobedient when wholly or partly trained to attack. Even mild misdemeanours, often stemming from nothing more than boisterous good humour, though excused in a smaller dog, may be regarded very differently when it is a German Shepherd Dog that offends.

Because a well-trained dog is well behaved and an advertisement for its breed, we strongly advise anyone who buys a German Shepherd Dog to join a training club and attend the classes.

The Kennel Club, 1–4 Clarges Street, Piccadilly, London W1, can supply addresses of clubs that offer instruction, for there are a great many and meetings are held in all parts of the country. Regular training sessions, plenty of patience plus daily practice at home, together with help and advice from a competent instructor, will not only prove interesting and open new horizons, but will certainly result in a dog that is a useful companion and a pleasure to take around under any conditions. While practical experience is always desirable, much invaluable information can be gained from reading Konrad Most's excellent book *Training Dogs*, which is published by Popular Dogs Publishing Company. There is also John Cree's *Training the Alsatian* (Pelham) which is easy to read and informative. As prices change frequently we recommend that Konrad Most's and John Cree's works can be obtained from: The Secretary, The German Shepherd Dog League, Silver Lee, Sparsholt, Winchester, Hants SO21 2NZ, where help and information are readily available. Another excellent book is Sylvia Bishop's *It's Magic*, which is regarded as a significant contribution to the art of dog training and can be obtained by post from *It's Magic*, The Office, 1-10 Arundel Mews, Arundel Place, Brighton BN2 1GO (£12.95 plus £1.50 p. & p.).

It is widely known that the Royal Air Force, even in peace time, continues to train German Shepherd Dogs and uses them in a variety of ways. In particular their guard dogs patrol huge airfields, a man and a German Shepherd Dog effectively doing a job that would entail ten men without the dog. Various stunts and tricks help to develop the dog's faculties and make it obedient and attentive, and so many of the R.A.F. demonstration teams can climb ladders, jump through hoops, and retrieve awkward and unusual objects such as eggs, chairs, metal buckets and other items awkward for dogs to pick up and carry. Any exercise that urges a dog to use its senses is of value.

The serving police dogs are often in the news and all too often have to demonstrate the practical worth of their training and to show that their prowess is by no means confined to the rather artificial conditions appertaining to working trials and competitions. Many a qualified police dog 'on the beat' regularly breaks up rowdy gatherings and street brawls, disperses hostile crowds, or makes arrests, and in many cases the constable would be quite unable to restore order without the dog. There are times when the 'long arm of the law' would be ineffective without the 'cold nose of the law'.

Another invaluable achievement is the method of identifying suspects by scent. Perhaps a glove is found at the scene of the crime, or maybe nothing more than a footprint in the damp earth beneath a window. The dog is given the glove to sniff, or shown the footprint. Then it is taken to the identity parade, where amongst a line-up of individuals is one thought to be connected with the crime. The dog moves along the line, sniffing each man, and if there is one connected with the glove or the spot on the ground, it immediately identifies him.

To train a dog to compete at working trials calls for easy access to the wide open spaces, and for certain items of equipment. Obedience can be taught in a back garden, but advanced exercises need country surroundings and seclusion. This is especially necessary when teaching a dog to track, and man-work, at least in the initial stages, should be taught on private land since for obvious reasons it would be exceedingly unwise to work half-trained dogs in public parks or on commons where casual passers-by or children at play might so easily become involved.

The equipment includes a leather or webbing tracking harness, and a line, apart from a wooden dumb-bell, and these things are relatively simple to acquire. Rather more of a problem are the regulation-size long jumps and high jumps, and the padded suit to protect the 'criminal'. These things are all expensive, and only a few training clubs are in a position to loan them to members.

These problems can be overcome, but because they make it harder for the 'man in the street' to train up to advanced 'P.D.' standards, the majority of people restrict their activities to obedience work, with tracking if the environment makes this possible. It is probably a good thing that attack and defence work is beyond the reach of a majority of amateur trainers, because, as has already been stated but which cannot be over-emphasised, advanced police work is not for the novice.

The popularity of obedience competitions is one of the great features of our time. Starting, in quite a small way, by having limited appeal to only a small section of German Shepherd Dog owners, the interest grew until it spread to other breed circles and now it is not uncommon to find 60 or 70 dogs of various breeds entered in one obedience class. As can be imagined, with so many competing and with the large numbers of very skilled trainers that abound today, competition is strong. Quite frequently a dog, working exceedingly well and making one very minor mistake (perhaps failing to sit absolutely squarely at the side of the handler) will obtain 99½ marks out of 100. One might imagine that it would be certain to qualify for a first, second, or at least a third prize. But no – it is more than likely that several entrants will have worked so perfectly that they have all gained full marks. This entails a 'run off', maybe several attempts to separate the top contenders, before the final placings can be made. Many breeds compete, and the Welsh and Border Collies are usually well to the fore, but there are invariably a great many German Shepherd Dogs taking part and they always hold their own against all comers.

Obedience tests are graded, and range from the Beginners and Novice classes through the stiffer Test B and Test C, the latter being very advanced.

The Kennel Club offers Obedience Certificates at selected shows, and handlers strive to win these most coveted awards in order to gain for their dogs the title of 'Obedience

Champion'.

The Obedience Championship at Cruft's Dog Show, held every year in February at Olympia in London, is always a special feature. The classes are unique since this is the only show at which the right to compete is by invitation only. The dogs invited are those which have won Obedience Certificates during the preceding year, and a win at Cruft's confers the title of Obedience Champion on the successful competitor. This means that every dog that performs at Cruft's is an acknowledged outstanding worker, and the rings are always packed with admiring spectators.

It was, for the writer, a memorable day when Obedience Champion Copyright of Rozavel C.D.ex. won the Cruft's Obedience Championship for her owner and trainer, Mrs I. Jones. As things turned out, it was no ordinary achievement, because Mrs Jones had been ill with a severe cold and, as a result, had completely lost her voice and was unable to speak. Olympia is an enormous building, and when the dog show is in progress, it houses some thousands of dogs. Consequently, the noise is frightful, and if they are not all barking at the same time, it certainly sounds to the casual visitor as if they are doing just that. Mrs Jones went into the ring with Copy, and with no chance at all of making her husky voice heard above the din, worked her entirely by signs – something she had not done before. If Copyright had performed at all under these adverse conditions it would have been surprising – that she won the class against the mass of top-class competitors and under such a handicap was miraculous. The judge, Mr F.K. Butler, said afterwards that he had never seen a more spectacular performance. It was all due to Mrs Jones's remarkable capabilities as a trainer and to the bond of affection that existed between Copy and herself – but we confess that we felt very proud to have bred Copy and thrilled at our good fortune in having sold her to such a brilliant handler.

It almost seems an anticlimax to recall, after such a great feat, that Copyright, when taking part in a demonstration of stunt-trained dogs, used to carry a tray of teacups round the ring and offer them to the audience! We only wish there were hundreds more like her to make friends for our breed.

Some training enthusiasts find obedience competitions a sufficient challenge, some do obedience and also working trials, a few are only interested in the latter. Certainly present-day standards call for perfection, and to achieve this, endless patience, a deep-seated love for dogs and a good deal of time are all needed. It is doubtful if time spent on training is ever wasted, however. Training is fascinating and also rewarding, as is proved by the numerous individuals who have started out enthusiastically showing dogs in the beauty ring, but have abandoned the struggle for the greater challenge of the obedience ring. And there are, happily, quite a number of people in that growing community of enthusiasts who aim to have the best of both worlds. They show their dogs in beauty classes and run them in obedience – and undoubtedly they are on the right lines. That is the German Shepherd Dog's true destiny – to look beautiful and work beautifully – no other dog can do this so easily or so well.

Working one's dogs is time-absorbing, but the time is never wasted. If the German Shepherd Dog can direct its intelligence into competitive channels, so can it utilise them in a different way. Because the breed is brainy and adaptable, it happened to be the first breed chosen by the founder of the original movement to train dogs to guide the blind. There was a time when, if one mentioned 'a blind man's dog', the image conjured up was that of a little mongrel terrier on a piece of string, trailing behind its master.

How different from the modern pair – the blind man and his dog, graduates from one of the Training centres maintained by the Guide Dogs for the Blind Association! The man steps out, walking briskly, and beside him walks his dog – possibly a German Shepherd Dog – which he holds by means of a hoop-shaped handle attached to a harness which the dog wears. The dog is thoroughly trained to lead him past obstacles, even to indicate obstructions such as low shop blinds which might hit the man but not the dog. The dog will pull back if a hazard – such as road works, a hole in the road, a bollard – is ahead.

The movement to train guide dogs got off to a very slow start. It was short of funds, and as things turned out, training a guide dog was to prove expensive. There was some public opposition

– certain people thought it was unkind to make the dogs do the work. Appeals or funds did not bring spectacular results, because the public seemed unable to understand what the scheme entailed; it was bemused by the chummy-little-terrier-on-a-leash idea. Somehow, the basic facts had to be got over. People needed to understand that a dog – and at that time, it was a German Shepherd Dog – can be taught to think for itself, to indicate when steps or stairs went up or down, to pull a man sideways when he looked like walking into a lamp-post. Somehow, the Guide Dog Movement survived. Thanks to the dedicated people who worked for it during its most difficult early days, it gradually extended the work until its marvellous achievements are now known and recognised everywhere – but this does not mean that it is still not in urgent need of donations for this valuable work.

It is very unfortunate that, with the extension of the Guide Dog Movement and the steady demand for dogs, the supply of suitable German Shepherd Dogs has fallen far below the demand in recent years. Experiments with various other breeds became necessary, and today the Association trains a number of dogs which include working collies of various types, and labrador retrievers, amongst others. The prospective guide dogs go to a collecting centre where they undergo exacting tests for character and trainability. A high percentage of the dogs offered are rejected for one reason or another. After all, the qualified guide dog – the finished article – will be responsible for a man's life, so it is clear that the utmost care is needed in choosing the dogs for this very special work. Even as training proceeds with the team of dogs that have been chosen, dogs are discarded at various stages as the course progresses. The final candidates which make the grade pass out and are then transferred to the care of the blind men and women who come to train with them, under supervision, over a period. Sometimes a particular dog does not get on well with a particular blind person, and adjustments and changes have to be made. Sometimes a blind person does not prove to be a suitable owner of a guide dog. Only experts with peculiar ability have proved suitable trainers for this most specialised work, and apart from understanding the mentality of the dog, these people need to be psychiatrists as well when it comes to fitting the man to the dog and vice versa.

It is a most inspiring sight when a guide dog and its owner are seen out walking together. Many blind people say that their guide dogs have completely revolutionised their lives. Whereas previously they were either completely house-bound or unable to go outside without – hesitantly – prevailing upon relatives or neighbours to lead them, they have suddenly acquired independence not unlike that of sighted persons. They want to go down to post a letter or do some shopping. The dog is at the ready, wagging tail, longing for the outing. On with the harness and away they go.

German Shepherd Dog breeders and lovers are very proud of the large part the breed has played throughout the evolution of the guide dog, but this pride could be shown in the most tangible fashion if more bitches of good temperament were offered to the movement. Certainly, service to man in this capacity is one of the best advertisements for the breed.

For a great many people of the writer's generation, at least, a first introduction to the German Shepherd Dog breed would have stemmed from the publicity surrounding the series of silent films starring the rival stars Strongheart and Rin-tin-tin. The handsome, accomplished dogs led us through a gamut of emotions, unequalled tear-jerkers as they were in a variety of situations. Their hair-brained adventures would keep us sitting on the edges of our seats, chewing our handkerchiefs or mopping our eyes as they escaped capture, downed the villains, rescued hero or heroine in the very nick of time, chewing through the cords that bound their wrists and generally organising matters so that good triumphed over evil and we all went home happy if exhausted. These clever dogs were very well trained, but as the films were silent, the handlers were able to talk to the dogs throughout the action and to give commands. The coming of the talking pictures put the trainers very much on the spot. Dog film stars have to perform without instruction or help while the camera is in action, for no commands can be given which would interfere with the sound track. Dogs must work on their own initiative or by signs.

The Rozavel kennels trained and supplied several German

Shepherd Dogs for British films, and in spite of these handicaps the dogs did what was expected of them.

We do recall one of the productions of *The Constant Nymph*, when our old Southwold-bred bitch named Jill was required to sit beside actor Lyn Harding as he played the piano. The director requested that she should look, soulfully, at his hands as he played, and seem to enjoy the music. We achieved this to everyone's complete satisfaction by planting tiny morsels of cooked liver on each of the ivory keys of the instrument! Jill was a greedy girl, and liver was again successful later in the film when she had to wander mournfully over her master's grave, sniffing the ground! Many of the effects involving dogs that seem so spectacular are really achieved by such simple means, but this in no way detracts from the ability of the dog and its eager co-operation. German Shepherd Dogs love to work, and can often, with patience, be taught most complicated stunts and tricks. They have been seen to 'count', to choose selected playing cards from packs, and pick out numbers, etc. Our own Unity of Rozavel C.D.ex. appeared on television, when she was asked to choose the Union Jack, placed at random amongst a mass of flags of different nations.

A more recent and much-loved star dog of film and television was Druidswood Anglo-Saxon (Saxon, to his friends) who, in the hands of the brilliant lady trainer, Dorothy Steves, performed in a wide variety of productions, among them Daphne du Maurier's *The Breakthrough*, *The Siege of Spaghetti House*, and the endearing family serial 'Let There Be Love' with Nanette Newman. He also appeared in episodes of 'All Creatures Great and Small' and 'Emmerdale Farm' – truly a versatile dog, with a response to his trainer which was the envy of everyone.

Mrs Uglione, an early and very successful trainer and breeder, used to put on a most amusing show for the public. This was quite an elaborate act, and involved the erection of a dummy 'house'. Clouds of smoke and a terrifying red glare would appear at the windows and door, and the fire alarm would be sounded. As smoke poured out, one of the 'Romana' German Shepherd Dogs would climb a ladder, dive through a window, and reappear with a large doll representing a child.

She would toss this out of the window, going back to rescue another and yet another, carrying the last one in her mouth as she descended the ladder carefully to a tumult of applause.

Sometimes training classes may be prevailed upon to stage demonstrations at fêtes and other gatherings, and these are often a wonderful means of showing the intelligence of the dogs taking part to a non-dog-show-going public which have few opportunities to see this. Such efforts do a lot to persuade the public that pedigree dogs are ultra-intelligent and well worth having, because there is really no end to the number of stunts these clever dogs can perform. They jump through hoops of fire (the most spectacular of stunts yet one of the easiest to teach and one which causes no harm or distress to the dogs). Teams of dogs jump over hurdles in unison, and individuals play 'leap-frog' and jump over the heads of their owners.

It was one of our dogs, Governor, who could scarcely be kept in any room or kennel. If we penned him in, no matter what sort of fastening there was on the door or the gate he would be out. He lifted latches, sometimes with his long nose, at other times with a paw. He turned door knobs with his teeth. He lifted bolts and then pulled them back, also with his foot. If he was left in a compartment of our long corridor kennel range he let himself out and then went down the line opening doors and releasing all his friends. Fortunately he only bothered to let the bitches out – never the males which was a mercy as it could have led to major incidents if a lot of rivals had met under those conditions. He did not particularly like the other dogs and so he ignored them. Governor also detested the dark. If ever we left him shut in the house with the lights out, he would find the switches, paw them, and when we came home we would find the place ablaze with electricity in every room to which he had access.

We once locked him in a darkened room because the bulb had fused. We know that he tried the switch because it was down when we came back, but he found it did not work. So he stood up on his hind legs and took the central pendant bulb out of its socket, and placed it, unbroken, on the floor. Just how he thought he could make it work we will never know, but clearly he was trying to fathom it all out somehow.

Governor was only one of many intelligent German Shepherd Dogs we have owned, but we always think that he was among the most brilliant of dogs. Having lived with him we feel sorry for the 'boffins' who maintain that dogs cannot think or reason. Our friends who knew him used to say that whenever they telephoned us they quite expected 'Gov' to answer the phone.

11

Common Ailments

CERTAIN ailments are liable to afflict dogs of all breeds, but good management goes a long way towards keeping them healthy, and it is probably true to say that in these respects the German Shepherd Dog is no different from any other working breed. Some years ago it was thought that one popular strain tended to produce a proportion of dogs which suffered recurrent attacks of wet eczema, and another from which descended some dogs liable to disorders of the kidneys. Both hereditary troubles were pinned on famous, much-patronised stud dogs, and it is only fair to say that in neither case was the accusation proved. Both dogs appear prominently in a great number of extended pedigrees of present-day dogs most of which are perfectly healthy externally and internally, and one feels that if these much-used pillars of the breed had really transmitted these troubles, they would be far more prevalent than they are today. However, certain animals produce dogs which are prone to suffer epileptic fits, and these bloodlines are well known to most established breeders. At all costs, inbreeding on any of the suspect lines should be avoided, since this is a particularly distressing ailment.

We do hear a great deal about hip dysplasia, which is a structural handicap. Despite much research, there is still no positive proof that the condition is hereditary, and at the same time there are well-qualified opinions that it might be a nutritional or deficiency problem. It is a condition which affects many breeds, and has only become noticeable in the past twenty years. It is, briefly, a deformity of the hip, whereby the socket is too flat to secure the ball-shaped bone at the end of the femur. This topic is more fully discussed under the heading *Hip Dysplasia* later in this chapter.

As regards a dog which falls sick, owners may be divided into two categories. Either they rush to the Veterinary Surgeon at the slightest provocation, bothering him unnecessarily and running up bills for themselves, or they doctor the animal at home, trying one so-called remedy after another, when possibly a prescription from the Veterinary Surgeon himself would clear up the trouble right away.

It is admittedly sometimes very difficult to know whether or not to call the Veterinary Surgeon especially if the dog becomes unwell late at night. On the whole, it is probably best to be safe rather than sorry and certainly most Veterinary Surgeons much prefer to be summoned at the onset of the illness instead of seeing the dog first when it has been ill for some days.

Naturally as the newer dog owner gains experience there will be many little day-to-day matters which can be safely treated at home, and even if it is deemed wiser to get the Veterinary Surgeon at all times, things happen when the Veterinary Surgeon is out or busy and the wise dog lover keeps a doggy first-aid box or cupboard at the ready. Obviously one cannot prepare for every imaginable eventuality, but the following list of items are useful stand-bys, and most keep fresh and usable almost indefinately excepting worm medicines which 'go off' and are best renewed from time to time.

USEFUL STAND-BYS

Eye-dropper
Cotton wool
2 or 3 gauze bandages, 2 in. and 3 in. widths
1 elastic bandage, 2 in. width
Curved, blunt-tipped scissors
Clinical thermometer (half-minute)
Peroxide of hydrogen
Dettol, and/or T.C.P.
Benzol-bensoate emulsion
Boracic powder
Permanganate of potash crystals
Milk of Magnesia, in liquid form

Chloromycetin eye ointment
Worm capsules
Tin of Slippery Elm food
Packet of arrowroot
Jar of honey
Packet of glucose
Aureomycin powder (from Veterinary Surgeon)

Other items may be needed and added from time to time, but everyone keeping dogs is likely to need some or all of the items on the list. If a dog is out of sorts or ill, such things will be wanted in a hurry, and a crisis invariably seems to occur when the shops are closed. It is at such times that the anxious owner blesses the foresight that prompted the stocking of a first-aid box.

The following list embraces some of the ailments which the average dog owner may encounter.

Abrasions

Dogs can tear themselves on wire, or when jumping walls or fences, and on accidentally stepping on broken glass or sharp pieces of metal hidden in long grass. Bathe the wound with a weak solution of T.C.P., taking care that any glass or metal is removed. Dab dry with cotton wool or clean linen, and apply some Aureomycin powder to the wound. If the cut is deep, or if an ear is torn, make haste to the Surgery to have it stitched, so that healing can commence.

Acid Milk

If puppies fail to thrive at birth, wail, and do not suck, it is possible that the dam's milk is to blame. Speedy action is called for, or they will all fade away and die. Get some blue litmus paper from a chemist, squeeze a drop of milk from a teat on to the paper. Normal milk makes a slightly mauvish stain, acid milk turns the paper bright pink. The puppies should be removed to a foster-mother or hand fed, and the dam dosed with milk of magnesia or bicarbonate of soda. If the litmus paper shows that the milk is normal, something else may be wrong and a

Veterinary Surgeon should see bitch and puppies without
delay.

Anal Glands

Active dogs do not suffer very much from impacted glands, but
occasionally older dogs, or dogs that through unsuitable feeding or lack of exercise have become constipated, need treatment. The dog drags itself along the ground in a sitting
position, tries to lick its rear end, holds the tail in an irregular
position, and is generally depressed and obviously uncomfortable. Examination will show that the glands – situated on either
side of the anus – are inflamed and suppurating. The Veterinary
Surgeon will show you how to squeeze the glands to empty
them of pus-like fluid, and will give you a small tube of special
ointment with instructions to apply it through the tiny nozzle
right into the nasty, sore little openings. The glands will be
extremely tender, it is sure to need two attendants – one to hold
the dog, and the other to attend to the sore places. A slight
modification of diet can help the healing process. Large pieces
of meat or hard rusk should be withheld for two to three weeks.
Cut the meat up into ¼-inch cubes and add a heaped tablespoonful of All Bran with a little wholemeal rusk and a teaspoonful of Olive Oil, mixing up well with a little stock to
moisten. Garlic capsules are also good, as they disinfect the
intestines and assist in the healing. Abels or Denes make
excellent capsules – dose according to instructions.

Appetite, Morbid

This is a distressing habit, where the dog devours excreta or
filth. It occurs sometimes in bitches in whelp, and is thought to
be a 'throwback' to the wild state, when they would seek to
cover-up traces of their condition against predators. In
puppies, it is supposed that the cause is indigestion or disturbance from teething. In all cases, one can only prevent the act
by removing all faeces before they can be devoured; and usually
a few days' supervision and scolding will give results. A tablespoonful of milk of magnesia for an adult, or a large teaspoon-

ful for a puppy, will help the indigestion. Repeat the dose for two days. As a last resort, liberally sprinkle pepper on a stool and let the dog sniff at it to discourage the habit.

Bad Breath

This usually indicates a stomach disorder or decaying teeth. Examine the dog's mouth, and if there is a bad tooth have the Veterinary Surgeon remove it, as decay spreads rapidly. Make sure there are no symptoms of worms, and if necessary dose accordingly. If there is a temporary digestive upset, give milk of magnesia, and use Amplex tablets to sweeten the breath. Sometimes the teeth are dirty during recovery from illness; they can be cleaned by gently rubbing with a piece of linen moistened with warm water and dipped in bicarbonate of soda.

Balanitis

This is the name given to the slight yellowish discharge which many stud dogs have on the prepuce. The dog removes it from time to time by licking itself, and though when noticeable it is not pleasant, it is not harmful. If treatment is thought necessary, the sheath may be syringed daily with a tepid solution of some bland antiseptic of the type used as a gargle.

Biliousness

Dogs frequently vomit froth and bile, especially if they have been eating grass, and sometimes for no apparent reason. There is no cause for alarm unless the vomiting is persistent, and this is always a worrying symptom of something badly wrong. A vomiting dog needs to be kept warm, food and water withheld, and nothing given by mouth excepting tablespoonfuls of egg-white and water until the Veterinary Surgeon arrives.

Bites

German Shepherd Dogs are not trouble-makers, and a ring full
of show dogs is invariably the quietest in the place. Jealousy
within a kennel is probably the most frequent source of dog-
fights, however, and once a German Shepherd Dog becomes
involved, the strong canine teeth can do a lot of damage. The
teeth can penetrate the thick fur, but usually most bites are
confined to the legs, thighs or ears. Dog bites rapidly become
septic if left untreated, and a deep wound or tear needs professional Veterinary attention. Penicillin ointment is usually
prescribed, and deep wounds should not be encouraged to heal
too fast but to remain open and drain. Bites on ears are always
spectacular, they bleed profusely and often look worse than
they really are. A torn ear must be stitched by the Veterinary
Surgeon with the minimum of delay. Small wounds can be
treated by bathing with peroxide of hydrogen and holding the
cotton wool plug against the bite until the bleeding stops, then
dusting with Aureomycin powder.

Bladder Irregularities

Bladder disorders are easily diagnosed. The dog or bitch tries to
urinate frequently, often with obvious effort and straining.
Sometimes it produces urine stained with blood, often a few
drops at a time only. Keep the dog quiet in a warm place,
withholding all solid foods. Give boiled water, cooled and with
a little glucose added. Seek Veterinary advice immediately.

Bowels

When a carefully fed, healthy dog passes a motion it should be
formed, dark yellow in the case of puppies, and brown in adults.
An occasional slightly loose motion can be due to a large
variety of causes and in general is nothing to worry about.
Consistently sloppy stools, bright yellow, greenish, grey, or
tinged with blood, are signs that the dog is unwell. Black stools,
often a cause for alarm, are quite normal when a dog is fed
entirely on raw meat, and always when a bitch passes the first

motion or two after her whelpings. Incessant straining presupposes an obstruction of some kind – perhaps a sharp piece of bone.

A dog in normal health should not require laxatives; but, above all, eschew human remedies. See also under the separate heading *Constipation*.

Diarrhoea is always a worrying symptom, especially if a puppy has not been inoculated. Never neglect the signs, and if it persists for more than a day seek the Veterinary Surgeon's help. If the motions contain blood, get him immediately.

Bronchitis

This presupposes that a dog has been allowed to lie around after a wetting, or that the kennel and/or the bedding are damp. Or the dog has been taken straight out of a centrally heated house or from the hearth-rug into a cold kennel or car. The dog needs treatment as advised by the Veterinary Surgeon and first-aid is rubbing the chest with 'Vick' or camphorated oil, boiling a steam kettle where the dog can inhale the humid air, and keeping it on a light diet and in warm quarters. Give small spoonsful of honey dissolved in warm water to soothe the throat; and always check the temperature twice daily.

Choking

A most distressing and dangerous emergency. It can be caused by a dog swallowing a piece of bone, a very large chunk of meat, or, in the case of a puppy, a stone or foreign body, or something with which it has been playing. One of our eight-months-old German Shepherd Dogs caught a tennis ball and swallowed it – mercifully it sicked it up again almost immediately, but many dogs have died through swallowing balls. If strong arms are nearby, hold the dog upside down and in its struggle it may vomit-up the obstruction. Or push your first finger down the throat and try to hook it up. It may be necessary to rush the dog to the Veterinary Surgeon but the time is short and everything possible must be done before the animal suffocates.

Chorea

A side-effect, following one of the virus diseases of the distemper-hard-pad-hepatitis group. The dog develops a decided twitch, sometimes on a foreleg, sometimes the jaw, sometimes it nods the head. Any nervous symptom of this type is serious, since it is difficult to cure and if it progresses as it often does, it may end in the dog having to be put to sleep. Chorea often heralds the arrival of convulsions, when the prognosis is very depressing. In mild cases, sedatives may help, and sometimes a dog will completely outgrow the trouble. If the twitch remains it is likely to prove an insuperable handicap in the show ring, and there are two opinions as to whether or not an animal suffering from chorea – however slight – is suitable for breeding.

Conjunctivitis

Any discharge from the eyes can be the onset of one of the highly contagious dog diseases, and the subject should be isolated, and the temperature taken. Normal temperature may mean that the dog has been out in a strong wind, or been allowed to hang its head out of the car window. A temperature over 101.2 may mean trouble. Some dogs suffer from a chronic eye discharge which is in no way associated with virus diseases. Frequent bathing with a tepid saline solution (one teaspoonful to a pint of water) or with a teaspoonful of Boracic powder in a pint of tepid water (Optrex is also very good) will be helpful. Dry the surface surrounding the eyes with cotton-wool. Eyes that water excessively may be bathed with strained cold tea. Chloromycetin ointment is useful, and the Veterinary Surgeon will prescribe something similar if the condition does not correct itself.

Constipation

A stoppage of the bowels is both painful and serious. If the dog strains when passing faeces, there may be a slight obstruction. A pessary, lubricated with olive oil, can be inserted into the anus, very gently and as far as the finger in a thin rubber glove can help it to penetrate. This will usually dislodge the material blocking the bowel and encourage a movement. Continue the treatment with a dessertspoonful of liquid paraffin each morning for three days, to establish regular evacuation.

Constipation is the root cause of a great deal of canine sickness; and modern prepared foods do not improve matters. Any food which is preserved or processed lacks the natural bulk and fibre so essential to the proper functioning of a dog's intestines. When owners feed tasty tit-bits of refined human foods as well, then you have the recipe for ruining a dog's digestion and making certain his bowel gets blocked. The daily evacuations should always be noted: the brown-coloured stool should be passed easily. Black or very dark stools over a period of more than 24 hours are a sign of a bowel haemorrhage, and this requires your Veterinary Surgeon's attention at once. Light or 'clay'-coloured stools indicate a liver disturbance and possibly a chill. If the dog shows no other symptoms (such as a rise in temperature or vomiting) and he is not listless or distressed, treat the liver condition by a change of diet as follows: stop all fats, oils and milk, and give 2-3 tablespoonsful of finely grated carrot incorporated in a pound of freshly minced raw meat. If he is hungry, he will not notice the carrot, since most dogs will readily eat this vegetable if it has been part of their puppy diet. Keep him on this diet for two or three days, and give him a course of Denes' parsley-and-watercress pills. If the dog is eager for more food, blend a carton of natural yoghurt with a small spoonful of honey and a tablespoonful of All Bran for his breakfast. An increase in his daily exercise will help to remedy the trouble considerably.

When treating constipation and allied ailments do not give the dog chicken cube broth (should this be recommended) as it contains artificial flavouring and spices which make it quite unsuitable. Instead, boil a chicken portion or an old boiling hen slowly for a couple of hours with garlic and carrot, adding a little *brown* rice for the last half hour. Then strain the liquid and give as a drink. The chicken and rice can be set aside for when the bowels return to normal. Also, avoid giving the dog cooked vegetables, as he will find these difficult to digest.

Convulsions

There is nothing more distressing than a dog in a fit. It twitches, looks wild-eyed and terrified, totters on its legs and falls to the ground, thrashing the limbs and struggling, sometimes whining or howling. Dogs rarely attempt to bite during convulsions. Slide a folded towel or blanket beneath the head, and if the jaws are champing, slip a wad of cloth between the teeth to prevent the tongue getting bitten. Stay with the dog, steadying it and, in so far as it is possible, prevent it from throwing itself about. As soon as it begins to regain consciousness talk to it and soothe it. Carry it to a quiet, dark place, and telephone the Veterinary Surgeon. If it is a puppy he may suggest a worm dose, and will probably prescribe bromide or phenobarbitone or other similar sedative. If a dog has not been inoculated, keep a careful watch for other symptoms as fits are sometimes associated with distemper and hard-pad diseases.

Coughs

Coughs may stem from bronchitis, from worms, or as a symptom of hepatitis. Isolate the coughing dog, keep it warm, feed it lightly and send for the Veterinary Surgeon.

Cuts

See Abrasions.

Dandruff

The German Shepherd Dog coat is easily kept healthy, but when a dog is moulting or out of condition the hair becomes dry and scurfy. A thorough dressing with olive oil, followed by a bath using a medicated shampoo, should dispose of the trouble. While the coat looks scurfy do not groom with too stiff a brush as this aggravates the condition.

Diarrhoea

See Bowels.

Dislocations

German Shepherd Dogs with thick, strong limbs should not suffer excepting when caused by a blow or a fall or similar accident. Keep the dog resting and get the Veterinary Surgeon.

Distemper

The old-fashioned distemper, such a scourge before the modern inoculations proved such valuable protectors, has largely disappeared, and so to a large extent has the not dissimilar disease named hard-pad disease. Both are invariably the cause of a high mortality, and it is difficult to understand people refusing to have their dogs injected against such devilish killers.

Wise dog owners – and that is the majority – have their dogs immunised. Ten to twelve weeks of age is favoured by some Veterinary Surgeons, and there are a number of vaccines on the market. Some of these require the one injection only, others more than one with intervals in between, but all give satisfactory results. It is but seldom that one hears of an inoculated dog contracting distemper or hard-pad. It is considered advisable to give booster shots every twelve months, and whilst a great many people do not do this, owners of valuable and greatly loved animals feel that any precaution taken against such dire infection is a wise one.

The symptoms of distemper are lassitude, loss of appetite, rising temperature, diarrhoea, and a yellowish discharge from the eyes. Injections are available which are both prophylactic and therapeutic, and the Veterinary Surgeon should be invited to inject both the sick animal and any contacts with the respective serums. He will advise treatment, and meanwhile the dog should be isolated, kept warm and comfortable, and provided with plenty of newspapers as a temporary 'lavatory'. In all but the warmest summer weather it is very unwise to allow a sick dog to go out of doors, apart from the likelihood of the infection being passed to others. Some German Shepherd Dogs are so fastidious that it is exceedingly difficult to persuade them to relieve themselves in the house or kennel under any circumstances. When this is the case, and when the dog is clearly uncomfortable, the Veterinary Surgeon may allow it to go outside for a minute or two if dressed in a warm coat. Coats can be contrived in emergencies from knitted sweaters or pieces of blanket.

Dysentery

See Bowels.

Earache

It is obvious when a dog has earache – it shakes the head, holds the head on one side, rubs the ear on the ground or scratches at it slowly and lazily, grumbling and groaning all the time. The sore ear should be treated immediately. Pour a few drops of sweet almond oil into the ear, and 'work' the ear to spread the oil at the base of the orifice. Wipe it out after 15 to 20 minutes with a cleansing tissue wrapped round a finger, and gently dislodge any dirt or discharge, renewing the tissue until completely dry and clean. Afterwards add drops of ear lotion as instructed on the bottle, and repeat the treatment each day (or twice daily if the infection is heavy). Cleaning the ears must be done very gently – never probe or push or great damage may be done. If in any doubt ask the Veterinary Surgeon for help.

Ears

In warm summer weather, especially when flies are prevalent, the edges of the ears may become crisp and sore, and the flies bite them so that they look most unsightly and worry the dog not a little. Gentle rubbing with benzol-bensoate removes the dirty, greasy deposit and discourages the flies. A German Shepherd Dog with soft ears looks sadly untypical. On page 117 we suggest some legitimate ways of encouraging the ears to stand erect, but these only apply to puppies and nothing can be done to improve an adult dog if its ears have not gone up.

Eczema

This is a fairly common complaint in most breeds, and stems from a variety of causes. A major cause of eczema are external parasites such as fleas or lice, in which case you find the dog has sudden bursts of enthusiastic scratching. Slow, rhythmic scratching usually indicates a blood disorder. In any case, lift the sufferer onto a bench or table, and carefully part the hair all over the body with a steel comb, inspecting under the elbows and flanks, and the underside of the tail, for any red or sore places. If fleas are present, treat with the powder available from pet shops, putting a little chloromycetin ointment into the eyes first to avoid irritation. Dab small patches of inflamed skin with calamine lotion; and take the dog for a walk immediately afterwards so that the lotion can dry and he will not be able to lick it, as this usually makes dogs sick. Repeat this treatment two or three times daily until the area is clear. If the trouble persists seek Veterinary advice.

Either way, the diet should be changed. A day's fast on water and glucose is advisable at the onset; then a diet of fresh meat with raw grated carrot. No milk should be given and only a little wholemeal bread rusk added to the meat. A course of Denes' Greenleaf tablets will be found helpful, and all bedding should be changed and the kennel properly sprayed with disinfectant each day.

This condition can appear in bitches when they are about to start their season or in any dog which is indulged with rich and unsuitable foods. Very sore or raw places (wet eczema) should be gently sponged with well-diluted peroxide of hydrogen – one part to four parts of warm water – and dabbed dry with a paper towel. It is advisable to cut all hair away from affected places.

Emetics

If the dog has swallowed a harmful substance, such as a putrid bird or animal, or a small object, and if the mouth has not been burnt or torn, then squirt salt and water (two tablespoonsful salt to half point of warm water) down the throat, or give a piece of washing soda the size of a *small* walnut. Administer this treatment outside as results can be sudden and uncontrolled.

Epilepsy

Fits and convulsions are really alarming, especially in a large breed such as ours, and we think it would be worthwhile if all owners would familiarise themselves with the immediate first aid, so that there is less risk of distress or damage to either dog or handler if this emergency arises. During a fit, a puppy (or dog) may snap, or throw himself about quite violently, so quickly cover his head with a towel or light blanket (or a jacket in an emergency) and remove at once into a darkened room or small kennel where there is nothing he can knock over to harm himself. Taking him out of direct bright light or sunshine is an important step in the first aid.

Fits can be caused by a heavy infection of worms, or from a dietary deficiency – also from sunstroke if the animal has been exposed for a long time under hot sun. Puppies may have convulsions during teething, or if they rapidly outgrow their strength and put a strain on the system – even from toxic-forming rubbish devoured when scavenging. If the puppy does not lose consciousness during the attack, one of the above causes could well be responsible for his condition, and he should make a good recovery once your Veterinary Surgeon has prescribed the medication suitable to his case.

An unconscious dog may have suffered brain damage from the virus-borne disease encephalitis, or from an accidental blow to the head. Here again, your Veterinary Surgeon will advise. If there is no history of similar illness in the dog's family, the nervous system may recover, although very slowly and with no certainty of a cure, since there is no way of assessing the extent of the damage caused by the attack. Keep the patient very quiet and away from playful companions during recovery, and feed a bland diet of semolina porridge (as recommended for puppy rearing), egg yolks and milk made into a custard and sweetened with honey, cottage cheese, and natural yoghurt sweetened with honey. A little fish cooked in milk and carefully boned, and a few wheatmeal digestive biscuits may be given if the patient seems hungry. A large, hard bone to chew helps to distract his attention from any pain and serves to relax his nerves. Attacks can be controlled by prescriptions from your Veterinary Surgeon. Dogs affected should not be used for breeding.

Fractures

When a fracture occurs it is commonly a front leg, a hind leg or hock bone. Dogs can break their legs scaling jumps, but in this day and age a great many accidents occur if a dog is allowed to run into the road. Make a splint by wrapping strips of cloth round a flat piece of wood, even a poker if nothing else is available, and using a crêpe bandage – the easiest for an amateur to handle – bandage firmly above and below the fracture, keeping the dog still and quiet until the Veterinary Surgeon comes, or until the dog can be carried – on an improvised stretcher – to the surgery.

Gastritis

Frequent vomiting, excessive thirst, and diarrhoea are the symptoms. Keep the dog quiet and warm, offer small pieces of ice to lick but do not allow water to drink. If the Veterinary Surgeon advises it, white of egg lightly beaten (not whipped until fluffy but just well stirred) in a little water, with or without glucose, is suitable. Small doses of bismuth must be prescribed and no solid food should be given until the Veterinary Surgeon orders a gradual return to a light diet.

Gums

Bleeding gums are a sign of pyorrhoea or caused by the teeth being in a state of decay – a condition found in old dogs. The Veterinary Surgeon will remove the teeth under anaesthesia, and the gums must be swabbed with saline solution.

Hard Pad

See Distemper.

Hepatitis

A serious disease with very variable symptoms. Temperature can be very high or very low, but either way the dog looks ill and miserable. Sometimes it vomits or has diarrhoea. In advanced stages, one or both eyes may turn turquoise blue, and when diagnosis has proved difficult this is considered an almost certain sign that the dog has been suffering from hepatitis.

Hepatitis is usually less infectious than distemper or hard-pad diseases, and sometimes it affects not more than one or two dogs in a big kennel. Those affected are usually the younger dogs. However, it is best to be on the safe side and isolate any sick dog, which in any event needs rest and quiet. It is most important to call the Veterinary Surgeon at once if hepatitis is suspected, as prompt treatment makes all the difference to the animal's chances of recovery.

Hernia

Many puppies develop small umbilical hernias, which feel soft and may be pressed flat with the thumb. These often disappear as the puppy grow up, and are quite harmless. If the hernia feels hard, or if it is at all large, the Veterinary Surgeon should be asked if an operation is advisable – if so this is simple and the dog recovers rapidly.

Hip Dysplasia

The first rumblings about this structural fault came in the late 1940s, and led to a considerable number of good animals being destroyed with only minor degrees of the condition. During the past twenty years or so the Germans, who are extremely thorough in these matters, have introduced a system of voluntary examination for most breeding animals, with rejection of those heavily affected. The examiners record the state of the hips after X-rays have been taken. In 1966, after much deliberation, the S.V. decided that dogs whose X-rays were satisfactory in the view of one of their breed surveyors should be tattooed on one ear with an identification number to correspond with their registration number, and this number was also recorded on the X-ray plates. It was then decided to institute gradings of the degree of dysplasia – 'A' signifying all clear. This system has brought about an improvement in hip soundness; but it is not a cure, since the *S. V. Zeitung*, the S.V.'s official magazine, records many heavily dysplastic animals bred from clear parents.

There is, as yet, no established pattern to show that the condition is directly hereditary. However, a serious breeder always looks for soundness in breeding subjects, and we must hope that the considerable research in progress will eventually help to eliminate the trouble. The German Shepherd Dog League has now instituted a voluntary scheme whereby X-ray plates can be professionally examined and 'scored' according to the results.

Hydrophobia

Also known as rabies, this is the disease, easily communicated to man, that prompts the authorities to insist upon a six-months' detention in quarantine for all dogs entering Britain from abroad. Rabies is unknown in this country as a result of these regulations, but common in many parts of the world. Rabies is transmitted by saliva from an infected animal – not necessarily a dog. Six weeks is considered to be the average incubation period but animals have been known to develop it more than six months after being bitten by a rabid animal. The symptoms are varied, but the dog usually demonstrates a complete change of character, a friendly and cheerful specimen becomes dull and morose and snappy. It suffers an agonising headache, followed by a painful spasm of the throat muscles when it attempts to drink. Shortly the very sight of water brings on this distressing symptom, hence the old theory that 'a mad dog fears water'. The dog is maniacal and dangerous, and if it is not put out of its misery, it becomes paralysed and death is sure. The inoculation treatment, long drawn out and, we are told, exceedingly painful, invented by Pasteur, offers the only hope of recovery to humans suspected of having been in contact with a rabid animal. We do not hear of dogs receiving treatment, perhaps because they are too dangerous to be handled throughout the process.

Hysteria

The old idea of a 'mad dog' (i.e. a rabid dog) is of the animal tearing through the streets or rushing round in circles, foaming at the mouth. In fact rabid dogs do not do this, they feel too ill and they sulk and hide away. A dog with hysteria does rush around howling and barking, often foaming and drooling, and we feel sure that hundreds of so-called 'mad dogs' were shot in days gone by when they were merely suffering from hysteria.

Hysteria can occur in dogs of all ages. When it is endemic in a kennel it is often a sign that the inmates are suffering from a suppressed form of distemper, and this is especially likely if the dogs have not been inoculated. It can also be due to wrong feeding, and experiments have shown that hysteria is produced in dogs fed entirely on biscuits or bread made from white flour.

Hysteria can also be caused by worms, and if one puppy is affected this might well be the reason and the attack need not occasion much alarm especially if other dogs in the litter are unaffected. Indigestion is another possible cause, especially if a greedy puppy gobbles more than its share of food. Dose the puppy with Milk of Magnesia, put it by itself in a dark kennel and ask the Veterinary Surgeon about a sedative if the attacks continue. There is no mistaking hysterical fits – the dog, with scarcely any warning, whines, looks wildly round, makes some sudden, jerky movements and starts to bark, howl or scream on a high-pitched note. During this, it seems deaf to the human voice and unaware of what goes on around it. Sometimes it bolts into the distance, or tears round in circles. Most dogs suffering from hysteria do not attempt to bite when captured, but occasionally when a dog is cornered and does not know what is happening to it, it will snap. Therefore care is needed and if a towel or coat can be thrown over the animal's head it makes it easier to secure.

The diet for a sufferer from this disease is very important, as the animal will be very weak indeed. No fats or milk of any kind should be given. Boiled rabbit, chicken and white fish – all carefully boned – may be fed lukewarm, and slices of wholemeal bread rusked in a cool oven and dotted with a little Marmite. Also home-made chicken broth (remove the fat with blotting paper when cool).

Impotence

German Shepherd Dogs are normally keen, reliable stud dogs, and if one should turn out to be impotent it is a great disappointment especially if it is a particularly good specimen. The Veterinary Surgeon can try a course of special injections, but in our experience these are rarely successful.

Jaundice

Usually leptospiral or caused by a chill, and always to be treated seriously. The dog is very thirsty, vomits quantities of colourless, watery fluid, and passes evil-smelling greyish-coloured motions. The whites of the eyes, and the skin, easily noticeable on the tummy and under the armpits, look yellow. The dog is extremely ill and urgent professional attention is essential if it is to recover.

Kidneys

Several kidney diseases are common among dogs, and old German Shepherd Dogs seem particularly liable to these once they get beyond the seven- or eight-years-old mark. Symptoms are scanty urine, frequent unsuccessful attempts to urinate, and incontinence. The dog may run a temperature, it arches its back, loses weight, and looks very unhappy. At times there is blood in the urine, and almost always excessive thirst. The most usual of these painful complaints is nephritis, where an additional symptom is sores around the mouth and lips. No condition as serious as this should be treated by a layman. Give the dog home-made barley water to drink, and call the Veterinary Surgeon.

Laxatives

See Constipation.

Meningitis

This is an inflammation of the brain, most usually met with in young puppies or dogs of any age which have been suffering from distemper or hard-pad disease. The dog has fits, during which it loses consciousness, or staggers about, usually in circles, struggles on the floor and froths at the mouth. When it regains consciousness it is dazed, unsteady on its legs, unable to focus its eyes, and will cry or whine. Unfortunately one fit tends to lead to another, and as they become more frequent and severe, so any hope of the animal's recovery diminishes. At this stage the Veterinary Surgeon will usually persuade the owner to have the dog put to sleep, for its sufferings are pitiful and the chances of it ever getting well are negligible. The onset of fits after an infectious illness are, for this reason, the most dreaded symptoms of all.

Nails

German Shepherd Dogs with good, thick, round cat-like feet rarely need a manicure. They manage to keep their toe-nails short by wearing them down on the ground. Flat, thin, or hare-shaped feet need constant attention as the nails almost always grow very long, and if they are not cut back they split, catch on rough ground, and even get torn from their sockets giving the dog a very sore and painful toe. Because dew-claws – the extra 'toes' occasionally found on the hind legs and always on the inside of the forelegs – also tear and cause nasty sores, those on the back legs are always removed within a few days of birth. There are some breeders who remove the front dew claws from German Shepherd Dog's legs, a custom normal with a great many other breeds. Generally these are left on, however, the custom having become normal practice through a questionable belief that they assist the dog to climb and scale jumps and fences.

Obesity

The lazy owner, not the dog, is to blame if a German Shepherd Dog is allowed to become too fat. Excess weight shortens the life of man or beast, leads to various ailments, and is a deterrent to the breeding potential of any dog or bitch. In most cases the animal is either under-exercised, over-fed, or is fed tit-bits or turned loose where it can steal them, and the remedy is obvious. Feed the German Shepherd Dog once daily on a small chunk of raw meat – about a pound – and nothing more. Dose daily with as much Epsom Salts as will go on a ½p coin. If results are not encouraging after a few weeks of this treatment, providing the dog is also getting plenty of brisk exercise, ask the Veterinary Surgeon to examine the dog in case it has a hormone deficiency which could be remedied by injections. None of these remarks apply to puppies, which should always be plump and well-covered; they usually fine down as they get older.

Parturient Eclampsia

This distressing condition is caused by the drain of calcium from the system during gestation. The bitch behaves oddly, seems very nervous, perhaps a little unsteady on her legs. Her eyelids twitch, she shivers and shakes, and may go into convulsions. It can happen at any time after the puppies are born, but the signs usually appear either in the first forty-eight hours or when the pups are two or three weeks old.

Swift action is necessary if mother and puppies are to survive. Send at once for the Veterinary Surgeon, who will inject a massive dose of calcium. If taken in time the calcium acts remarkably quickly and recovery is rapid; but the bitch can collapse and die if prompt measures are not taken. Meanwhile, remove the puppies. Keep them warm and away from direct heat and draughts. If they are new-born, feed them at hourly intervals with small quantities of a warm drink given from a dropper. This should be made up from two teaspoonsful of evaporated milk and a heaped teaspoonful of glucose dissolved in a half pint of warm water and stirred well. This is intended to prevent dehydration and keep the family warm until the mother is well enough to take over.

Any bitch can develop eclampsia; but nervous or highly strung ones are particularly at risk. The condition has a nasty habit of running in families – and if a bitch is subject to it, it is not improbable that some of her daughters may suffer from it after parturition. Once a bitch has had eclampsia she is very likely to have it whenever she whelps, especially if she breeds large litters. A recent idea is to treat bitches with parathyroid, and it is well worth discussing this possibility with the Veterinary Surgeon.

Pills

Some dogs are very good about being dosed, others struggle and fight and make it a most exhausting process for all concerned. The best way, with a gentle dog, is to prise open the jaws – but be careful not to squeeze the lips over the teeth and hurt it – drop the pills on the back of the tongue and give them a good push with the first and middle fingers of the right hand. If the dog resents this, crush the pills and tip the resultant powder on to the back of the tongue either from a teaspoon or from a small piece of folded paper. If neither method works, let the dog get hungry and conceal the tablets, one by one, inside a ball of tasty chopped meat or other well-liked tit-bit – and the best of luck!

Purgatives

See Laxatives, and Bowels.

Pymetria

This is a chronic inflammation of the womb, which can fill with pus. The sufferer is extremely ill, has a high temperature, will vomit, and there may or may not be an unpleasant discharge from the uterus. The Veterinary Surgeon will decide whether to try to treat the condition or whether an immediate hysterectomy is essential to save the life of the bitch.

Rabies

See Hydrophobia.

Rheumatism

Elderly dogs, however well cared for, can suffer from this, but if young German Shepherd Dogs develop this painful ailment it is often because they have been put into their kennels wet, or allowed to lie about on damp cement or stone floors. The dog is stiff, and it cries out in pain when it tries to rise from a recumbent position. Warmth and comfort are essentials, the bowels should be kept open, and one aspirin tablet (and one only) may be given morning and night to ease the pain. A course of garlic capsules is recommended to clear the bloodstream.

Rickets

German Shepherd Dogs suffer badly from rickets if they are not well fed, well exercised and well housed during puppyhood. Any large breed needs plenty of nourishing food, the maximum amount of sunlight obtainable in this wretched climate of ours, freedom, and fresh air. Puppies need all these things at the same time. Even well-fed puppies kept in clean kennels can become rickety if they do not have enough room to exercise themselves. The first signs are of turned-out forelegs and turned-in hind legs. The joints look lumpy, the puppies walk or run with a lumbering gait, and often cry when playing or when touched. If the puppies appear to have all they require, the condition might be due to worms, and they should be dosed at once. Be sure the puppies have ample raw meat, seaweed tablets and Vitamin D supplements, warm, dry beds and gentle exercise on gravel and not on cold, wet concrete or in long, damp grass. Treatment under these conditions will bring about considerable improvement, but although the legs will strengthen and straighten it is usually impossible to remove the signs of rickets completely, and a knowledgeable dog breeder or judge can generally see at a glance that the dog has had rickets at some time or other.

Saline

Normal saline solution is one teaspoonful of common house-hold salt to a pint of tepid water. This is used to bathe wounds, as a mouth-wash, and for several other purposes.

Shock

Shock can be caused by a fall, by an accident, or by contact with an electric cable. There have been many cases of puppies chew-ing the flex of a TV or electric lamp. The extensions of electric railways, easily transversed by dogs, have also led to tragic acci-dents which are often fatal. If the dog is merely unconscious, remove it from contact with the wire or cable with the hands encased in rubber gloves or wrapped in dry cloth, or with thick sticks held in each hand. The breathing will be shallow and feeble and the limbs cold. Place the dog on a comfortable bed and pack it round with hot-water bottles (wrap these in old jumpers or sweaters, or squares of blanket to make certain they cannot burn or scald the patient). Cover the dog with blankets, and get the Veterinary Surgeon – fast.

Stretcher

The German Shepherd Dog is a big heavy dog to move if it has been immobilised by illness or accident. A stretcher can be improvised by turning the sleeves of a tough overcoat or burberry-type raincoat inside, buttoning the coat, and then slipping the handles of two brooms down inside the sleeves. The dog can be eased on to the 'stretcher' and held steady by one person while two more carry it out to the car, or into the kennel or room where it is to be nursed. The dog may be moved more easily this way than if one or more individuals try to carry it in their arms.

Stings

Wasp stings are very common and very frightening. Bee stings are rather less common but equally unpleasant. One of our

German Shepherd Dogs discovered a hole in a bank, containing a wild bee's nest – we will never forget what she looked like when she staggered home. It was several days before she could eat or drink and the swelling began to go down. She was treated by the Veterinary Surgeon with anti-histamine injections. Stings on the mouth, neck or tongue are particularly dangerous and need Veterinary care. Ordinarily the sting should be removed with tweezers and the spot dabbed with half a cut onion, clean cotton soaked in vinegar, or T.C.P. Keep the dog warm and quiet.

Tablets

See Pills.

Teeth

German Shepherd Dog puppies cut their teeth normally, neither very early nor very late. During teething the gums get quite sore and inflamed and this often affects the ear carriage. Puppies which have had erect ears for the first few weeks drop their ears while they are changing their teeth. Sore gums make puppies disinclined to eat, and if puppies go off their food, yet seem well and lively, just examine the mouths – therein may lie the reason.

German Shepherd Dogs need their teeth cleaned as do all dogs. A small hard toothbrush, a few scraps of soft, clean rag, a tin of smoker's tooth powder (yes, really!) and a saucer-full of peroxide of hydrogen, and the job is easily done. With a piece of the rag wrapped round the finger, dip it in the saucer and then in the tooth powder. Rub the teeth well, then finish with the brush dipped in warm water. If tartar has been allowed to accumulate a proper surgical tooth scaler will be needed. These are not difficult to use, but it is important to ask a Veterinary Surgeon or an experienced dog owner to demonstrate. A diet that includes an occasional big, hard biscuit helps to keep teeth clean. We 'sit on the wall' as regards bones which are also considered to be effective tooth-cleaners. We think that big shin and marrow bones are ordinarily harmless and greatly enjoyed by the dogs, but our Veterinary Surgeon tells us that a large part of his work is devoted to treating dogs which have succeeded in swallowing chips of bone and he considers all bones should be barred.

Temperature

The dog in health has a temperature of 101.2°F. A very small deviation is rarely a cause for anxiety, especially where puppies or nervous dogs are concerned. An incident such as an unaccustomed car ride can send a temperature up. A very sudden rise or drop in temperature for no obvious reason, especially if it is accompanied by the smallest sign of malaise, is a danger sign. The dog should always be isolated from others, and seen by a Veterinary Surgeon. To take a temperature, smear the end of the clinical thermometer with vaseline and insert gently into the rectum. Hold it there a little longer than the half-minute, and be sure the mercury is shaken down into the bulb before insertion. Get someone else to hold the dog while you take the temperature. Remove the thermometer, wipe it clean with cotton-wool and move it about until you can see exactly what the mercury registers. Then dip in Dettol, wipe dry, shake down and slip it back into its metal case. If the temperature is high or low, keep the dog warm and quiet until the Veterinary Surgeon arrives.

Tonsillitis

The dog usually runs a temperature, the throat is red and inflamed, and the animal is off colour and disinclined to eat. Tonsillitis is generally regarded as a contagious infection and the Veterinary Surgeon should see the patient and advise treatment.

Vomiting

See Biliousness and Gastritis.

Worms

German Shepherd Dog puppies suffer from round worms as do most youngsters, older dogs are sometimes troubled by tape-worms. If puppies' stomachs swell considerably after eating, and also if their breath smells unpleasant at four or five weeks of age it is wise to weigh them, and ask the Veterinary Surgeon to prescribe their medicine according to weight and age. Six- to eight-weeks-old puppies may be wormed with any of the prop-rietary worm cures, but follow the directions carefully. Do not dose young puppies on a particularly cold day nor if they have been in any way off colour or upset inside.

Tape-worms call for special preparations, and some of these expel the worms in their entirety while others dissolve the worms inside the dog. Both are effective but while you do know that your efforts have been successful when you see results, if you do not shovel up worms you do not know if the dog had them at all, and if the medicine has worked or not. In any case, with tape-worms it is essential that the heads are passed, other-wise the revolting things can grow again. Tape-worms are formed from flat segments joined together rather like a string of beads, and the heads are thin like little pieces of string.

APPENDIX A

THE KENNEL CLUB BREED STANDARD

(Reproduced by kind permission of The Kennel Club)

General Appearance Slightly long in comparison to height: of powerful, well-muscled build with weather-resistant coat. Relation between height, length, position and structure of fore and hindquarters (angulation) producing far-reaching, enduring gait. Clear definition of masculinity and femininity essential, and working ability never sacrificed for mere beauty.

Characteristics Versatile working dog, balanced and free from exaggeration. Attentive, alert, resilient and tireless with keen scenting ability.

Temperament Steady of nerve, loyal, self-assured, courageous and tractable. Never nervous, over-aggressive or shy.

Head & Skull Proportionate in size to body, never coarse, too fine or long. Clean cut; fairly broad between ears. Forehead slightly domed; little or no trace of central furrow. Cheeks forming softly rounded curve, never protruding. Skull from ears to bridge of nose tapering gradually and evenly, blending without too pronounced stop into wedge shaped powerful muzzle. Skull approximately 50% of overall length of head. Width of skull corresponding approximately to length, in males slightly greater, in females slightly less. Muzzle strong, lips firm, clean and closing tightly. Top of muzzle straight, almost parallel to forehead. Short, blunt, weak, pointed, overlong muzzle undesirable.

Eyes Medium sized, almond-shaped, never protruding. Dark brown preferred, lighter shade permissible, provided expression good and general harmony of head not destroyed. Expression lively, intelligent and self-assured.

Ears Medium sized, firm in texture, broad at base, set high, carried erect, almost parallel, never pulled inwards or tipped, tapering to a point, open at front. Never hanging. Folding back during movement permissible.

Mouth Jaws strongly developed. With a perfect, regular and complete scissor bite, i.e. upper teeth closely overlapping lower teeth and set square to the jaw. Teeth healthy and strong. Full dentition desirable.

Neck Fairly long, strong, with well developed muscles, free from throatiness. Carried at 45 degrees angle to horizontal, raised when excited, lowered at fast trot.

Forequarters Shoulder blades long, set obliquely (45 degrees) laid flat to body. Upper arm strong, well muscled, joining shoulder blade at approximately 90 degrees. Forelegs straight from pasterns to elbows viewed from any angle, bone oval rather than round. Pasterns firm, supple and slightly angulated. Elbows neither tucked in nor turned out. Length of foreleg exceeding depth of chest.

Body Length measured from point of breast bone to rear edge of pelvis, exceeding height at withers. Correct ratio 10 to 9 or 8 and a half. Under-sized dogs, stunted growth, high-legged dogs, those too heavy or too light in build, over-loaded fronts, too short overall appearance, any feature detracting from reach or endurance of gait, undesirable. Chest deep (45%-48%) of height at shoulder, not too broad, brisket long, well developed. Ribs well formed and long; neither barrel-shaped nor too flat; allowing free movement of elbows when gaiting. Relatively short loin. Belly firm, only slightly drawn up. Back between withers and croup, straight, strongly developed, not too long. Overall length achieved by correct angle of well laid shoulders, correct length of croup and hindquarters. Withers long, of good height and well defined, joined back in smooth line without disrupting flowing top-line, slightly sloping from front to back. Weak, soft and roach backs undesirable and should be rejected. Loin broad, strong, well muscled. Croup long, gently curving downwards to tail without disrupting flowing top-line. Short, steep or flat croups undesirable.

Hindquarters Overall strong, broad and well-muscled, enabling effortless forward propulsion of whole body. Upper thighbone, viewed from side, sloping to slightly longer lower thighbone. Hind angulation sufficient if imaginary line dropped from point of buttocks through lower thigh just in front of hock, continuing down slightly in front of hind feet. Angulations corresponding approximately with front angulation, without over-angulation, hock strong. Any tendency towards over-angulation of hindquarters reduces firmness and endurance.

Feet   Rounded toes well-closed and arched. Pads well-cushioned and durable. Nails short, strong and dark in colour. Dewclaws removed from hindlegs.

Tail   Bushy-haired, reaches at least to hock – ideal length reaching to middle of metatarsus. At rest tail hangs in slight sabre-like curve; when moving raised and curve increased, ideally never above level of back. Short, rolled, curled, generally carried badly or stumpy from birth, undesirable.

Gait/Movement   Sequence of step follows diagonal pattern, moving foreleg and opposite hindleg forward simultaneously; hind foot thrust forward to midpoint of body and having equally long reach with forefeet without any noticeable change in backline.

Coat   Outer coat consisting of straight, hard, close lying hair as dense as possible; thick undercoat. Hair on head, ears, front of legs, paws and toes short; on back, longer and thicker; in some males forming slight ruff. Hair longer on back of legs as far down as pasterns and stifles and forming fairly thick trousers on hindquarters. No hard and fast rule for length of hair; mole-type coats undesirable.

Colour   Black or black saddle with tan, or gold to light grey markings. All black, all grey, or grey with lighter or brown markings referred to as Sables. Nose black. Light markings on chest or very pale colour on inside of legs permissible but undesirable, as are whitish nails, red tipped tails or wish-washy faded colours defined as lacking in pigmentation. Blues, livers, albinos, whites (i.e. almost pure white dogs with black noses) and near whites *highly undesirable*. Undercoat, except in all black dogs, usually grey or fawn. Colour in itself is of secondary importance, having no effect on character or fitness for work. Final colour of a young dog only ascertained when outer coat has developed.

Size   Ideal height (from withers and just touching elbows): Dogs 62.5 cm (25 ins). Bitches 57.5 cm (23 ins). 2.5 cm (1 in) either above or below ideal permissible.

Faults   Any departure from the foregoing points should be considered a fault and the seriousness with which the fault should be regarded should be in exact proportion to its degree.

Note   Male animals should have two apparently normal testicles fully descended into the scrotum.

POST-WAR KENNEL CLUB REGISTRATIONS

1946	—	11,045	1968	—	14,958
1947	—	11,787	1969	—	16,546
1948	—	10,433	1970	—	16,834
1949	—	10,334	1971	—	13,857
1950	—	10,056	1972	—	15,078
1951	—	9,050	1973	—	15,185
1952	—	7,533	1974	—	14,936
1953	—	6,984	1975	—	11,357
1954	—	6,720	1976	—	5,167
1955	—	7,170	1977	—	3,191
1956	—	7,416	1978	—	9,907
1957	—	7,121	1979	—	16,725
1958	—	7,797	1980	—	18,127
1959	—	7,486	1981	—	18,127
1960	—	7,877	1982	—	16,068
1961	—	8,337	1983	—	18,124
1962	—	8,841	1984	—	20,593
1963	—	9,887	1985	—	21,009
1964	—	10,773	1986	—	21,649
1965	—	12,572	1987	—	19,309
1966	—	12,180	1988	—	14,650
1967	—	14,081			

The drop in figures for 1976/77/78 was caused by the adoption of the active and basic registration system whereby it was possible to provide a figure for active registration only. Therefore the figures are not indicative of the total number of German Shepherd Dogs registered with the Kennel Club during the period when this system was in operation (April 1976–October 1978).

APPENDIX C

BREED CLUBS

Before we list the large number of Clubs in the British Isles, we would like to give a few details concerning the Parent Club, the Verein für Deutsche Schäferhunde – known generally as the S.V. It is a huge organisation, with membership approaching 150,000 (1985). Based in Germany, it exercises a degree of control over the breed that our own freedom-loving breeders would take some years to accept – if ever!

The Headquarters and central administration are in Augsburg, with local branches in every area who ensure that the strict rules concerning breeding are upheld. Despite this vigilance, the Parent Club recognises that, for most of us, breeding and owning German Shepherd Dogs is a hobby; and only when it is absolutely necessary do they enforce regulations to safeguard the dog and protect its reputation as the world's Number One dog for service.

The annual show is a masterpiece of organisation, attracting some 1,500 entries, with an Open Dog Class of around three hundred. The judging takes three days; and the sight of so many top-class animals, with plenty of time to assess and admire them, is a delight for all who attend. It is also a great social occasion, with delegates from German Shepherd Dog Clubs from every corner of the globe present.

Allertonshire German Shepherd Dog Club
Alsatian German Shepherd Dog Club of Bristol
Birmingham & District German Shepherd Dog Association
Blackburn & District Alsatian & Dog Training Club
Bolton & District German Shepherd Dog Club
British Association for German Shepherd Dogs
British German Shepherd Dog Training Club
Caledonian German Shepherd Dog & All Breeds Training Club
Clyde Valley German Shepherd Dog Club
Crewe, North Staffordshire German Shepherd Dog (Alsatian) Club
Derbyshire German Shepherd Dog Club
Fife Alsatian Club
The German Shepherd Dog (Alsatian) Club of United Kingdom
German Shepherd Dog Club of Devon

German Shepherd Dog Club of Essex
German Shepherd Dog Club of Hertfordshire
German Shepherd Dog Club of Northern Ireland
German Shepherd Dog Club of Kent
German Shepherd Dog Club of Scotland
German Shepherd Dog Club of Suffolk
German Shepherd Dog (Alsatian) Club of Wales
German Shepherd Dog (Alsatian) Club of United Kingdom
German Shepherd Dog League of Great Britain
Grampian German Shepherd Association
Heads of the Valley German Shepherd Dog Club
Humberside German Shepherd Dog Club
Iceni German Shepherd Dog Training Club
Leicestershire German Shepherd Dog Club
Liverpool German Shepherd Dog Training Club
Lowland Counties Alsatian and Belgian Shepherd Training Club
Midland Counties German Shepherd Dog Association
Norfolk Alsatian Association
Northern Alsatian Training Society
North Wales Alsatian Club
North Eastern German Shepherd Dog Club
Northumberland & Durham German Shepherd Dog Training Club
North Yorkshire & South Durham German Shepherd Dog Club
Preston & Fylde Alsatian Club
Reedyford Dog Training & German Shepherd Club
Scottish Western Alsatian Club
Sheffield German Shepherd Society
Southern Alsatian Club
Southern Alsatian Training Society
South of Scotland German Shepherd Dog & All Breeds Training
   Club
South Western German Shepherd Dog Club
South Yorkshire Alsatian Association
Tonbridge German Shepherd Dog Training Club
Tyne Valley German Shepherd Dog Training Club
West Yorkshire German Shepherd Dog Club
Wigan Alsatian Club

The names and addresses of secretaries can be obtained on application
to the Kennel Club, 1–4 Clarges Street, London W1Y 8AB.

APPENDIX D
POST-WAR CHAMPIONS

Name	Sex	Sire	Dam	Breeder	Born
Brian of Aravon	D	Hero of Roslin	Benita of Aravon	W. R. McCammon	24.2.42
Yvo of Ravenscar	D	Ch. Gerolf of Brittas	Ch. Biene of Dellside	The Very Rev. Canon Farrar	9.3.40
Southdown Adora	B	Ch. Southdown Hettel	Ch. Southdown Jeanetta	Mrs Leslie Thornton	7.10.40
Walston Sentinel	D	Perfection of Rhamin	Greta of Astolat	Mr W. M. Stone	6.5.45
Monti of Welham	D	Jerry of Robscott	Gipsy of Welham	Mrs F. N. Pickett	7.8.45
Jacqueline of Rigi	B	Southdown Jeremy	Silva of Rigi	Miss D. Homan	13.6.43
Hamish of Letrualt	D	Victor of Erol	Frieda of Letrualt	Dr A. M. Girvan	5.9.44
Arno of Saba	D	Ingosohn of Erol	Empress of Leeda	Mrs I. Gauntlett	14.9.45
Jet of Seale	D	Southdown Jeremy	Helen of Seale	Mrs M. Howard	14.10.45
Karaste Karenina av Hvitsand	B	Orest of Brittas	Quella of Brittas	Mrs J. D. Hart	16.8.40
Russet Kiska of Danver	B	Knight Batchelor of Roslin	Russet Chrystel	Mr W. Mason	1.8.44
Fidala of Cranville	B	Etzel of Brittas	Belveda of Cranville	Mrs R. H. Barker	2.7.45
Daga of Templefields	B	Etzel of Brittas	Quella of Brittas	Mr and Mrs J. Parr	1.11.44
Fleur de Lis of Rowley	B	Gottfried of Coulathorne	Irmgard of Coulathorne	Mrs W. Rider	6.2.46
Squire of Rowley	D	Southdown Jeremy	Shene of Rigi	Mr L. W. Charles	21.11.45
Southdown Karda	D	Southdown Jeremy	Southdown Queen Bee	Mrs Leslie Thornton	8.2.44
Hillsman of Ivel	D	Tribesman of Ivel	Fair Maid of Ivel	Mrs Jeeves	12.2.45
Indigo of Brittas (Irish Ch.)	D	Vagabond of Brittas (Irish Ch.)	Katia of Brittas	Mrs G. M. Barrington	25.2.46
Apollo of Saba	D	Ingosohn of Erol	Empress of Leeda	Mrs I. Gauntlett	14.9.45
Danko v. Menkenmoor of Hardwick	D	Lex Preussenblut	Bionda v.d. Buchenhöhe	Mr A. Moelsen	5.8.46
Honey of Druidswood	B	Gottfried of Coulathorne	Francesca of Druidswood	Mrs Pickup	31.5.46
Cingla II a.v. Trebergsklippan	B	Ch. Rosenhovs Muck	Faiy a.v. Trebergsklippan	Mr H. Borjesson	29.5.43
Mistress of Melandra	B	Chorltonville Consol	Chorltonville Calonne	Mr and Mrs L. Beever	10.5.44
Pamela of Whiteville	B	Janitor of Whiteville	Kola of Whiteville	Mrs E. M. Pike	15.3.44
Neva of Coulathorne	B	Gottfried of Coulathorne	Ingrid of Coulathorne	Mrs V. E. Dyer	28.7.45
Erhwald Penny of Southlore	B	Viking of Coulmony	Shene of Rigi	Mr L. Charles	27.7.44
Avon Prince of Alumvale	D	Ch. Arno of Saba	Briarville Crystal	Mr E. Carver	12.8.48
Hella Secretainerie	B	Ch. Arno of Saba	Frivolity of Peak Hill	Mr J. Schwabacher	3.7.47

198

Name	Sex	Sire	Dam	Breeder	Born
Artemis of Iada	B	Ch. Arno of Saba	Iada Gerta of Celebre	Mrs Babcock-Cleaver	12.8.48
Abbess of Saba	B	Ingosohn of Erol	Empress of Leeda	Mrs I. Gauntlett	4.9.45
Nantes of Leimar	B	Quest of Peak Hill	Alona of Playways	Mr T. Leitch	30.12.43
Vikkas Delsa av Hvitsand	B	Ch. Vagabond of Brittas (and Irish Ch.)	Ch. Karaste Karenina av Hvitsand	Mr and Mrs P. Elliot	18.7.47
Reginella Romana	B	Mario Romana	Ghita of Ingon	Mrs G. Uglione	29.1.47
Vagabond of Brittas (Irish Ch.)	D	Ch. Gerolf of Brittas	Ellengart of Brittas	Mrs G. M. Barrington	11.1.44
Letton My Hero	D	Hero of Roslin (Irish Ch.)	Maureen of Brittas	Mrs J. P. Beck	26.6.48
Sonja of Highcarrs	B	Damon of Highcarrs	Europa of Iada	Mr M. Turpin	30.3.47
Barrie of Buckthorn	D	Trumpeter of Ivel	Una of Copthill	Miss U. M. Heslop	20.12.45
Alise Tadellos	B	Gottfried of Coulathorne	Delhia Romana	Mrs V. Egger	20.10.45
Anna Karenina Vitalis	B	Ch. Danko v. Menkenmoor of Hardwick	Freda of Oxhey	Mr W. R. Russell	13.8.49
Edana of Combehill	B.	Ludo of Druidswood	Sara of Redbyville	Mr H. E. Johnson	9.10.48
Ischka of Brittas	B	Ch. Vagabond of Brittas (and Irish Ch.)	Katia of Brittas	Mrs G. M. Barrington	25.2.46
Jalcon Adela of Vesetta	B	Caruso of Croftholme	Vesta of Croftholme	Mrs S. and Miss M. Wightman	4.11.58
Ranee of Karda	B	Ch. Southdown Karda	Blondie of Karda	Mrs K. L. Godson	1.1.46
Rola of Brittas (Irish Ch.)	B	Ch. Vagabond of Brittas (and Irish Ch.)	Vesta of Ivel	Mrs G. M. Barrington	7.2.48
Sabre Secretainerie	D	Ch. Danko vom Menkenmoor of Hardwick	Frivolity of Peakhill	Mr J. Schwabacher	22.8.49
Axel von Lubbecker Land	D	Rolf vom Osnabruckerland	Thea vom Hermannsland	Mr F. Rullmann	8.7.49
Lyric of Southavon	D	Mario Romana	Isla of Brittas	Mrs J. Macpherson	9.5.49
Poultonoire Artist	D	Ch. Arno of Saba	Delia of Glendaire	Mrs R. C. Adamson	14.5.48
Romana Peppino	D	Breuse Tadellos	Romana Micheline	Mrs G. Uglione	13.2.50
Sabre of Surtayne	D	The Master of Eggerness	Sheila of Rossmere	Mr W. B. Stant	25.10.43
Sergeant of Rozavel	D	Galliard of Brittas	Goody of Rozavel	Mrs T. Gray	29.5.48
Uisgebeata of Brittas	B	Mario Romana	Iola of Brittas	Mrs G. M. Barrington	27.5.48
Bromholm Beda of Croftholme	B	Caruso of Croftholme	Lola of Croftholme	Mr and Mrs N. Bancroft	14.2.48
Drakemyre Amber	B	Ch. Indigo of Brittas (and Irish Ch.)	Magali of Croftholme	Mr A. Brown	19.1.49
Harmony of Druidswood	B	Gottfried of Coulathorne	Francesca of Druidswood	Mrs M. Pickup	31.5.46
Nannette of Clodien	B	Ch. Monti of Welham	Maid of the Taff	Mr A. G. Elliott	22.1.50

Name	Sex	Sire	Dam	Breeder	Born
Vitalis Amazon	B	Ch. Danko vom Menkenmoor of Hardwick	Freda of Oxhey	Mr W. R. Russell	13.8.49
Cip of Lynrowe	D	Ch. Danko vom Menkenmoor of Hardwick	Rampa of Karda	Mrs L. Rowland	28.4.49
Norn Johann of Tenbury	D	Grey Boy of Norn	Sophia of Ravenscar	Mrs S. Lockwood	7.3.46
Southdown Nireus	D	Ch. Danko vom Menkenmoor of Hardwick	Ch. Ranee of Karda	Mr B. C. Dickerson	4.9.50
Terrie of Glenvoca	D	Ch. Danko vom Menkenmoor of Hardwick	Ch. Abbess of Saba	Messrs G. Crook and J. Schwabacher	26.1.50
Altania of Poultonoire	B	Ch. Arno of Saba	Delia of Glendaire	Mrs R. C. Adamson	14.5.48
Ansa of Bolivar	B	Ch. Indigo of Brittas	Bolivar Anna of Holtwood	Mr H. E. Roberts	11.3.49
Filesca of Brittas	B	Sentinel of Brittas	Uriel Princess du Clos des Loups	Mrs G. M. Barrington	3.8.50
Fiona of Sirdar	B	Chorltonville Consol	Iada Jamima of Arnold	Mr J. Evans	12.3.47
Laurel of Wambrook	B	Knight's Errant of Leimar	Ranee of Lanka	Mr W. Ravenscroft	5.8.46
Reddicap Felicity of Dondoran	B	Brande of Howbar	Anna of Dondoran	Mrs D. Corkindale	19.11.48
Walgunde of Brittas	B	Ch. Indigo of Brittas	Edrika of Brittas	Mrs G. M. Barrington	9.9.48
Baron of Celebre	D	Chesney of Woodforte	Ch. Artemis of Iada	Mr D. T. Williams	5.8.51
Cito von der Meerwarcht	D	Donner Vom Gerbergarten	Gunda vom Schloss Rauschenstein	Mr F. Bernecker	8.3.52
Danki of Glenvoca	D	Ch. Terrie of Glenvoca	Ch. Sabre Secretainerie	Mr G. Crook	14.2.52
Koenig of Knowlebank	D	Ceiriog Siriol	Bridget of Ivel	Mrs E. Adams	5.8.49
Chota of Glandoreen	B	Ambassador of Wil-Muir	Krista of Wolfhill	Mr R. McCullough	5.4.51
Grizel of Combehill	B	Ch. Danko vom Menkenmoor of Hardwick	Sara of Redbyville	Mr H. E. Johnson	14.2.50
Perdita of Kentwood	B	Ch. Indigo of Brittas	Nerissa of Kentwood	Miss S. H. Godden	4.3.52
Southdown Sapphire	B	Ch. Southdown Nireus	Southdown Jacynth	Mr B. C. Dickerson	30.4.52
Arlene of Bolivar	B	Ch. Indigo of Brittas (and Irish Ch.)	Bolivar Anna of Holtwood	Mr H. E. Roberts	11.3.49
Arthemis of Glenvoca	B	Ch. Jet of Seale	Ch. Abbess of Saba	Mr G. Crook and Mr J. Schwabacher	15.4.51
Carissima of Bolivar	B	Mario Romana	Bolivar Anna of Holtwood	Mr H. E. Roberts	15.5.51
Cefne of Eveley	B	Tadellos Uno of Brittas	Longbrook Efne of Eveley	Mrs M. E. Tidbold	8.2.51
Dora of Eveley	B	Ch. Danko vom Menkenmoor of Hardwick	Lady of Littlebrook	Mr F. Holland	12.3.51

Name	Sex	Sire	Dam	Breeder	Born
Empress of Eniswen	B	Iada Themistocles	Duchess of Eniswen	Mr D. Parry	10.5.51
Gitana of Combehill	B	Ch. Danko vom Menkenmoor of Hardwick	Sara of Redbyville	Mr H. E. Johnson	14.2.50
Invader of Eveley	D	Ch. Avon Prince of Alumvale	Walda of Brittas	Mrs M. E. Tidbold	14.5.52
Iona of Eveley	B	Ch. Avon Prince of Alumvale	Walda of Brittas	Mrs M. E. Tidbold	14.5.52
Lodo of Bucklebury	D	Ch. Danko vom Menkenmoor of Hardwick	Ilse Secretainerie	Miss M. Langer	16.10.49
Quixotic of Huesca	D	Quixotic of Isk	Danae of Huesca	Miss S. J. Kozhevar	6.8.51
Rebecca of Byenroc	B	Ch. Avon Prince of Alumvale	Alone of Byenroc	Miss J. C. Miles	13.12.51
Riot of Rhosincourt	D	Ch. Danko vom Menkenmoor of Hardwick	Rhoda of Rhosincourt	Miss V. G. Madder	27.10.51
Allegro of Seacroft	D	Yokel of Aronbel	Helina of Eveley	Miss A. M. Bendle	8.7.54
Bruno of Seale	D	Mario Romana	Sonia of Seale	Mrs M. Howard	29.5.52
Carol of Perfection	B	Ch. Avon Prince of Alumvale	Karen Tadellos	Mrs R. Wallace	17.7.53
Celebrity of Jackfield	D	Ch. Avon Prince of Alumvale	Adele of Tunstall	Mrs M. Lancett	18.1.55
Chiquita of Kelowna	B	Ch. Avon Prince of Alumvale	Helim of Kelowna	Miss M. O'Grady	25.10.51
Cimlan Phoana	B	Ch. Avon Prince of Alumvale	Jassy of Brinton	Miss B. J. Drake	14.4.53
D'Arcy of Lustyglaze	D	Laird of Cranville	Grizelda of Lustyglaze	Miss M. O'Gerry	5.1.54
Jaguar of Stranmillis	D	Lodo of Bucklebury	Aileen of Stranmillis	Mrs D. Beach	28.1.52
Letton Duskie Despot	D	Ch. Letton my Hero	Vitalis Philomela of Eveley	Mrs J. Beck	12.4.53
Letton Rola of Alsaren	D	Ch. Indigo of Brittas	Eroica of Templefields	Mrs E. G. Renouf	28.6.51
Lucien of Highcarrs	D	Ch. Avon Prince of Alumvale	Ch. Sonja of Highcarrs	Mr M. Turpin	17.5.53
Marquita of Eveley	B	Ch. Danko vom Menkenmoor of Hardwick	Walda of Brittas	Mrs M. E. Tidbold	17.4.53
Querida of Cranville	B	Ch. Avon Prince of Alumvale	Jandy of Cranville	Mrs R. H. Barker	29.3.53
Quince of Southavon	D	Ch. Romana Peppino	Isla of Brittas	Mrs J. Macpherson	3.2.53
Ransome of Byenroc	D	Ch. Avon Prince of Alumvale	Ilona of Byenroc	Miss J. C. Miles	13.12.51
Vikkas Donna av Hvitsand	B	Ch. Avon Prince of Alumvale	Ch. Vikkas Delsa av Hvitsand	Mr and Mrs P. Elliott	27.6.54
Yokel of Aronbel	B	Ch. Avon Prince of Alumvale	Kerry Dancer of Aronbel	Mr E. Aaron	20.1.53
Jaguette of Stranmillis	B	Lodo of Bucklebury	Aileen of Stranmillis	Mrs D. Beach	28.1.52
Asoka Ardent	B	Jonty of Jonquest	Vikkas Alela av Hvitsand	Mrs M. J. Litton	18.5.55
Hortondale Pointsman	D	Terrie of Glenvoca Ch. Ob. Ch.	Cimlan Phoanna Ch.	Mr W. Ginzel	8.2.55
Beowulf of Seale	D	Bruno of Seale Ch.	Seale Amanda of Ararat	Mrs M. Howard	12.2.55

Name	Sex	Sire	Dam	Breeder	Born
Ilex of Brittas	D	Atlas of Brittas	Rola of Brittas Ch. Irish Ch.	Mrs G. M. Barrington	6.5.55
Sparky of Aronbel	D	Allegro of Seacroft Ch.	Yasmin of Aronbel	Mr I. E. Aaron	2.8.55
Helina of Eveley	B	Tadello Uno of Brittas	Longbrook Efne of Eveley	Mrs M. E. Tidbold	13.5.52
Glenvoca Shauna	B	Danki of Glenvoca Ch. Ob. Ch.	Chota of Glandoreen	Mr J. W. Thompson	27.4.56
Diane of Shraleycarr	B	Avon Prince of Alumvale Ch.	Chanson Val Dassa	Messrs A. & G. R. Mason	22.8.55
Duchess of Shraleycarr	B	Avon Prince of Alumvale Ch.	Chanson Val Dassa	Messrs A. & G. R. Mason	22.8.55
Mignonette of Huesca	B	Romana Peppino Ch.	Dagmar of Huesca	Miss S. J. Kozhevar	13.9.56
Ansa of Hamel	B	Cimber of Friarsbush	Avocet of Hamel	Mr R. Jackson	25.5.55
Moonraker of Monteray	D	Monteray's Juggernaut of Jonquest	June of Eveley	Mr J. Wilson	31.12.54
Letton Tregiskey Eloquence	B	Quince of Southavon Ch.	Letton Dusky Delight	Miss J. C. Lane	17.3.56
Asoka Cherusker	D	Crusader of Evesyde	Vikkas Alda av Hvitsand	Mrs M. J. Litton	10.9.57
Cimlan Plainsman	D	Danko vom Menkenmoor of Hardwick Ch.	Kiku of Huesca	Mrs B. J. Drake	14.2.54
Demetrius of Kentwood	D	Quince of Southavon Ch.	Perdita of Kentwood Ch.	Miss S. H. Godden	18.6.56
Harmony of Llanyravon	B	Cecil Secretainerie	Casamina of Llanyravon	Mrs N. Evans	26.2.54
Hortondale Priscilla	B	Terrie of Glenvoca Ch. & Ob. Ch.	Cimlan Phoana Ch.	Mr W. Ginzel	8.2.55
Nobel of Swansford	D	Swansford Hussan of Bolivar	Jeanette of Jonquest	Mr A. D. Swann	17.2.57
Tackleway Kyrie	D	Kings Ransome of Eveley	Tackleway Barcarolle	Lt.-Col. and Mrs J. F. H. Clare	31.10.57
Ulbert of Brittas Irish Ch.	D	Ilex of Brittas Ch. & Irish Ch.	Querida of Brittas Irish Ch.	Mrs G. M. Barrington	4.12.56
Ursula of Brittas	B	Ilex of Brittas Ch. & Irish Ch.	Querida of Brittas Irish Ch.	Mrs G. M. Barrington	4.12.56
Crusader of Evesyde	B	Quince of Southavon Ch.	Janine of Jonquest	Mr S. Greaves	29.4.56
Asoka Caprice	B	Crusader of Evesyde	Vikkas Alda av Hvitsand	Mrs M. J. Litton	10.9.57
Athena of Dalmeith	B	Avon Prince of Alumvale Ch.	Karen Tadellos	Mrs R. Wallace	12.8.57
Churlswood Cautious	B	Avon Prince of Alumvale Ch.	Fancy Free of Charavigne	Mr and Mrs L. A. Collins	13.2.57
Dusty of Alanmoordale	D	Fearless of Alanmoordale	Pixie of Hamel	Mrs I. Page	23.2.56
Gorsefield Khahn	D	Crusader of Evesyde	Gorsefield Cingla	Mrs W. R. Kinsman	21.8.57
Joyciel Adela of Hastingsdene	B	Arno of Glenvoca	Ann of Hastingsdene	Mr W. Hastings	12.4.54
Lynwulf Juno	B	Beowulf of Seale	Honesty of Eveley	Mr V. Woodward	23.6.57
Sabre of Glandoreen	B	Arno of Glenvoca	Chota of Glandoreen	Mr R. McCullough	12.3.55
Vesta of Gossops	B	Sandyman of Noblehurst	Vanity of Hardwick	Mr J. W. Kinge	26.5.56
Vikkas Chiefton of Deanthorpe	D	Moonraker of Monteray Ch.	Jalna of Jonquest	Mr F. A. Bell	17.10.57

Name	Sex	Sire	Dam	Breeder	Born
Francesca of Lexter	B	Yokel of Aronbel Ch.	Cara of Eveley	Mrs A. M. Winter and Mrs M. E. Tidbold	29.8.56
Arghan Anton of Glanford	D	Yokel of Aronbel Ch.	Gloxinia of Huesca	Mr C. A. Harrison	7.11.57
Clintonville Fascinator	B	Crusader of Evesyde Ch.	Clintonvilles Biky of Elbruz	Mr and Mrs C. D. Griffiths and Miss T. Patel	22.8.58
Kondor of Brittas (Irish Ch.)	D	Condor v. Hohenstamm	Pia Wikingerblut of Brittas	Mrs G. Barrington	12.7.58
Fenella of Goss	B	Sandyman of Noblehurst	Lavender of Charavigne	Mrs B. Scarratt	19.11.57
Fiona of Shraleycarr	B	Avon Prince of Alumvale Ch.	Chanson Val D'Assa	Messrs A. & E. R. Mason	24.2.57
Francesca of Kentwood	B	Demetrius of Kentwood Ch.	Rosalind of Kentwood	Miss S. H. Godden	12.1.58
Francesca of Silverlands	D	Quest of Cranville	Sonnett of Silverlands	Mrs V. Berdoe Wilkinson	17.8.59
Gorsefield Granit	D	Crusader of Evesyde Ch.	Gorsefield Carousel	Mr R. Hall	28.12.58
Hortondale Asoka Felicity	B	Asoka Cherusker Ch.	Asoka Ardent Ch.	Mrs M. Litton	18.2.59
Hycap Delilaha	B	Lucien of Highcarrs Ch.	Rhapsody of Reddicap	Mrs V. Towers	13.9.57
Makabuse Otto	D	Peter Pan of Eveley	Barilla of Byenroc	Mrs M. F. Marshall	26.5.58
Saba of Llanyravon	D	Hortondale Pointsman Ch.	Harmony of Llanyravon Ch.	Mr and Mrs E. C. Scammell	7.6.59
Ulele of Silverlands	B	Kings Ransome of Eveley	Marquita of Eveley Ch.	Mrs V. Berdoe Wilkinson	23.7.57
Vasco of Brinton	D	Hortondale Pointsman Ch.	Eveleys Happy of Charavigne	Mr and Mrs B. M. Lindsay	27.10.57
Harper of Oldway	B	Marshall of Oldway	Victoria of Oldway	Mrs G. Bartlett	27.4.58
Juno of Annarene	B	Sparky of Aronbel Ch.	Annette of Annarene	Mr N. Cameron	9.5.58
Neroli of Huesca	B	Shadow of Huesca	Melisande of Annarene	Miss S. J. Kozhevar	11.1.59
Churlswood Tosca of Brinton	B	Archer of Brinton Ch.	Zena of Brinton	Mrs J. Tabor	3.4.61
Clintonville Joy	B	Crusader of Evesyde	Clintonvilles Biky of Elbruz	Mr & Mrs C. Griffiths	15.3.59
Eveleys Ailsa of Brinton	B	Asoka Cherusker Ch.	Eveleys Vanity of Brinton	Mr & Mrs B. Lindsay	19.8.59
Fair Lady of Charavigne	B	Cherusker of Evesyde Ch.	Ellina of Eveley	Mr I. Dummett	2.2.59
Fenton of Kentwood	D	Asoka Cherusker Ch.	Francesca of Kentwood Ch.	Miss S. H. Godden	30.10.60
Hortondale Drover of Brinton	D	Asoka Cherusker Ch.	Eveleys Happy of Charavigne	Mr & Mrs E. Lindsau	21.2.60
Janice of Alanmoordale	B	Arghan Anton of Glanford	Asta of Hamel	Mr C. Barrett & Mrs I. Page	26.8.59
Rosetta of Lexter	B	Eveleys Grimm of Charavigne	Genevieve of Lexter	Mrs A. M. Winter	5.10.58
Sabu of Vosta	D	Odin of Glenvoca	Oscodas Vokelle of Vosta	Mr & Mrs D. Foster	26.7.58
Swansford Kay of Bolivar	B	Nobel of Swansford	Carissimar of Bolivar Ch.	Mr H. E. Roberts	22.9.58
Archer of Brinton	D	Asoka Cherusker Ch.	Eveleys Vanity of Brinton	Mr & Mrs Lindsay	19.8.59
Atstan Asta	B	Cent Zu Den Funf Giebeln	Atstan Sabena of Noblehurst	Mrs P. Stanley	29.6.59
Churlswood Cossack of Brinton	D	Vasco of Brinton Ch.	Ellina of Eveley	Mr and Mrs B. Lindsay	18.2.60

Name	Sex	Sire	Dam	Breeder	Born
Eureka of Chervanna	B	Ludwig of Charavigne Ch.	Capri of Chervanna	Mrs F. Walsh	13.1.63
Harmony of Eveley	B	Ludwig of Charavigne Ch.	Eveleys Ailsa of Brinton Ch.	Mrs Tidbold and Miss Lankester	30.6.62
Hortondale Marteen	B	Asoka Cherusker Ch.	Hortondale Priscilla Ch.	Mr W. Ginzel	12.2.61
Ludwig of Charavigne	D	Cent Zu Den Funf Giebeln	Hella of Charavigne	Mrs I. Dummett	26.11.59
My Gal of Hildesheim	B	Asoka Cherusker Ch.	Hildesheim Anna of Wrenhall	Mr T. Allbeury	18.4.62
Stavanna Sultan of Evesyde	D	Sparky of Aronbel Ch.	Asoka Buena of Evesyde	Mr and Mrs Hayward	17.10.61
Anabella of Norloch	B	Asoka Cherusker Ch.	Karen of Northmeols	Mr and Mrs Kinloch	3.2.63
Atstan Impresario	D	Celebrity of Jackfield Ch.	Atstan Uma	Mrs P. Stanley	10.7.61
Connoisseur of Sheracyn	D	Ramacon Buccaneer	Brunella of Noblehurst	Mr and Mrs T. V. Rankin	3.9.62
Empress of Peadron	B	Asoka Cherusker Ch.	Collette of Peadron	Mr and Mrs G. Teanby	4.7.62
Eveleys Quill of Lexter	D	Atstan Impresario Ch.	Flicka of Lexter	Mrs A. M. Winter	24.12.62
Oldway Vivacious of Charavigne	D	Maverick of Stranmillis	Hella of Charavigne	Mrs I. Dummett	14.2.61
Vondaun Juno	B	Ludwig of Charavigne Ch.	Eveleys Jenny of Silverlands	Mrs Y. D. J. Daunton	6.3.62
Churlswood Jason	D	Hortondale Drover of Brinton Ch.	Churlswood Aleeta of Stephendell	Mr and Mrs L. A. Collins	10.1.63
Tackleway Rock of Novem	D	Ludwig of Charavigne Ch.	Tackleway Kyrie Ch.	Lt-Col and Mrs Clare	22.2.62
Kristin of Dunmonaidh Irish Ch.	B	Chanooka of Hawtop	Dunmonaidh Karen of Shraleycarr	Miss Moncreiffe	7.7.62
Eureka of Amulree	B	Sir Galahad of Seacroft	Harobel of Shraleycarr	Mr and Mrs Anderson	17.3.62
Adonis of Lanayeen	D	Gorsefield Granit Ch. (and Irish Ch.)	Serene of Lanayeen	Mr G. F. Taylor	9.11.62
Candella of Ansville	B	Kim of Shraleycarr	Amanda of Lynnville	Mrs D. Evans	15.8.62
Churlswood Olddean Isobel	B	Churlswood Cossack of Brinton Ch.	Olddean Anna Leisa of Brinton	Mrs M. F. Hewitt	2.6.61
Donna of Ansville	B	Chanooka of Hawtop	Janet of Evansville	Mrs D. Evans	22.8.63
El Halcon of Brittas	D	Kondor of Brittas Ch. (and Irish Ch.	Ursula of Brittas Ch. (and Irish Ch.)	Mrs G. M. Barrington	10.9.61
Fantasia of Chervanna	B	Ludwig of Charavigne Ch.	Eveleys Lilt of Huesca	Mrs F. Walsh	29.9.63
Hendrawens Tackleway Rigoletto	D	Ludwig of Charavigne Ch.	Tackleway Kyrie Ch.	Lt Col and Mrs J. F.H. Clare	22.2.62
Melissa of Shraleycarr	B	Asoka Cherusker Ch.	Duchess of Shraleycarr Ch.	Messrs A. and G. R. Mason	24.10.61
Rossfort Curcao	D	Ludwig of Charavigne Ch.	Rossfort Vikkas Lucilla Av. Hvitsand	Mrs S.M. Hunter	11.11.63

Name	Sex	Sire	Dam	Breeder	Born
Shootersway Persephone	D	Atstan Impresario Ch.	Shootersway Lucretia of Stranmillis	Mr and Mrs R. A. Allan	1.2.63
Uschi von Affecking	B	Edo vom Haus Geltinger	Pura von Affecking	Kurt Schneider	18.1.60
Vondaun Querida of Flawforth	D	Vondaun Quantock	Vondaun Jani of Kesley	Mrs Y. D. T. Daunton	1.10.64
Vondaun Ulric of Dawnway	D	Archer of Brinton Ch.	Eveleys Jenny of Silverlands	Mrs Y. D. T. Daunton	13.4.64
Agnes of Norloch	B	Asoka Cherusker Ch.	Karen of Northmeols	Mr and Mrs N. Kinloch	3.2.63
Archduke of Rozavel	D	Ludwig of Charavigne Ch.	Twilight of Rozavel	Mrs Thelma Gray	29.8.64
Athena of Anderkris	B	Archer of Brinton Ch.	Sonnet of Amberwell	Mr and Mrs K. Anderson	31.5.62
Brockdale Avenger	D	Terrie of Brinton	Madam Lulu of Brooksbill	Mrs S. Wolfson	12.1.65
Cherrods Fine Fella	D	Clintonville Noble Sir	Clintonville Karen	Mr and Mrs W. Cherry	17.12.62
Condor vom Schiefen Giebel (Irish Ch.)	D	Klodo Aus Der Eremitenklausse	Berri vom Lustjagen (Ger. Ch.)	Herr Georg Fass	6.11.63
Cosalta Fiona	B	Ludwig of Charavigne Ch.	Siren of Charavigne	Mr and Mrs P. Swigeiski	14.12.46
Dunmonaidh Graff of Lexter	D	Atstan Impresario Ch.	Flicka of Lexter	Mrs A. Winter	14.4.65
Elsa of Wodenbury	B	Ludwig of Charavigne Ch.	Lyn of Shraleycarr	Mr J. Harrison	16.7.62
Hendrawens Wendling Cascade	D	Vasco of Brinton Ch.	Astrid of Byenroc	Mrs J. Early	17.4.63
Leo of Llanyraven	D	Saba of Llanyraven	Makabusi Rosella	Mrs N. Evans	7.6.63
Syrious Bassett Griselda	B	Ludwig of Charavigne Ch.	Bassett Joyous Greetings	Mrs D. Ellis	28.6.64
Atstan Luke	D	Lorenz of Charavigne	Thoros Atstan Asta Ch.	Mrs P. Stanley	8.7.62
Baron of Baileyhill	D	Baileyhill Moonlight Lord	Garnet of Eveley	Mr and Mrs E. P. Geary	10.6.61
Churlswood Arno of Hanslor	D	Churlswood Jason Ch.	Bella of Hanslor	Mr and Mrs A. G. Deamer	25.6.45
Claydonhill Heatherette	B	Lethams San Antonie	Claydonhill Dominic	Mrs L. C. Dace	12.6.65
Flawforth Electra of Milbas	B	Ludwig of Charavigne Ch.	Barbara of Milbas	Mr and Mrs E. T. Turner	29.6.65
Lisa Romana	B	Ludwig of Charavigne Ch.	Susina Romana	Mr G. Uglione	17.10.64
Yvette of Eveley	B	Connoisseur of Sheracyn Ch.	Aeronica of Eveley	Mrs M. Tidbold	5.10.65
Gye of Lexter	D	Atstan Impresario Ch.	Flicka of Lexter	Mrs A. Winter	14.4.65
Shootersway Bragaina	B	Churlswood Jason Ch.	Shootersway Phaedra	Mr and Mrs R. A. Allan	2.9.66
Hendrawen's Nibelung of Charavigne	D	Hendrawen's Quadrille of Eveley	Vikkas Debbie Av Hvitsand	Mrs I Dummett	18.5.66
Athena of Hatherton	B	Guardsman of Ansville	Duchess of Ansville	Mr and Mrs T. E. Millington	16.3.66
Don Juan of Norloch	D	Vondaun Ulric of Dawnway Ch.	Anbella of Norloch Ch.	Mr and Mrs Kinlock	11.3.66

Name	Sex	Sire	Dam	Breeder	Born
Grania of Zighallen	B	Gorsefield Granit Ch. and Irish Ch.	Corina of Arnhem	Mr R. Mitchell	11.8.64
Hendrawens Garry of Wilindrek	D	Ludwig of Charavigne Ch.	Hildesheim Anna of Wrenhall	Mrs J. Wilkinson	25.4.64
Lucille of Keyna	B	Ludwig of Charavigne Ch.	Marydowns Vista of Eveley	Miss Z. Pearce	25.11.66
Seinn Feiner of Muckross	D	Larigan Kerrygo	Camay of Skegby	Mrs E. Scawthon	25.12.65
Shootersway Cressida	B	Eveley's Quill of Lexter Ch.	Shootersway Lucretia of Stranmillis	Mr and Mrs R. Allan	14.2.66
Venitta of Emmevale	B	Archer of Brinton Ch.	Blanka of Edcliffe	Mr H. Emmett and Mr L. Heseltine	7.1.66
Zia of Marlish	B	Derby von der Schinklergrenze	Quality Street of Marlish Am. Ch.	Mrs S. A. Coates	15.10.64
Alverry Dark Rosaleen of Elpyk	B	Ludwig of Charavigne Ch.	Molly of Clonbeg	Mrs E. Pyke	13.2.65
Coolree's Enchantment of Eveley	B	Hendrawen's Charade of Charavigne	Marydown Little Venus of Eveley	Mrs M. Tidbold and Miss L. Pearce	10.2.67
Cosalta Franklyn	D	Ludwig of Charavigne Ch.	Siren of Charavigne	Mr and Mrs P. Swigciski	14.12.64
Eclipse of Eveley	D	Hendrawen's Charade of Charavigne	Marydown Little Venue of Eveley	Mrs M. Tidbold and Miss L. Pearce	10.2.67
Efne of Eveley	B	Hendrawen's Charade of Charavigne	Marydown Little Venue of Eveley	Mrs M. Tidbold and Miss L. Pearce	10.2.67
Hargret Rivercroft Nylon	B	Condor Vom Schiefen Giebel	Vondaun Gennetta of Rivercroft	Mrs E. M. Harrison and Dr M. Gibson	28.9.67
Joll Vom Bemholt	D	Bodo Vom Lierberg	Esta Vom Friedlichenheim	Mr W. Schlusen	9.10.64
Hendrawen's Syrious Norge	D	Hendrawen's Quadrille of Eveley	Syrious Bassett Griselda	Mrs D. A. Wingate	12.6.66
Laura of Sanbiase	B	Ludwig of Charavigne Ch.	Wascana Irma of Sanbiase	Mrs D. P. Fulcher	5.4.66
Nevada of Sheracyn	D	Hendrawen's Quadrille of Eveley	Hathaway of Sheracyn	Mr and Mrs T. V. Rankin	23.5.67
Hendrawen's Tackleway Troubadour	D	Ch. Ludwig of Charavigne	Ch. Tackleway Kyrie	Lt Col and Mrs Clare	22.1.65
Peregrine of Dunmonaidh	D	Condor Von Schiefen Giebel Ch. and Ir. Ch.	Olga of Dunmonaidh	Miss Moncreiffe of Moncreiffe	4.12.66
Ramacon Swashbuckler	D	Ramacon Philanderer	Ramacon Nanette	Mr W. Rankin	23.9.68

Name	Sex	Sire	Dam	Breeder	Born
Rolf of Dunmonaidh	D	Condor Von Schiefen Giebel Ch. and Ir. Ch.	Rilla of Dunmonaidh	Miss Moncreiffe of Moncreiffe	19.3.67
Rossfort Rissalma	B	Rossfort Curaco Ch.	Gleam of Littlefleet	Mrs S. M. Hunter	20.5.68
Imemma of Grafmere	B	Clintonville Milord	Toplady of Meccamoor	Mr and Mrs F. Hunter	4.8.68
Burgomaster of Brittas	D	Billo V. Saynbach	Alamander of Brittas	Mrs G. M. Barrington	11.2.66
Evely's Bunessa of Flawforth	B	Hendrawen's Charade of Charavigne	Ionia of Eveley	Miss M. V. Hind	26.3.68
Khyberi of Coolree	B	Vondaun Nantes of Flawforth	Vondaun Parthenos of Coolree	Mrs H. B. Rawson-Mackenzie	22.1.67
Knotrom's Emile	B	Hendrawens Charade of Charavigne	Kystorm of Knotram	Mrs O. Morton	14.5.68
Ramacon Philanderer	D	Ludwig of Charavigne Ch.	Bernadene Ramacon Ireina	Mrs M. V. Ambrose	19.2.67
Eros of Lyrenstan	D	Dunmonaidh Drummond of Charavigne	Athena of Anderkris Ch.	Mr and Mrs S. Gillon	7.5.68
Rossfort Premonition	D	Lex of Glanford	Vondaun Belsima of Brinton	Mrs S. M. Hunter	21.8.69
Druidswood Consort	D	Dromcot Quadra of Charoan	Druidswood Yasmin	Mrs M. Pickup	15.4.68
Ramadan Red Silk	B	Eclipse of Eveley Ch.	Melody of Dawnway	Mesdames J. Bingham and J. Stokes	19.2.69
Shootersway Hermione	B	Shootersway Bacchus	Shootersway Persephone Ch.	Mr and Mrs R. A. Allan	26.3.69
Starhope's Mireille of Charavigne	B	Hendrawen's Charade of Charavigne	Vondaun Querida of Flawforth Ch.	Mrs I. Dummett and Mrs K. Watts	1.11.68
Cheryll of Emmevale	B	Eclipse of Eveley Ch.	Venitta of Emmevale	Messrs. L. Heseltine and H. Emmett	12.3.70
Tarquin of Dawnway	D	Eclipse of Eveley Ch.	Masquerade of Dawnway	Messrs W. and R. Cartwright	2.7.70
Kingsmens Witchcraft	B	Hendrawen Syrious Norge Ch.	Kingsmen Naomi of Jugoland	Mrs S. Butland	16.9.69
Juno of Anjou	B	Anjous Marquis of Flawforth	Bracken of Anjou	Mrs G. Cheetham	12.6.69
Tramella's Innsbrook Jonty	D	Innsbrook Northedge Bandido	Duxella of Mynstonmoor	Mr and Mrs W. Crawshaw	1.6.68
Naldera of Amulree	B	Vondaun Ulric of Dawnway Ch.	Harobel of Amulree	Mr and Mrs H. Anderson	16.2.67
Ramacon Virginia	B	Ramacon Philanderer Ch.	Ramacon Nanette	Mr W. Rankin	28.5.70
Elaina's Kingsmens Ransome	B	Dunmonaidh Kirk of Shraleycarr	Kingsmens Zeimtah of Jugoland	Mr & Mrs P. Butland & Mrs M. Callam	17.7.67
Emmevale Majestic	D	Vondaun Ulric of Dawnway Ch.	Sarella of Emmevale	Mr H. Emmett & Mr L. Heseltine	1.4.71

Name	Sex	Sire	Dam	Breeder	Born
Gorsefield Shah	D	Vondaun Ulric of Dawnway Ch.	Gorsefield Meerbrook Gaytime	Mrs M. J. Pilling	19.10.66
Honddu Cita	B	Clintonbille Milford	Deborah of Clonbeg	Mr B. R. Stockwell	24.2.69
Melony Bethune	B	Ilk Von Den Eschbacher Klippen	Melony Wyoming	Mrs B. Lines	13.10.70
Norwulf Enchantment	B	Hendrawens Syrious Norge Ch.	Vikkas Debbie Av Hvitsand	Mrs I. Dummett	18.6.69
Olivia of Eveley	B	Vondaun Ulric of Dawnway Ch.	Efne of Eveley Ch.	Mrs M. Tidbold	18.8.70
Iota of Rondetto	B	Cosalta Franklyn Ch.	Rondetto Anasasia	Mr & Mrs A. V. Ruff	29.6.69
Kelowna Winged Feet	B	Druidswood Consort	Garonne of Kelowna	Miss M. O'Grady	28.3.70
Marchael Suhaili	B	Hendrawen's Syrious Norge Ch.	Marchael Box of Tricks	Mrs B. F. Marshall	21.9.70
Novem Bolero	B	Rossfort Premonition Ch.	Andromeda of Novem	Mr Woods & Mr Dunkly	7.3.71
Shootersway Eros	D	Ramacon Philanderer Ch.	Shootersway Eurydice	Mr & Mrs R. Allan	5.2.69
Commisar of Antalon	D	Ramacon Swashbuckler Ch.	Wraith of Hilrada	Mr B. Hulme	17.6.71
Shootersway Xanthos of Colgay	D	Druidswood Consort Int. Ch.	Shootersway Eurydice	Mr & Mrs R. Allan	3.1.72
Dieter of Charvorne	D	Nautilus of Huesca	Chanda of Charvorne	Mrs J. Charteris	1.12.71
Dermark Kari	B	Rossfort Premonition Ch.	Octavia of Royden	Mr & Mrs D. W. G. Fenton	20.5.71
Davendens Barbarella	B	Cosalta Fidel of Davendens	Dermark Irena	Mr & Mrs Page	3.3.72
Gailsmoor Carousel	B	Emmevale Majestic Ch.	Asta of Gailsmoor	Mr E. W. Morton	23.6.72
Wauchopes Francesca	B	Rossfort Premonition Ch.	Wauchope's Amanda	Mr & Mrs Gribben	14.3.72
Spartacist of Hendrawen	B	Ramacon Swashbuckler Ch.	Flicka of Brinton	Mr A. Husain	7.11.72
Gilden Adonis	D	Lynwulf Musician	Quidora of Dunmonaidh	Mrs G. A. Denham	12.9.71
Gregrise Velveteen	D	Ramacon Philanderer Ch.	Gregrise Nemesis	Mrs E. Day & Miss Ash	20.7.72
Ritz of Hanslor	D	Opportunist of Upland	Bella of Hanslor	Mr M. Bethell	10.6.68
Peerless of Norloch	D	Gorsefield Granit Int. Ch.	Donnabella of Norloch	Mr & Mrs Kinloch	5.6.71
Ronet Nina	B	Druidswood Consort Ch.	Vikkas Ibis Av Hvitsand	Mrs & Mr R. A. Firth	22.1.70
Witch of Wyeview	B	Atstan Lucifer	Wyeview Donnabella	Mrs K. Lewis	23.8.67
Bedwins Caroline	B	Anjou's Pimpernel	Bonzelham Thundersky	Mr M. L. Griffiths	29.1.72
Ullswood Folly	B	Eclipse of Eveley Ch.	Marquita of Dawnway	Mr & Mrs M. J. Blackhurst	30.12.70
Tramella's Honddu Bechan	B	Clintonville Milord	Honddu Sasha	Mr & Mrs B. Stockwell	23.5.68
Vonjen Nijinski	D	Vonjen Lorenzo	Vonjen Princes Zona	Mrs A. Jenkins	11.4.70

Name	Sex	Sire	Dam	Breeder	Born
Rossford Oran of Kenmil	D	Rossfort Premonition Ch.	Moonbeam of Rossfort	Mrs S. Hunter	26.4.71
Aerokens Debonair	B	Eclipse of Eveley Ch.	Eveley's Cinderella of Kenya	Mr & Mrs J. Langhorn	7.4.71
Nyta of Duconer	B	Quartrain of Amulree	Brena of Duconer	Mrs D. P. Mitchell	23.12.69
Turnstyle Chalice	B	Ferdl Von Den Eschbacher Klippen	Ronsbourne Canby	Mr & Mrs Turner & Mr G. Ward	13.3.69
Unisca Ricardo	D	Ramacon Swashbuckler Ch.	Unisca Pick O'The Pops	Mrs E. Sutton	10.10.71
Vornhill Vigilante	D	Vikkas Scipio Av Hvitsand	Ayeshazk of Jugoland	Mrs Brocklehurst	27.7.72
Eveley's Fancy Free	B	Emmevale Majestic Ch.	Coolree Sabina	Mrs M. Tidbold	22.9.72
Cedarsdean Montana	D	Lex of Glanford	Bonnie of Cedarsdean	Mrs M. Stephenson	10.6.73
Cellie Von Herzogtum Franken	B	Jorg Vom Neuborn	Tuja Von Der Elisabethan	Walter F. Grull	12.10.72
Charminone of Brittas	B	Rossfort Premonition Ch.	Landa of Brittas	Mrs G. M. Barrington	3.8.72
Daval Lynaka of Lexicade	B	Alstan Cordoba Tan	Ursa of Huesca	Mr T. K. Greenow	8.3.73
Delridge Erhard	D	Vecrin Erhard	Delridge Camilla	Mesdames B. K. Budd & E. F. Wilson	12.10.73
Glenteall Cesaer	D	Mandarin of Coolree	Glenteall Miranda	Mr H. Teall	10.4.72
Kenmils Oransgirl	B	Rossfort Oran of Kenmil Ch.	Kenmil's One and Only	Dr K. Sames	4.10.72
Norwulf Treasure Trove of Chaddyford	D	Tramella's Innsbruck Jonty	Norwulf Meditation Ch.	Mrs E. M. Barron	9.2.73
Norwulf Meditation	B	Patraliza's Lord Jim from Hendrawen	Norwulf Enchantment Ch.	Mrs E. M. Barron	15.5.71
Shedocast Condor	D	Druidswood Consort Ir. Ch.	Rossfort Rafika	Mrs S. Whittaker	8.7.72
Tanfield Delfie	B	Orsof Vom Besucher Schloss	Tanfield Anja	Miss A. Greaves	22.6.73
Kenmils Orangina of Scratchard	B	Rossfort Oran of Kenmil Ch.	Kenmil's One and Only	Dr K. Sames	4.10.72
Kingsmens Mere Magic of Greenveldt	B	Kenmil Montana of Charavigne	Kingsmens Sbrigani of Jugoland	Mr & Mrs J. Johnson	2.12.72
Delridge Indigo	D	Druidswood Consort Ir. Ch.	Delridge Camilla	Mesdames B. K. Budd & E. F. Wilson	26.11.74
Eveley's Bonnie Prince Charlie	D	Commisar of Antalon Ch.	Gina Mia of Eveley	Mrs M. Tidbold	3.3.75
Jacnel Philados	D	Rossfort Premonition Ch.	Rossfort Angelola	Mr & Mrs J. Wright	12.7.72
Letton Premium	D	Rossfort Premonition Ch.	Letton Shootersway Scylla	Mrs J. Beck	17.5.73
Mikorr Aquarius	D	Rossfort Premonition Ch.	Freida of Mikorr	Mr M. J. Orr	2.1.72
Norwulf Virgil	D	Tramellas Innsbrook Jonty Ch	Norwulf Enchantment Ch.	Mrs E. M. Barron	4.8.73

Name	Sex	Sire	Dam	Breeder	Born
Paulinous Dusalka	D	Paulinous Buccaneer	Jacqlyndon Reina	Mr P. Smith	6.5.74
Zanto Zu Den Stocken of Emmevale	D	Mutz Zu Den Stocken	Rieke v.d. Friehelt Westerholt	Herr H. Dostmann	7.8.73
Banja Vom Hil-Ka Forst	B	Reza v.d. Wienerau	Welle Vom Kopenkamp	Mr F. R. Eskander	1.5.74
Emmevale Natasha	B	Rossfort Premonition Ch.	Vanessa of Emmevale	Mr & Mrs H. Emmett	1.7.73
Luxol Bewitched	B	Eros of Lyrenstan Ch.	Enchantress of Tunnley	Mr & Mrs M. J. Creighton	30.3.75
Marydown Oranella	B	Rossfort Oran of Kenmil Ch.	Marydown Dianella	Mr & Mrs G. D. Tucker	24.7.74
Mystonmoor Victoriana	B	Rossfort Premonition Ch.	Questa of Mystonmoor	Mrs O. M. Evan & Mr & Mrs L. A. Thompson	7.3.73
Patraliza's Bronte	B	Merriveen Dominic of Bruderkern	Patraliza's Ariaden	Mr & Mrs J. Marshall	11.11.73
Rondeaux's Kanasta	B	Rossfort Oran of Kenmil Ch.	Marchael Njangah	Mrs J. C. Blackman	24.9.74
Rosehurst Andre	B	Druidswood Consort Ch.	Gorsefield Mattie Brown	Mr E. Broadhurst	29.9.73
Sionhouse Pirouette	B	Sionhouse Ibila	Sionhouse Kesdemona	Mr J. Gossage	19.9.72
Aerokens Tristar	D	Spartacist of Hendrawen Ch.	Aerokens Debonair Ch.	Mr & Mrs J. Langhorn	14.8.75
Nepeans Tambourlaine	D	Spartacist of Hendrawen Ch.	Tamzin of Nepean	Miss P. Wills	5.10.74
Ramadan Jacobus	D	Delridge Erhard Ch.	Zelda of Sanbiase	Mr J. Bingham	14.2.76
Royvons Giaconda	D	Hendrawens Sagittarius of Aeroken	Royvons Prima Donna	Mr & Mrs R. James	31.3.76
Royvons Red Rum	D	Delridge Erhard Ch.	Caemaen Kendra of Bridgecroft	Mr & Mrs R. James	3.6.77
Fairycross High Society	B	Rossfort Siradus	Tamara of Faircross	Mrs A. Adam	16.3.75
Grafmere Parlez-Vous	B	Grafmere Nimrod	Imemma of Grafmere	Mr & Mrs F. Hunter	3.5.74
Kenhope Octinski	B	Rossfort Oran of Kenmil Ch.	Natinski of Kenhope	Mr H. Blom	19.2.73
Lynlee Cherokee of Hendrawen	B	Lynlee Castaway	Rossacre Golden Myth	Mrs S. C. Douglas	18.3.77
Marchael Tarjipanya	B	Rossfort Oran of Kenmil Ch.	Marchael Sumaili Ch.	Mrs B. Marshall	2.10.74
Nepeans Eloquence of Byrdel	B	Nepean Saratoga	Nepean Regalia	Miss P. Wills	18.8.75
Olivia of Shootersway	B	Peerless of Norloch Ch.	Shootersway Xenia	Mr & Mrs R. A. Allan & Mr & Mrs F. H. Bennett	15.5.74
Aronbel Leading Lady of Cyard	B	Rossfort Premonition Ch.	Dorvaak Dawns of Aronbel	Mr E. Aaron	22.3.74
Voirlich Amigus	D	Ramadan Jacobus Ch.	Castlamaine Mercedes	Mrs J. E. Warner	25.1.77
Amulree's Heiko	D	Dorvaak Jarro	Robuna's Black Diamond	Mr & Mrs H. Anderson	19.8.76
Rintilloch Havoc of Amulree	B	Emmevale Zarroff	Listondene Fancy Pants	Mr J. Hendrie	29.8.77

Name	Sex	Sire	Dam	Breeder	Born
Sadira Paulette	B	Delridge Erhard Ch.	Sadira Francine Ch.	Mr R. Winfrow	7.5.77
Cresswell's Caroline	B	Ramacon Swashbuckler Ch.	Cresswell's Kingsmen's Festival	Mr & Mrs G. Thomas	27.5.74
Fairycross Made to Measure	B	Delridge Erhard Ch.	Tamara of Fairycross	Mrs A. Adam	29.7.76
Graloch Amorous	B	Charavignes Marbello of Starhope	Dorvaak Kleopatra of Graloch	Mrs P. A. G. McCulloch	15.4.75
Gregrise Liquid Fire	B	Spartacist of Hendrawen Ch.	Gregrise Antique Lace	Mrs E. Day & Miss G. Ash	2.10.76
Hendrawen's Ingot	B	Nepeans Tambourlaine Ch.	Flicka of Brinton	Mr & Mrs E. J. White	30.5.76
Labrasco Chica	B	Rossfort Premonition Ch.	Labrasco Amanda	Mrs P. H. E. Scott	1.7.75
Zoe of Sanbiase	B	Rossfort Premonition Ch.	Quella of Sanbiase	Mr & Mrs Smith	1.7.73
Langfaulds Amos	B	Donar v. Fiemereck	Langfaulds Zany	Mr H. de Zutter	1.12.77
Manven-Oriel of Ravenways	D	Tarquin of Dawnway Ch.	Manven Muna	Mr R. H. Walker	7.1.76
Greenveldt Big Benn	D	Delridge Erhard Ch.	Knightbird of Stranmillis	Mrs J. A. Green	1.6.77
Voirlich Amigus	D	Ramadan Jacobus Ch.	Castlemaine Mercedes	Mrs J. E. Warner	25.1.77
Katja v Haus	D	Va Lasso Di Val Sole	Anka v.d. Seracher Heide	Herr K. Engelfried	12.11.77
Labrasco Dulce	B	Vikkas Tanfield Caro	Labrasco Amanda	Mrs P. H. E. Scott	13.7.77
Rina Vom Hasenborn	B	Negus v. Kirschental	Bora v.d. Nussallee	Herr W. Maxein	17.4.77
Beruhen Lady Jane of Bedwin	B	Dirk Vom Clausenhang of Bedwin	Shooterssway Ceres	Mr B. Blades	24.5.78
Double Eclipse of Allunstown	B	Karl of Lyrenstan	Oldway Sari Shooting Star	Mr A. J. Freeman	20.9.77
Glentaff Georgette of Cresswell	B	Ramacon Swashbuckler Ch.	Creswells Natasha	Mr & Mrs P. R. Day	25.8.75
Royvons Danielle	B	Royvons Red Rum Ch.	Royvons Kara	Mr & Mrs R. James	2.6.78
Sadira Petite Fleur of Bedwin	B	Delridge Erhard Ch.	Sadira Francine Ch.	Mr R. J. Winfrow	7.5.77
Whodunnit of Stranmillis	B	Thunder of Stranmillis	Rufflette of Stranmillis	Mrs D. Beach	18.6.76
Jaybeez Apollo	D	Neapeans Tambourlaine Ch.	Tunnleys Patrina	Mr J. L. Best	3.4.77
Jonimay Devil Dick	D	Donar Von Fiemereck	Jonimay Martello Charm	Mr & Mrs T. J. Hannen	30.10.77
Medlock Cai	D	Vikkas Tanfield Caro	Leska v. Anger	Mr & Mrs R. Saunders	15.2.77
Rothick Invictor	D	Rothick Ezra	Mona v. Adeloga	Mr & Mrs R. Ringwald	13.8.78
Dunmonaidh Gytha	B	Chicko Von Gut Friedburg	Dunmondaidh Oak Beauty	Miss Moncreiffe of Moncreiffe	2.1.79
Dermark Prinda	B	Satan v.d. Ajaxklause	Dermark Gal	Mr & Mrs D. W. G. Fenton	20.6.78
Druidswood Sapphire	B	Vikkas Tanfield Caro	Druidswood Jemina	Mr M. Pickup	18.9.76
Fairycross Salina	B	Delridge Erhard Ch.	Fairycross High Society Ch.	Mrs A. Adam	30.4.77
Fascination of Ariom	B	Spartacist of Hendrawen Ch.	Ariom Arnica	Mr H. Lloyd	19.5.77

Name	Sex	Sire	Dam	Breeder	Born
Greenveldt Dallas	B	Dirk v. Clausenhang of Bedwin	Taralan Tralen of Greenveldt	Mrs J. A. Green	4.7.78
Judamie Nevada	B	Barry v. Status Quo	Judamie Efne	Mrs J. Lloyd	12.7.79
Karleby Gay Lady	B	Rondorkris Revelation	Karleby Antasia	Mr A. Bowman	21.11.78
Kurtlee Seffe of Delridge at Fairview	B	Emmevale Zarroff	Kurtlee Minnisota	Mesdames Lee & Budd	29.9.78
Renygar How's Zat	B	Renygar Tomahawk	Renygar Rowena	Mrs I. Garlick	16.6.78
Wyecrest Dominic	D	Eros of Lyrenshan Ch.	Wyecrest Bountiful	Mr & Mrs T. D. Syers	22.5.74
Aerokens Breda	B	Aerokens Tristar Ch.	Tramella's Kola	Mr & Mrs Langhorn	23.2.77
Marydown Oranella	B	Rossfort Oran of Kenmil	Marydown Dianella	Mr & Mrs G. D. Tucker	24.7.74
Fanto vom Bayerischen Wald	D	Casar von Arminius	Beggi vom Bayerischen Wald		26.4.75
Tarik of Ellindale	D	Amulree's Heiko	Allankey Twopence	Mrs P. Gilmour	9.12.78
Elsaville Artful Dodger	B	Emmevale Zaroff Australian Ch.	Rockverne Mazurka	Mr & Mrs Tilley	12.1.79
Maik von Holtkampersee	D	Yasso v. Steppenbrunnen	Inda v. Brockenblick	Herr Niedergassel	5.11.79
Starhopes Kassi	B	Starhopes Lido	Starhopes Sapphire	Mrs McGilvray	4.7.80
Virane Chantilly Lace	B	Virane Alexis	Josdan Gemma of Virane	Mr & Mrs Smith	3.3.79
Dermark Esis	B	Dunmonaidh Faber of Markinch	Dermark Kari Ch.	Mr & Mrs Fenton	2.7.75
Fairycross High Society	B	Rossfort Siradus Australian and N.Z. Ch.	Tamara of Fairycross	Mrs Ann Adams	16.3.75
Alsahurst Raconteur	D	Maik vom Holtkampersee Ch.	Alsahurst Odette	Mrs M. Wiper	18.7.81
Alshvar Schultz	D	Cito v. Königsbruch Ch.	Alshvar Rhythm and Blues	Mr & Mrs Withy	20.6.82
Amulree Hassan	D	Amulree Heiko Ch.	Rintilloch Havoc of Amulree Ch.	Mr & Mrs Anderson	18.4.80
Ariomwood High 'N Mighty	D	Cito v. Konigsbruch Ch.	Fascination of Ariomwood Ch.	Mrs M. Garwood	15.8.83
Charvorne Dielander	D	Dieter of Charvorne Ch.	Charvorne Elander	Mrs J. Charteris	16.10.79
Colthurst Warlord	D	Rothick Echo	Colthurst Starshine	Mr & Mrs Sanderson	2.9.81
Fanto vom Diemelbergland	D	Eros v. Humbachtal	Grilla von der Ederfelsburg	Mr & Mrs Bradley	2.4.79
Kenmils Bellisima of Danalas	B	Eveleys Avrom Star of Kenmils	Kenmils Cleo	Dr K. Sames	15.5.79
Lewshar Corriander of Creswell	B	Kingsmens Captain Fantastic	Gregrise No Robbery at Kenmil	Mr & Mrs P. Lewis	9.12.79
Marvid Marianna	B	Lornaville Ambassador	Lornaville Selina	Mr R. Brandon	12.7.80

Name	Sex	Sire	Dam	Breeder	Born
Ramona di Casa Ossola	B	Lasso di Val Sole	Cilli vom Badsee	Signor G. Ossola	15.1.79
Senjo Yashika of Janshar	B	Barry v. Status Quo Australian Ch.	Senjo De Dum De Dum	Messrs Jones & Bowden	29.12.79
Silberwald Ischka	B	Donar von Fiemereck	Silberwald Beth	Mrs Goodhead & Mr J. Stokes	14.3.79
Moonwinds Golden Cumulus	D	Emmevale Zaroff Australian Ch.	Moonwinds Golden Showers	Miss P. Meaton	11.8.78
Muscava's Flint	D	Tramella's Catastrophe	Tramella's O'Patsy	Mrs P. Harvey	26.2.80
Muscava's Rocky	D	Muscava's Flint Champion	Seravonne's Minuet from Muscava	Mrs P. Harvey	16.3.83
Alf vom Quengelbach	D	Quai v.d. Boxhochburg	Tanja vom Quengelbach	Herr H. Griesbach	3.3.81
Ralymin Caligula	D	Spartacist of Hendrawen Ch.	Ralymin Sasparilla	Mrs M. Fletcher	11.8.77
Reneric Scarlet Chieftan	D	Royvon's Red Rum Ch.	Reneric Golden Gleam	Mr & Mrs Somerfield	8.2.80
Sansarc Navigator	D	Jutones Alf	Hazelcourts Oriana of Sansarc	Mrs L. Benton	3.4.82
Meik v.d. Talquelle	D	Barry vom Rauber Lippold	Sonja vom Bultenweg	Herr J. Stapel	16.8.79
Vorlante Magnum	D	Cito vom Königsbruch Ch.	Incrani of Vorlante	Mr & Mrs Bradley	10.1.82
Calform Angelina of Parojoy	B	Royvon's Red Rum Ch.	Ramacon Demoiselle	Mr & Mrs Ashton	8.6.79
Donzarra's Erla	B	Cito vom Königsbruch Ch.	Trevons Wild Alliance of Donzarra	Mr & Mrs Disney	14.1.82
Emmevale Lara	B	Cito vom Königsbruch Ch.	Emmevale Emmaline	Mr & Mrs Emmett	3.4.82
Allankee's Heini	B	Amulree's Heiko Ch.	Amulree's Ambergris	Mrs M. Ellison	30.8.79
Bedwins Fantasia	B	Natan v. Pelztierfarm *Double Sieger*	Lirka v. Asbacher Land	Mr & Mrs Griffiths	2.2.81
Bedwins Onyx of Judamie	B	Iro v. Pigersberg Canadian Ch.	Anja v. Komtureihof	Mr & Mrs Griffiths	5.9.77
Victoria Bygoly	B	Delridge Erhard	Ursula Bygoly	Mr & Mrs Hadley	25.4.79
Gregrise Alice Blue Gown	B	Royvon's Red Rum Ch.	Gregrise Quilted Satin	Mrs E. Day & Miss G. Ash	22.12.79
Gavington Arikara	B	Zambo vom Königsbruch	Bedwins Zerlina at Gavington	Mr & Mrs Miller	10.9.81
Iolanda Britta	B	Rothick Invictor	Iolanda Marena	Mr & Mrs Miller	31.8.80
Janshar Island Mist	B	Vicksburg Fero	Albra Firespite of Janshar	Mrs Thompson	5.11.82
Karashea's Amorous	B	Manven Oriel of Ravenways Ch.	Quintessence Quowonder	Mrs K. Pye	not known
Kayards Dixie	B	Herzog von Adeloga	Flamme v.d. Herrnweide	Mr & Mrs Wileman	1.8.80
Kimwell Whatagel of Greenveldt	B	Greenveldt Big Ben Ch.	Shelly Syrna of Samworth	Mrs Hale	2.6.80

Name	Sex	Sire	Dam	Breeder	Born
Cito von Königsbruch	D	Nick v.d. Wienerau	Biene v. Entlebuch	Herr W. Glutting	7.7.79
Lord v.d. Krautschneise	D	Karat v.d. Berg-Wilbringen	Aster v.d. Salzbergen	Herr Georg Hoffmann	23.7.74
Marchael Match-Maker	D	Royvon's Red Rum Ch.	Marchael Tajipanya Ch.	Mrs B. Marshall	21.1.79
Labrasco Infanta	B	Delridge Erhard Ch.	Labrasco Chica Ch.	Mr & Mrs Scott	not known
Meadlodge Harvest Princess	B	Eveleys Bonnie Prince Charlie Ch.	Meadlodge Wheat Harvest	Mr & Mrs K. Smith	25.7.78
Mowview Fancy Pants	B	Manven Oriel of Ravensways Ch.	Mowview Miss Exquisite	Mr V. Bentley	29.4.79
Kitti v.d. Platt	B	Yoll vom Adeloga	Hella v.d. Platt	Herr P. Dumont	4.5.80
Reneric Scarlet Ribbons	B	Royvon's Red Rum Ch.	Reneric Golden Gleam	Mr & Mrs Somerfield	8.2.80
Nadia v.d. Talquelle	B	Quino v. Hylligen Born	Gera v. Farbenspiel	Herr J. Stapel	23.10.80
Rosehurst Chris	D	Sieger Uran v. Wildsteigerland	Rosehurst Ramana	Mrs A.T. Broadhurst	25.7.86
Norwulf Fabian	D	Lido v. Hambachtal	Norwulf Liebestraum	Mrs C.M. Barron	1.7.83
Carliston Zeus	D	Ch. Reneric Scarlet Chieftain	Royvons Red Rhumba	Mrs C. Wileman	16.10.81
Acresway Gundo	D	Australian Ch. & Spanish Sieger Ogus de Colombo	Ronet Lana of Acresway	Norma Brown	17.9.83
Alix of Aronbel	D	Aronbel Parisian	Aronbel Francine	Mrs Wilson	7.3.80
Canlake Igor	D	Quanto v. Kopenkamp	Chanell v. Feidhoekerland	Mr & Mrs G. Davis	14.11.83
Chrisno's Vanoc	D	Ch. Spartacist of Hendrawen	Chrisno's Osaka	Mrs C. Taylor	29.9.77
Hebrus Buccaneer	D	Ch. Alsahurst Raconteur	Withenshaw Anastasia of Hebrus	Mr & Mrs Skevington	24.11.82
Janus v. Insel Wehr	D	Igor v. Harberg	Cessie v. Königsbrüch	Werner Brethaver	Unknown
Jonal Basko	D	Ch. Cito v. Königsbrüch	Bushvale Alicia of Jonal	Mr & Mrs J. Young	10.6.83
Tell de la Maison Bauer	D	Eno v. Sulzberg	Natacha de l'Alsace du Nord	J. Bauer	27.3.82
Lornaville Spartan General of Beaubroor	D	Spartacist of Hendrawen	Lornaville Adelaide	Mr R. Brandon	29.9.80
Longvale Legacy	D	Longvale San Diego	Dvella Elation	Mrs J.M. Farnell	10.11.83
Kerson Kyerk	D	Ch. Amulree Heiko	Eumor Delight of Kerson	Messrs A. & S. Kerr	15.5.80
Moonwinds Harrier	D	Ch. Cito v. Königsbrüch	Moonwinds Golden Cloudburst	Miss P.A. Meaton	12.12.82
Patjustons Jack the Lad	D	Ch. Greenveldt Big Ben	Yusmydear of Stranmillis	Mrs P. Wright	1.4.80
Rampisham Tumack	D	Ch. Cito v. Königsbrüch	Rarity of Rampisham	Miss C. de Battista	26.2.83
Salenze's Dexi	D	Ch. Cito v. Königsbrüch	Limburg Carina of Salenze	Ms P. Holland	22.11.83
Iwo vom Seyenvenn	D	Quax vom Bubenlachring	Quinni vom Wendelinsturm	Richard Fengler	26.10.81

Name	Sex	Sire	Dam	Breeder	Born
Shootersway Lido	D	Reza vom Hylligen-born	Shootersway Solaria	Mr & Mrs R. Allan	30.4.82
Bedwins Kokarde	B	Quai von der Boxhochburg	Mausi von Seebachtal	Mr & Mrs Griffiths	12.11.81
Catja vom Elizabethan Klaus	B	Xaran von Grezland	Kendie von Haus Schwizier	Herman Kling	15.4.82
Jacnel Nacale	B	Gero of Jonimay	Vanda vom Monchberg	Mr & Mrs J. Wright	23.2.85
Kelnik Anika	B	Albra Jareborg	Delmonic Hella of Kelnik	Mrs B. Fahy	4.1.84
Kemjon Biene	B	Int Ch. Rothic Invictor	Ch. Judamie Nevada of Kemjon	Mrs M. Kemp	27.12.81
Langfaulds Fancy	B	Masuta Paicite	Langfaulds Chloe	Mr H. de Zutter	26.3.81
Malkris Kristel	B	Ch. Maik v. Holtkampersee	Rossfort Minnie Mouse	Mrs M. Bryan	13.7.82
Moonwinds Golden Mirage	B	Ch. Cito von Königsbrüch	Moonwinds Golden Cloudburst	Miss P. Meaton	12.12.82
Godika von der Mürrenhütte	B	Xito von der Mürrenhütte	Anka von Saunergraben	Mrs S. Hadley & Mr R. Byrne	7.6.82
Myzak Beguilin	B	Caemaen Beethoven	Gayville's Declare	Mr & Mrs G. Edwards	18.8.81
Neppits Copperglow of Lynchwood	B	Tadellos Warro von Unterhain	Gregrise Tawny Owl	Mr & Mrs C. St John	28.10.80
Patenza Bella Donna	B	Tremillon Khan of Patenza	Tremillon Gay Celebration	Mrs P. McCabe	4.10.82
Renygar Pandora	B	Renygar Daredevil	Renygar Spun Gold	Mrs I. Garlick	30.6.81
Salvest Silver Bangle	B	Caemaen Beethoven	Ambers Petite of Annkev	Mrs A.K. Hoyland	2.9.80
Charlie's Girl of Shercoz	B	Shercoz Checkmate Charlie	Edensmuir Golden Girl	Mr C. Bell	21.6.84
Shercoz Sorrenna	B	Ch. Meik v.d. Talquelle	Devansa Dream Machine	Mrs A.L. Zivers	25.10.83
Strco Kerry Gold	B	Cirguy Chipaway of Chavorne	Strco Chantilly Lace	Mrs N. Strange	18.7.85
Teyves Copycat	B	Gorrets Jasper	Rintilloch Legacy	Mrs S. Auld	26.1.84
Aphelion Byrony of Emmaglen	D	Dorndale Pergusa	Tanfield Gilda	Mrs S. Jaggers	12.1.79
Gayvilles Canti	D	Ch. Cito von Königsbrüch	Gayvilles Lorraine	Mr & Mrs D. Hall	12.1.85
Kemjon Lex	D	Tell from Bygoly at Kemjon	Ch. Kemjon Biene	Mrs M. Kemp	29.10.85
Panja vom Loherstein	B	Zaffo vom Arminius	Innes vom Loherstein	Herr Grubl	25.1.85
Longvale Nadia	B	Ch. Cito von Königsbrüch	Longvale Fantasy	Mrs J.M. Parnell	26.12.84
Lornaville Mr Bee	D	Lornaville Ambassador	Lornaville War Lady	Mr R. Brandon	24.12.83
Jezebel of Patjuson	B	Ch. Patjuson's Jack the Lad	Lady of Bradville	Mr J. Shannon	23.6.82
Renygar Mighty Quinn	D	Ch. Tuffleys Sparky	Ch. Renygar How's Zat	Mrs I. Garlick	1.10.82
Royvons Quando of Paroba	D	Royvons Grando	Royvons Tonja	Mrs Y. James	14.9.84
Lissie of Sieba	B	Lido v. Humbachtal	Bygoly Kissy	Mr D. Bignall	22.12.84
Nickel v. Unterhain Tadellos	D	Nick v.d. Wienerau	Sadra v. Unterhain	Herr Pillimeir	9.11.82
Bedwins Pirol	D	Uran von Wildsteigerland	Ch. Panja v. Loherstein	Mrs J. Griffiths	31.10.86
Lauser vom Hasenborn	D	Erk vom Holtkampersee	Hatje vom Hasenborn	Herr Maxein	29.5.84
Longvale Octavius	D	Ch. Cito v. Königsbrüch	Longvale Fantasy	Mrs Farnell	15.12.83

215

Name	Sex	Sire	Dam	Breeder	Born
Cas v.d. Molenakker	D	Dan v.d. Bärenschlucht	Jennie v.d. Molenakker	Herr Stipoonk	5.4.85
Royvons Arab	D	Ch. Cito v. Königsbrüch	Royvons Kara	Mrs Y. James	25.1.83
Amulree Tisn't	B	Ch. Longville Octavius	Amulree Hullabaloo	Mr & Mrs Anderson	14.5.86
Wham Fantastic of Copybush	B	Ogus de Columbo	Bedwins Hannah	Mr & Mrs Appleby	24.11.83
Deswar Narshadesh of Nidibed	B	Rothic Vinoble	Labrasco Katarina	Mr A.D. Debidin	27.12.83
Gayville Dixie	B	Ch. Meik v.d. Talquelle	Trethvane Barbrann of Gayville	Mr & Mrs Hall	2.7.85
Kayjon Zanadoo	D	Uran v. Wildsteigerland	Illushin Latisha	Mr & Mrs Rogers	Unknown
Kemjon Inka	B	Rothic Atilla	Ch. Judamie Nevada of Kemjon	Mrs M. Kemp	16.6.84

APPENDIX E

POST-WAR WORKING TRIAL CHAMPIONS

Name	Sex	Sire	Dam	Breeder	Born
Rockswall Bello Romana	D	Amigo Seehim W.T. Ch.	Ghita of Ingon	Mrs G. Uglione	24.5.41
Loki of Hatherlow	D	Erich of Bucklebury	Anna of Avondale	Mr H. Darbyshire	20.10.46
Sigurd of Jotunheim	D	Yvo of Ravenscar Ch.	Lyn of Harith	Mr H. Woods	13.4.43
Mountbrowne Largo	D	Philemon von Ruhstadt	Lydia of Bucklebury	Chief Constable, Surrey	10.2.51
Amaryllis of Helmdon Ob. Ch.	B	Southdown Nireus Ch.	Wanda of Nonington	Mrs V. Wibberley	12.6.53
Mountbrowne Shaun	D	Cito von Schaferleben	Mountbrowne Nienas Sicki	Chief Constable, Surrey	30.6.53
Mountbrowne Umbra	B	Philemon von Ruhstadt	Mountbrowne Nienas Sicki	Chief Constable, Surrey	21.6.54
Emma of Woffra	B	Shepherdon Statesman	Lassie of Montiwell	Mrs M. Nicholson	22.5.54
Southdown Caspia Ob. Ch.	B	Southdown Nireus Ch.	Southdown Gitana	Mr B. C. Dickerson	30.10.54
Mountbrowne Ullah	B	Philemon von Ruhstadt	Mountbrowne Nienas Sicki	Chief Constable, Surrey	21.6.54
Quest of Pasha	D	Letton Pasha of Combehill	Glennis Antoisich	Mr D. W. Ruthwell	22.4.56
Mountbrowne Vague	D	Cito von der Meerwacht Ch.	Southdown Raider	Mr A. S. George	2.8.54
Dunelm Jamie P.D.Ex	D	Pedigree unknown			unknown
Quest of Ardfern P.Ex	D	Cresta of Aronbel P.D.Ex	Letton Questionaire	Mr J. A. Allen	1.3.58
Rolph of Friarsbush	D	Czar of Friarsbush	Danae of Helmdon	Mr R. C. D. Robertson	13.3.60
Pressburg Zorro	D	Ex von Bronninghausen	Bowesmoor Zyxa	Mr G. M. Smith	20.6.60
Hankley Andromeda	B	Danki of Glenvoca Ch. and Ob. Ch.	Amaryllis of Helmdon W.T. Ch. and Ob. Ch.	Mrs D. Foreman	15.2.58
Dianton Taurus	D	Bruce of Seale	Diana of Kempton	Mrs R. Wlodarczyk	19.3.59
Zenda of Stroan	B	Beowulf of Seale Ch.	Suzanne of Windfalls	Mrs D. Thomson	30.8.58
Ballerina of Hankley	B	Hortondale Pointsman Ch.	Amaryllis of Helmdon W.T. Ch. and Ob. Ch.	Mrs D. J. Foreman	11.7.59
Farnrae Rusty	D	Jip Unregistered	Shula Unregistered	Mr J. Bradley	26.4.61
Vikkas Niall av Hvitsand	D	Vikkas Rando av Hvitsand	Vikkas Tanias Superior av Hvitsand	Mr and Mrs P. Elliott and Mr and Mrs J. Hirst	9.4.58
Halan Jill	B	Cito von Der Meerwacht Ch.	Ginney of Pilchards Cove	Mrs J. C. Williams	10.5.61
Mountbrowne Wotan	D	Ex von Brohninghausen	Mountbrowne Freya	Chief Constable, Surrey	8.3.60
Jacopo of Aycliffe	D	Alf vom Haus Happel	Ilse vom Abtshof	Chief Constable, Durham	15.4.62
Mountbrowne Ajax	D	Mountbrowne Vagus W.T. Ch.	Mountbrowne Netta	Chief Constable, Surrey	22.11.60

Name	Sex	Sire	Dam	Breeder	Born
Mountbrowne Doron	D	Drummer Boy of Dromcot	Pressburg Greta	Chief Constable, Suurey	18.5.62
Glenroyal of Callander	D	Overend Esspresso	Clarendown Alwyn	Mr J. C. Morris	22.12.61
Hero of Hastehill	D	Roon Zu Den Sieben-Faulen	Ballerina of Hastehill	Mrs P. Harris and Mr L. Pagliero	8.3.64
Mountbrowne Huntz	D	Drummer Boy of Dromcot	Pressburg Greta	Chief Constable, Surrey	29.7.63
Dirk of Caddam	D	Gorsefield Granit Ch.	Ionia of Shraleycarr	Mr and Mrs W. Moncur	18.7.62
Victor of Aycliffe	D	Jacopo of Aycliffe W.T. Ch.	Assi von der Rheingegend	Chief Constable, Durham	17.10.65
Arkwood of Amberwell	D	Astan Luke	Ardent of Amberwell	Dr H. Hein	14.8.66
Astan Outlaw	D	Astan Impresario	Jewel of Shraleycarr	Mrs D. Stanley	10.4.64
Invader of Hankley	D	Marcus of Hankley	Hankley Sindi of Hindrick	Mrs D. Foreman	26.3.65
Wesmid Bowesmoor Gerald	D	Bowesmoor Rock Tadellos	Charm of Bishopsmarston	Mrs J. Stovin	13.9.65
Beedawn Liza	B	Falcon of Rockverne	Juma of Snittles	Miss H. I. Addyman	11.10.64
Barrimline Saba	D	Gustav of Jugoland	Mepal Lucky Lassie	Mr R. Burbridge	9.6.66
Moorglen Hope of Druderkern	B	Asoka Cherusker Ch.	Lady of Bruderkern Obed Ch.	Mr W. Core	30.6.63
Kikki Av Foss	B	Kilmore Lad	Sheena Dawn of Brighouse	Mr and Mrs Alderson	28.12.64
Kenbellas Joody	B	Silver Dollar Prince	Pride of Erin	Mr and Mrs W. Reilly	21.9.66
Turo of Eurony	B	Int. Ch. Ilex of Brittas	Cheyene of Eurony	Mr T. Rooney	7.10.58
Nikki of Hankley	D	Astan Luke Ch.	Ballerina of Hankley W.T. Ch & Obed. Ch.	Mrs D. Foreman	11.12.66
Tanfield Millflash Parro	D	Ilk Von Den Eschbacher Klippen	Stavens Gitta	Mrs Jeggo	29.7.69
Bois of Limbrook	D	Wilindrek Gustav of Jugoland	Laila of Limburg	Messrs D. & B. Thomas	2.1.70
Bowesmoor Falk	D	Quick Vom Eningsfeld	Bowesmoor Konya	Mr E. Glaisher	23.5.69
Tanfield Wystan	D	Ilk Von Den Eschbacher Klippen	Goldoak Jandora	Miss S. Cook	7.2.70
Night Raider of Invajendra	D	Shane of Invajendra	Abbess of Invajendra	Miss J. J. Allen	27.4.69
Lance of Amberwell	D	Astan Luke	Lynda of Amberwell	Dr H. Hein	17.11.69
Taypol Amalga	D	Mancraie of Auchansheen	Tina (unregistered)	Mrs J. Brennan	11.8.72
Bowesmoor Hugo	D	Bowesmoor Inky	Hondsruck Gault Echo	Mr H. Darbyshire	7.8.69
Burnaway Freia	B	Ilk Von Den Eschbacher Klippen	Burnaway Chiquita of Creslac	Mr W. Hardaway	1.8.70
Dalynmar Admiral	D	Perham Wayfarer	Zara of Dalynmar	Mr & Mrs R. J. Smith	28.1.71
Burnaway Igor	D	Verus v.d. Ulmer Felswand	Burnaway Freia W. T. Ch.	Mr W. Hardaway	2.3.74

218

Name	Sex	Sire	Dam	Breeder	Born
Metpol Fang	D	Fredarchris Brindon	Metpol Janet	Commissioner of Police of The Metropolis	12.5.70
Olderhill Serpa	D	Tanargo Aeolus	Olderhill Solo	Mrs A. Butler	23.2.75
Tony of Kenstaff	D	Unknown	Unknown	Unknown	Unknown
Vonfisk Argo	D	Orsof Von Busecker Schloss	Giggi Von Michelstadter-Rathaus	Mr W. H. Wilson	24.8.74
Aycliff Countess	B	Silhouette of Charavigne	Pauline of Aycliffe	Chief Constable of Durham Constabulary	1.12.73
Kara Kara	B	Solo of Kerady	Helga of Perrycourt	Mr J. Hudson	24.4.72
Kabeyun Digby	D	Impuls Aus German7	Kabeyun Banda	Mrs M. Topping	11.6.75
Vonfisk Bandit	D	Nestor Vom Haus Mussnafen	Giggi Vom Michelstradter-Rathaus	Mrs Y. Fisk	13.7.75
Kabeyun Enne	B	Vikkas Quartz	Kabeyun Banda	Mrs M. Topping	22.5.76
Newshamvale New Year Tex	D	Eros of Lyrenstan Ch.	Amberhaze Helen	Mr V. M. Gaines	1.1.77
Druidswood Quintas		Amenable of Druidswood	Druidswood Lustre	Mrs M. Pickup	
Borderfame the Victor		Donar v. Fiemereck	Borderfame the Fanfare		
Denarjo Joby		Olderhill Gerbil	Olderhill Jillian		
Overhills Stylistic		Sabo v.d. Dorheimer Hohe	Overhills Solitaire	Mrs M. Parnell	27.5.79
Jonimay Drusus		Donar v. Fiemereck	Jonimay Martello Charm	Mr & Mrs T. Hannan	
Gefni Carbon Copy		Kabeyun Digby W.T. Ch.	Aberdare of Kent		
Jacinffo's Shalako		Falk v. Haus Edelflor	Olderhill Geisha		
Burnaway Quints	B	Ch. Fanto von Bayerischen Wald	W.T. Ch. Burnaway Maricer	Mr W. Hardaway	20.3.82
Burnaway Molto	D	Ch. Delridge Erhard	Kenstaff Athena of Burnaway	Mr W. Hardaway	24.8.78
Burnaway Maricer	B	Ch. Delridge Erhard	Kenstaff Athena of Burnaway	Mrs S. Hardaway	24.8.78
Appinslight Arran	D	Ch. Langfaulds Amos	Knockindu Ophelia	Mrs N. Carmichael	13.12.81

APPENDIX F

POSTWAR OBEDIENCE CHAMPIONS

Name	Sex	Sire	Dam	Breeder	Born
Sappho of Ladoga	B	Pericles av Hvitsand	Viola of Brittas	Mr C. J. Graham	16.5.46
Ennice of Mossville	B	Reddicap Winston of Dorsida	Lady Olflame	Mrs H. Blackband	14.8.48
Raf of Schone	D	Romana Gerry	Schone	Mrs N. Condon	14.5.48
Croftholme Whilemina	B	Balgin of Cranville	Jenifer of Croftholme	Mr and Mrs N. Bancroft	11.5.46
Siegfried of Jotunheim	D	Kuno of Vendor	Crumstone Prudence	Mr and Mrs C. E. Frinker	13.4.43
Merlinsvale Crystal	B	Chorltonville Classic	Gillian of Merlinsvale	Messrs L. and G. Thomas	29.1.46
Della of Gipton	D	Rex of Brackenedge	Grey Lady of Mahlew	Mr A. C. Welham	2.2.46
Prince of Barmouth	D	Ricky of Shuttleworth	Judy of Orbel	Mr W. S. Cameron	14.11.48
Brutus of Anglezarke	D	Pilot Secretainerie	Amy Secretainerie	Mrs L. Greenhalgh	10.8.47
Magda of Adarvon	B	Hero of Roslin (Irish Ch.)	Atlanta of Adarvon	Mr C. T. Powley	23.4.50
Jane of Seale	B	Jet of Seale	Devotion of Seale	Mrs M. Howard	27.9.50
Angus of Heronsmoor	D	Seppel vom Scheuerbusch of Rozavel	Faun of Hand	Mrs V. E. Porter	18.7.50
Hassan of Navrig	D	Ameer of Marack	Nada of Whiteville	Mrs F. D. Girvan	7.1.48
Joy of Quainton	B	Southdown Irorro	Sheila of Ladoga	Miss E. K. Jones	26.5.49
Diligent Blackboy	D	Unknown	Unknown	Unknown	Unknown
Tackleway Fantasia	B	Tackleway Finch	Paprika of Karda	Mr and Mrs J. F. H. Clare	11.9.51
Franz of Combehill	D	Baron of Combehill	Nobel Empress	Mr S. Gilbertson	8.5.49
Terrie of Glenvoca Ch.	D	Danko vom Menkenmoor of Hardwick Ch.	Abbess of Saba Ch.	Mr G. Crook and Mr J. Schwabacher	26.1.50
Shepherdon Spun Gold	D	Avon Prince of Alumvale Ch.	Letton Gaiety	Mrs M. E. Porter	9.12.51
Ariel of Swansford	B	Danko vom Menkenmoor of Hardwick Ch.	Jennifer of Alderley	Mr A. D. Swann	5.11.52
Rajah of Cymru	D	Major of Theobalds	Lady of Tilldene	Miss P. Till	8.1.50
Danki of Glenvoca Ch. (and Irish Ch.)	D	Terrie of Glenvoca Ch. and Ob. Ch.	Sabre Secretainerie Ch.	Mr G. Crook	14.2.52
Tarzan of Rainier	D	Hardwick Cosalta of Lynrowe	Susan of Longbridge	Mr J. R. Turner	28.5.51
Amaryllis of Helmdon W.T. Ch.	B	Southdown Nireus Ch.	Wanda of Nonington	Mrs V. Wibberley	12.6.53

220

Name	Sex	Sire	Dam	Breeder	Born
Belle of Kilmaurs	B	Alex of Dalvrogit	Catriona of Aragon	Mr W. Howitt	21.3.51
Greyvalley Chloe	B	Norn Rollicking Fun	Merlinsvale Crystal Ob. Ch.	Miss B. U. Pindar	25.5.51
Vaqueel of Kelowna	D	Avon Prince of Alumvale Ch.	Helium of Kelowna	Miss M. O'Grady	25.10.51
Silver Dandy	D	Prince of Greenvale	Raydor Panda	Mr J. A. Holley	1.8.49
Lassie of Venrom	B	Don of Ayr	Rachael of Morton	Mr D. Burgoyne	7.8.50
Lupo di Lombardia	D	Gnome of Milngavie	Elfenben Kimina	Mr S. Callaghan	28.5.53
Son of Silvershan	D	Silvershan of Guildhall	Judy of Trenome	Mr J. Dion	31.5.51
Copyright of Rozavel	B	Seppel vom Scheuerbush of Rozavel	Miss Argus of Rozavel	Mrs T. Gray	27.7.51
Vicki of Knockindu	B	Maxwell of Ledasa	Bambi of Greyshiels	Mr J. A. J. McNulty	8.1.51
Stormy Susanah	B	Thor of Pesth	Misty	Mrs P. Reader Harris	29.5.52
Della of Glenvoca	B	Terrie of Glenvoca Ch. and Ob. Ch.	Sabre Secretainerie Ch.	Mr G. Crook	14.2.52
Southdown Caspia W. T. Ch.	B	Southdown Nireus Ch.	Southdown Gitana	Mr B. C. Dickerson	30.10.54
Rafina of Schone	B	Raf of Schone Ob. Ch.	Stormy Susanah Ob. Ch.	Mrs P. Reader Harris	10.9.54
Amphion of Palermo	D	Danko vom Menkenmoor of Hardwick Ch.	Oldfields Pride	Mr J. A. Deegan	5.5.50
Boyd of Wellenk	D	Frederik of Ordmuir	Anita of Wellenk	Mr W. Chadwick	31.1.54
Isabelle of Rozavel	B	Ludo of Druidswood	Darkness of Rozavel	Mr T. Gray	24.2.53
Christel of Llanyravon	B	Ingo Secretainerie	Pia Secretainerie	Mrs J. N. Evans	4.7.51
Michelsen of Charaon	D	Whiteville Axel	Chitra of Charoan	Mr and Mrs C. Forman-Brown	2.2.56
Iliad of Tollhurst	D	Riot of Rhosincourt Ch.	Averil of Akela	Mr A. J. Adams	19.6.53
Amanda of Jumaral	D	Brevet of Perando	Reena of Eveley	Mr J. Prior	21.7.55
Rosemary of Ockendon	B	Axel von Lubbecker Land Ch.	Rosalind of Rhosincourt	Mr B. Dexter	13.6.55
Glenvoca Curracloe Grania	B	Danki of Glenvoca Ch.	Chota of Glandoreen Ch.	Mr J. W. Thompson	27.4.56
Sea Holly	B	Vaqueel of Kelowna Ob. Ch.	Isabelle of Rozavel Ob. Ch.	Mis U. M. Ogle	14.10.56
Roys Choice of Elmtree	B	Rex Prince of Foresthill	Lassie	Mr W. N. R. Politick	29.10.51
Orpheus of Combehill	D	Cito von der Meerwacht Ch.	Grizel of Combehill Ch.	Mr H. E. Johnson	11.9.54
Greyvalley Franzi	B	Cito of Maco	Greyvalley Chloe Ob. Ch.	Miss B. V. Pindar	30.3.57
Alex of Janpermaz	D	Terrie of Glenvoca Ch. and Ob. Ch.	Shepherdon Katinka of Janpermaz	Mr and Mrs Mazur	24.10.57
Black Cloud	D	Dagger of Swyn	Anniss of Swyn	Mr J. P. Coult	25.11.53
Carlo of Perrycroft	D	Trojan of Corvedell	Corvedell Etherow Elegant	Mr R. Biggs	23.11.53
Laurel of Vagorlex	D	Breuse of Seale	Lalique of Kelowna	Mr G. W. Carpenter	5.3.57

Name	Sex	Sire	Dam	Breeder	Born
Victor of Baltera	D	Cuno of Elanbriach	Odette of Combehill	Mrs M. S. Bodman	6.7.58
Sheba of Dale	B	Pan of Mistral	Geraldine of Putland	Mr R. F. Trew	5.4.56
Bruno of Mendin	D	Karl of Mendin	Shane of Perrycroft	Mr J. T. Hudson	13.11.55
Holmflow Rebel	D	Letton Duskie Despot Ch.	Token of Vosta	Mr W. Homer	8.8.57
Aniela of Janpermaz	B	Terrie of Glenvoca Ch. & Ob. Ch.	Sheperdon Katinka of Janpermaz	Mr and Mrs J. Mazur	24.10.57
Lady of Bruderkern	B	Arno of Glenvoca	Alona of Haydock	Mr R. Lloyd	7.3.60
Eager Major	D	Unknown	Unknown	Mr D. Chalkey	Unknown
Caroline of Hankley	B	Orpheus of Hankley	Southdown Fidelia	Mr T. Wiggins	11.2.61
Bright Future	B	Eveleys Grimm of Charavigne	Jokenhill Jewel	Mr J. H. Cockman	18.6.60
Jhettanund Daycross	D	Cuno of Elenbriach	Jacqualine of Wolverdene	Mrs M. S. H. Bodman	1.8.58
Enjakes Kim	B	Southdown Nireus	Angelica of Codicote	Mr N. Stephens	9.7.58
Flak of Ardgye	D	Aldo of Monasteryhill	Odette of Combehill	Mrs M. S. Bodman	11.7.60
Valerie of Cremas	B	Iliad of Tollhurst	Sheila of Newington	Mr G. F. Harris	14.10.57
Apollo of Hawkswood	D	Quixotic of Huesca Ch.	Antoinette of Dawnhill	Mr J. M. Stokes	8.11.58
Ballerina of Hankley W.T. Ch.	B	Hortondale Pointsman Ch.	Amaryllis of Helmdon W.T. Ch. & Ob. Ch.	Mrs D. J. Foreman	11.7.59
Hankley Andromeda W.T. Ch.	B	Danki of Glenvoca Ch. & Ob. Ch.	Amaryllis of Helmdon W.T. Ch. & Ob. Ch.	Mrs D. J. Foreman	15.2.58
Jill of Broster	B	Avranger of Bryngoleu	Bonnie of Woodlark	Mr J. Brough	4.5.58
Ricky Royalist	D	Carl of Notwen	Playful Sheba	Mr S. J. Morley	10.8.58
Benhooks Zeena	B	Tregiskey Daylight	Benhooks Vanda	Mr P. Cox	12.3.59
Cordo of Perrycourt	D	Letton Cordo of Brittas	Keyra of Shalgar	Mr J. T. Hudson	20.12.61
Silvershan of Guildhall	D	Prince of Glenvoca	Cerrig Snow	Mrs W. M. Allen	17.10.59
Halan Jill	B	Cito Von Der Meerwacht Ch.	Ginney of Pilchards Cove	Mrs J. C. Williams	10.5.61
Bwana of Terony	D	Bruno of Seale Ch.	Jennifer of Jonquest	Mr and Mrs F. Brown	30.8.57
Janie of Hawgrove	B	Quest of Jesvale	Frieda of Hawgrove	Mr R. Plumpton	29.11.61
Trudie of Hyhefield	B	Turpin	Nima	Mr C. Dyos	14.5.60
Grinstede Ranger	D	Vasco of Brinton Ch.	Norwulf Kelpie	Mrs E. Wallis	29.6.64
Heelaway Bestone	D	Gorsefield Granit Ch.	Heelaway Cora of Hankley	Mr C. M. Wyant	1.12.63
Inge Shah of Westonvale	B	Shah of Danrose	Piddington Sally	Mr J. M. Reeve	15.7.62
Hellaway Amon	B	Wickesfield Gordon	Caroline of Hankley Ob. Ch.	Mr C. M. Wyant	23.11.63
Iliad of Cremas	D	Peniskys Samuel of Noble Hurst	Cleo of Janpermaz	Miss M. S. Lomax	24.8.65

Name	Sex	Sire	Dam	Breeder	Born
Odin of Kentera	D	Monarch of Morachdale	Ava of Monastery Hill	Mr M. S. Bodman	9.4.65
Bandino of Roseavon	D	Rossfort Curacao Ch.	Bracken of Gipsyville	Mr and Mrs J. W. Malone	16.1.66
Blondell of Jakalede	B	Amego of Jakalede	Viikas Bellona Av Hvitsand	Mr J. Jones	23.12.65
Lowenbournes Krystal of Greyvalley	B	Lorenz of Charavaigne	Lowenbournes Dustup	Mrs D. M. Sandland	20.4.63
Prince Firecave	D	Bruce (unr.)	Hilda of Sutherland	Mr T. L. Wornham	19.2.66
Shadowsquad Teal	B	Billo Vom Saynbach	Shadowsquad Sonata	Miss M. Drown	28.11.66
Kinder Syde Raven	B	Rossfort Curacao Ch.	Vanella of Brinton	Mr T. Taylor	24.11.67
Ranvic Gerda	B	Terrie of Brinton	Hankley Aquila	Mr H. Randall	30.3.66
Greyvalley Honey	B	Ace Higin	Lowenbournes Krustal of Greyvalley	Mrs B. V. Hill	12.9.68
Daintree Debutante of Hallowmas	B	Observer of Lexter	Gregrise Gay Garland	Mrs B. Hallett	30.8.68
Hellaway Cora of Hankley	B	Ludwig of Charavigne Ch.	Hankley Andromeda	Mrs D. J. Foreman	31.1.62
Schultz of Valhalla	D	Golden Boy of Brunton	Tara Tigress	Mr A. Wilson	13.3.69
Meiklestane Moondust	B	Rossfort Curacao Ch.	Meiklestane Heirloom	Mr & Mrs Fletcher	29.1.70
Sabre Potters Pride of Brynbank	D	Bryndale Harlow	Coral Queen	Mrs Seaber	27.5.76
Springfarm Quiver	B	Buster	Springfarm Nikki	Mrs E. S. Johnson	7.11.66
Garnaza Stefan	D	Vondaun Ulric of Dawnway Ch.	Melony Ziguener	Mr & Mrs P. Garner	17.7.72
Craigdallie Politician	D	Dorvaak Crack O'Dawn	Craigdallie Masquerade of Monarchdale	Mr & Mrs F. Schofield	18.1.72
Hellaway Usher	D	Heelaway Unit Ob. Ch.	Heelaway Zena	Mr C. Wyant	4.8.71
Prince of Ormsby	D	Cortez of Framley	Lady (unregistered)	Mr D. Wilkinson	20.12.68
Stenghari Cyclops	D	Atstan Luke Ch.	Stenghari Tnutah of Jugoland	Mr A. Byrne	5.9.69
Ginthersun Amber	B	Hero of Hastehill W.T. Ch.	Leading Lady of Baileyhill	Mr P. M. Ostick	30.7.70
Playboy of Troy	D	Pedro of Acrevale	Acrevale Huesca	Miss I. A. Barker & Mr H. Reading	26.2.74
Schatten Sa Meday	D	Zypher of Huesca	Iona of Amulree	Miss E. Johnstone	5.6.72
Yvo Yvonne	B	Odin of Kentara Ob. Ch.	McGregors Rhonda Valley	Miss E. Reid	14.3.74
Rintilloch Gingham	B	Rossfort Premonition Ch.	Karenberg Ella	Mr & Mrs Hendrie	23.6.74
Yvo Yvonne		Odin of Kentara Ob.\Ch.	McGregor's Rhondda Valley	Unknown	Unknown
Benjo Dustybin of Siltewk		Petrel of Amberwell	Wopey of Llewynteg	Unknown	Unknown
Shadowsquad Tsara at Romeno	B	Rhinestone of Brittas	Shadowsquad Cilicia	Mrs M. Paul	Unknown

223

KENNEL CLUB WORKING TRIAL REGULATIONS
1st July 1988

GENERAL REGULATIONS

1. Eligibility.
   a. Working Trial licences will be issued to registered or affiliated Societies only.
   b. Dogs entered at Kennel Club licensed Working Trials must be registered at the Kennel Club in accordance with Kennel Club Regulations for Classification and Registration B.
   c. Dogs under eighteen calendar months of age are ineligible for entry at Kennel Club licensed Working Trials, except Bloodhounds which may be entered for Bloodhound Trials at 6 months.
   d. If, in the opinion of the General Committee, a dog is of a savage disposition it shall be ineligible for entry at any Working Trial held under Kennel Club Regulations.
   e. Persons disqualified or suspended under Kennel Club Rules are not eligible to take part in any Kennel Club licensed event.

2. Licensed Working Trials.   Licensed Working Trials held under Kennel Club Rules and Regulations are those held under Licence granted by the General Committee of the Kennel Club, and are:
   a. Championship Working Trials – Open to all competitors, except where a qualification for entry has been approved by the General Committee of the Kennel Club and at which Kennel Club Working Trial Certificates are offered.
   b. Open Working Trials – Open to all competitors.
   c. Members Working Trials – Where entry is limited to Members of the Societies.
   d. Matches – Where entry is limited to Members of the Societies.

3. Permission to Hold Working Trials.
   a. The General Committee shall have the power to grant,

withhold or cancel permission to hold any licensed Working Trials.

b. Any cancellation or abandonment of a Trial without prior permission of the General Committee must be reported in writing to the Kennel Club without delay.

4. Undertaking.   Applications to hold Working Trials must contain the signatures of such Officers of the Society as are required on the forms and full names and addresses must be given. The application form signed by such officers shall be an undertaking by each of them to bind themselves jointly and severally to hold and conduct the Working Trial in accordance with the Rules and Regulations of the Kennel Club, to guarantee the due payment of all prize money and to abide by and adopt any decision of the General Committee or any authority to whom the General Committee may delegate its powers.

5. Application.   The application for a licence to hold a Working Trial must be made to the Secretary of the Kennel Club, 1-5 Clarges Street, London W1Y 8AB, on an official form which must be properly completed, together with the appropriate licence fee, at least 60 days before the date of the Working Trial.

6. Documentation.   At every Working Trial the following documents must be available:
   a. The licence for the Trial.
   b. A copy of Kennel Club Rules and relevant Working Trials Regulations.
   c. A copy of the Schedule and Catalogue for the Trial.
   d. The completed entry forms for the Trial.

7. Disqualification of Dogs.   A dog shall be disqualified and removed from the Trial if it is:
   a. A bitch which is in season.
   b. Suffering from any infectious or contagious disease.
   c. Interfering with the safety or chance of winning of an opponent.
   d. Of such temperament or is so much out of control as to be a danger to the safety of any person or other animal.
   e. Likely to cause suffering to the dog if it continues competing.

8. Objections.
   a. An objection to a dog must be made to the Secretary of the

Show in writing at any time within seven days of the last day of the meeting upon the objector lodging with the Secretary the sum of £25.00. The deposit may be returned after the General Committee of the Kennel Club has considered the objection. Should any objection be made other than under Regulation 7, the dog should be allowed to compete and a full report made to the Kennel Club.

b. When an objection is lodged the Secretary of the Society must send to the Kennel Club:
   (1) A copy of the objection
   (2) The name and address of the objector
   (3) The name and address of the owner of the dog
   (4) All relevant evidence

c. The objection will then be referred to the General Committee of the Kennel Club for a ruling.

d. No objection shall be invalidated solely on the grounds that it was incorrectly lodged.

e. If the dog objected to is disqualified, the prize to which it would otherwise have been entitled shall be forefeited, and the dog or dogs next in order of merit shall move up and take the prize or prizes.

f. No spectator, not being the owner of a dog competing, or his accredited representative has the right to lodge any objection to a dog or to any action taken at the meeting unless he be a member of the Committee of the Society or of the General Committee of the Kennel Club or a Steward of the meeting. Any objection so lodged will be disregarded.

9. Fraudulent or Discreditable Conduct at Working Trials. The Secretary of a Trial must immediately report to the Secretary of the Kennel Club any case of alleged fraudulent or discreditable conduct, or any default, omission or incident at or in connection with the Trial which may come under his notice, even where parties concerned have indicated that they intend taking no action and at the same time forward to the Secretary of the Kennel Club all documents and information in connection therewith which may be in his possession or power. If evidence is placed before the General Committee to its satisfaction that undue influence has been exercised by any person(s), or that any improper means have been used to influence the appointment of a Judge or interfere with the competition of a dog at any Trial held under Kennel Club Rules and Regulations, the General Committee may require all correspondence and evidence in connection with the case to be produced in order that it may deal with the offender(s) under Kennel Club Rule 42.

10. Penalty for Infringement of Kennel Club Rules by Working Trial Managements. The General Committee shall have power to fine the Officers of the Society holding the Working Trial who have broken Kennel Club Rules and Regulations in the conduct of the Trial.

11. Unlicensed Trials. Notwithstanding the provisions of these Regulations, certain events which are not licensed by the Kennel Club may from time to time be recognised by the General Committee of the Kennel Club.

The General Committee shall have power to grant permission for Kennel Club registered dogs to be entered for such events. The standing of a judge, exhibitor or promoter will not be prejudiced by participation in these special unlicensed events.

12. Working Trial Certificates.
 a. A Kennel Club Working Trial Certificate will be awarded to any dog winning a T.D. or P.D. Stake at a Championship Working Trial provided that it has obtained 70% or more marks as indicated in the Schedule of Points and has also been awarded the qualification 'Excellent' by obtaining at least 80% of the possible total marks for the stake. A Reserve Working Trial Certificate will be awarded to the dog placed second in the Stake provided it is similarly qualified.
 b. A Kennel Club Working Trial Certificate will be awarded to a Bloodhound winning a Senior Stake without assistance at a Championship Working Trial for Bloodhounds as if it has clearly identified the runner to the satisfaction of the Judge or Judges. A hound will be considered to have made a satisfactory identification if it is seen to approach and clearly select the runner from a group of three people at the end of the line.
 c. Certificates will be awarded by the Judge or Judges at a Championship Working Trial P.D. (Patrol Dog), T.D. (Tracking Dog), W.D. (Working Dog), U.D. (Utility Dog), and C.D. (Companion Dog) Stake to dogs which have entered, provided that the dog has complied with any additional requirements for that Stake. The added qualification 'Excellent' shall be awarded should the dog also obtain

80% or more marks of the total for the Stake.

d. The Judge or Judges at Open Working Trials shall award Certificates of Merit for those dogs whose marks would have gained them a qualification 'Excellent' at a Championship Working Trial, provided that the Certificate contains the following words: 'This Certificate does not entitle the dog named thereon to any qualification recognised by the Kennel Club except entry in appropriate Stakes at Championship Working Trials.' Such Certificates of Merit must contain the name and breed of the dog, the name of the owner, the title of the Society and date of the Trial, the Stake and the marks awarded.

e. Societies may issue Qualification Certificates in Championship Stakes to their own design, subject to the approval of the Kennel Club, but they must contain the name and breed of the dog, the name of the owner, the title of the Society and the date of the Trials, the qualification and marks awarded and signature of the Judge(s) and Working Trial Manager.

13. Working Trial Championships.

a. The Kennel Club Working Trial Championships at which Patrol Dog (P.D.) and Tracking Dog (T.D.) Stakes shall be scheduled are held annually.

b. The responsibility for organising the Championships each year will normally be delegated to a Working Trial Society approved to hold Championship Working Trials, such Society to be selected by the Working Trials, Obedience and Agility Committee from applications submitted by Societies.

c. The Secretary of the host club will, unless otherwise specified, be the Working Trial Secretary for the event, the Society scheduling the Championships appointing a Trials Manager.

d. The following shall be the method of selection of judges for the Championship:

(1) Nominated by Working Trial Societies which have been granted Championship Working Trial status for balloting by the Working Trial Council.

(2) Recommendation by the Working Trials, Obedience and Agility Committee.

(3) Final approval by the General Committee.

e. Dogs eligible for entry in the Championships qualify as follows.

(1) T.D. Championship: A dog must have been placed 1st in

Championship T.D. Stake with the qualification 'Excellent' in the Stake during the period 1st October – 30th September preceding the Championships.

(2) P.D. Championship: A dog must have been placed 1st in Championship P.D. Stake with the qualification 'Excellent' in the Stake during the period 1st October – 30th September preceding the Championships.

(3) Dogs which qualify as above in both P.D. and T.D. Championship Stakes may be entered in both Championship Stakes.

(4) The Winners of the previous year's Championship Stakes qualify automatically.

(5) No other dogs are eligible for entry in the Championships except by special permission of the General Committee of the Kennel Club.

f. The Championships will normally be held during the third weekend in October each year.

g. The Working Trial Society selected to hold the Championships may forego holding one Open Working Trial during the year in which they hold the Championships without affecting their status to hold other Championship Trials.

14. Schedules.

a. The Society holding a Working Trial must issue a schedule which shall form the basis of a contract between the Society and those entering dogs. No modifications may be made to the schedule before the date of the Trial, except by permission of the Kennel Club and such modifications must be advertised.

b. Two copies of the schedule must be lodged with the Kennel Club when published and at least 30 days before the date of the Trial.

(Above Amendment to paragraph 14b. effective 1st January, 1990.)

c. The schedule must contain:

(1) The date and place of the Working Trial.

(2) The latest date for applying for entry at the Trial.

(3) The amount of entry fees and any prize money.

(4) A statement that a draw will be made for the order of running.

(5) The conditions and qualifications for making entries and for intimating acceptance or refusal of entries.

(6) An announcement that the Working Trial is held under

Kennel Club Working Trial Regulations with such exceptions as the Committee of the Society may decide. Such exceptions and conditions must have received the approval of the General Committee of the Kennel Club prior to publication of the schedule.

(7) The definition of each Stake, together with the qualification and limitations for entry in that Stake.

(8) The names of the Judges. An announcement that if the entries in the Companion Dog (C.D.) Stake exceed 20, a second Judge may be appointed to judge the Group IV exercises and the competitors notified accordingly.

(9) A statement that spayed bitches and castrated dogs may compete.

(10) An announcement that, except for Bloodhound Trials, dogs under the age of 18 months are not eligible for entry.

(11) A regulation which prohibits Judges at the Trial entering a dog which is recorded in their ownership or part ownership.

(12) A separate official entry form which must include the 'declaration' to be signed by the entrant as on the specimen entry form issued by the Kennel Club.

(13) A statement that should circumstances so dictate the Society, in consultation with the Judges, may alter arrangements as necessary. Such changes and the circumstances surrounding them must be reported to the Kennel Club.

15. Entry Forms. Such forms must be in accordance with the approved form issued by the Secretary of the Working Trial.

a. All entries must be made on the official entry from and each competitor must use a separate form.

b. All entry forms must be retained by the Committee of a Working Trial for at least twelve months from the last day of the Trial, and must be forwarded to the Kennel Club if requested, together with any other documents.

16. Catalogue. The Society must publish a Catalogue for the Trial containing:

a. The name of the Society holding the Trial.

b. The date and place of the Trial.

c. The names and addresses of competitors.

d. The registered name of each dog entered, the Stake in which

it is entered together with its full particulars as recorded on
the entry form.

   e. The name of the Judge(s) for each Stake.

The Secretary of a Working Trial shall send (within 7 days of the
Trial) the Judges' certification and two marked catalogues to the
Kennel Club indicating the prize winners and those dogs to which
the Judges have awarded Certificates.

17. Management.

   a. Societies must schedule one other tracking stake in addition
to the Working Trial Certificate Stake.

   b. A Working Trial Manager must be appointed by the
Committee of the Society who shall be responsible for
ensuring that the regulations are observed but he may not
interfere with the judges' decisions which shall be final. He
shall decide upon any matter not related to judging and not
provided for in the Rules and Regulations and may call upon
the Judge or Judges to assist with the decision which will be
final. The Working Trial Manager may not compete at the
Trial and should be present throughout.

   c. The Working Trial Manager and the Judges should assess the
weather conditions and should they consider the weather
unfit for holding the Trial the commencement may be
postponed until such time as it is considered necessary for the
Trial to be abandoned and the entry fees returned.

   d. When a Judge is prevented from attending or finishing a
meeting which has commenced, the Working Trial Manager
shall decide what action is to be taken.

   e. The order of running tracks shall be determined by a draw
and competitors notified accordingly by post of their
reporting time prior to the day of the Trial.

   f. The winner of the Stake shall be the dog that has qualified
with 70% or more marks in each group of the Stake and has
obtained most marks. No dog that has not so qualified shall
be placed in the prize list above a qualified dog. If no dog has
qualified the dog with the highest number of marks may be
awarded the prize, but Judges are also empowered to withold
any prize if in their opinion the dogs competing do not show
sufficient merit. Nothing in this Regulation shall apply to the
award of 'Special' prizes. At an Open Working Trial the
winner of the Stake shall be the dog that had qualified in all
groups even where the total mark was less than that for a dog

that had not so qualified. Where no dog had qualified in all groups, that with the highest mark shall win.

g. The Committee may reserve to themselves the right to refuse any entries.

h. Working Trials for Bloodhounds shall be exempt from the Definitions of Stakes and Schedules of Exercises and Points. The Schedule for each Bloodhound Working Trial shall be submitted to the Kennel Club for approval before publication.

i. Replacement judges appointed in an emergency must have previously judged the stake they are to judge.

18. Approval of Judges.

a. Working Trial Societies must apply to the General Committee for the approval of all judges at Championship Working Trials twelve months before the date of the Trial.

b. The following minimum conditions apply for the nomination of Judges for Championship Working Trials:

(1) For C.D. Stake – Must have judged at least two Open Working Trials and have as a handler qualified a dog 'Excellent' in a Championship C.D. Stake.

(2) For U.D. Stake – Must have judged U.D. or W.D. Stakes at two Open Working Trials, have judged C.D. Stake at a Championship Working Trial and have as a handler qualified a dog 'Excellent' in a Championship W.D. Stake.

(3) For W.D. Stake – Must have judged U.D. or W.D. Stakes at two Open Working Trials, U.D. Stake at a Championship Trial and have as a handler qualified a dog 'Excellent' in a Championship W.D. Stake.

(4) For P.D. and T.D. Stakes – Must have judged W.D. Stake at a Championship Trial, must have judged two or more Open Working Trials, including T.D. Open for T.D. Judges and P.D. Open for P.D. Judges and qualified a dog 'Excellent' in the Stake nominated to judge and must not have judged a Championship T.D. or P.D. Stake in the previous six months.

To have 'Judged' means to have Judged all groups of a Stake.

c. Service and Police Judges are eligible to judge U.D. Stake at a Championship Trial provided they have qualified a dog W.D. 'Excellent'. They must qualify for approval for other Stakes as above, except that those who have judged all parts at Regional or National Police Dog Trials will not have to qualify as a civilian handler.

Judges at open Working Trials – Before a person is appointed to judge at an open Working Trial, they must satisfy the Committee of the Society holding the Trial that they have qualified a dog 'Excellent' in the Stake they are to judge or in a higher Stake. Police and Service judges are exempt from this provided that, if they have not qualified a dog 'Excellent' in the Stake they are to judge, they have judged all parts at Regional or National Police Dog Trials.

19. Judging.

a. Judges at Kennel Club licensed Working Trials must Judge in accordance with Kennel Club Rules and Regulations.

b. Judges at Working Trials may not enter a dog which is recorded in their ownership or part ownership at the Trial at which they are Judging.

c. The Judge(s) shall certify on a form provided by the Kennel Club that in their opinion the Stake was held in accordance with the Schedule and with Kennel Club Regulations.

d. The Judge or Judges in consultation with the Working Trial Manager may arrange for dogs to be working singly or together in any numbers. All dogs entered in a Stake shall be tested as far as possible under similar conditions.

e. All awards made by the Judge or Judges at a Working Trial shall be in accordance with the agreed scale of points approved by the General Committee of the Kennel Club. Equal awards are prohibited, where there is equality of marks the award must be decided by a 'run off'.

20. Competing.

a. An owner or handler may handle the dog; once the dog has commenced work an owner must not interfere with his dog if he has deputed another person to handle it.

b. The Working Trial Manager shall announce the specific time at which a dog or group of dogs may be called for any exercise or group of exercises. Each dog must be brought at its proper time. The times and order may be changed if necessary at the discretion of the Working Trial Manager with approval of the Judge or Judges provided that no hardship is thereby caused to any competitor. If absent when called, the dog shall be liable to be disqualified by the Judge or Judges.

c. A person handling a dog may speak, whistle or work it by hand signals as he wishes, but can be called to order by the Judge or Judges for making unnecessary noise, and if he persists the Judge or Judges can disqualify the dog. Punitive correction or harsh handling of the dog is forbidden.

d. No dog entered for competition and at the meeting may be withdrawn from competition without notice to the Working Trials Manager. No dog shall compulsorily be withdrawn from a Stake by reason of the fact that it has obtained less than 70% of the marks in any one group.

e. Failure to participate in any exercise in a group in any Stake shall result in failure to qualify in that group.

f. No competitor shall impugn the decision of the Judge or Judges.

21. Delegated Powers of the Scottish Kennel Club. For the purpose of these Regulations, all powers of the General Committee relative to Working Trials held in Scotland and licensed by the Scottish Kennel Club are delegated to the Executive Council of the Scottish Kennel Club. Applications for licences, objections and allegations of fraudulent or discreditable conduct relative to Working Trials licensed by the Scottish Kennel Club must be made to the Secretary General of the Scottish Kennel Club, 6b Forres Street, Edinburgh EH3 6BJ.

For the purpose of paragraph 2 of this Regulation, the power to grant, withhold or cancel permission to hold any licensed Working Trial in Scotland, other than a Championship Working Trial, shall be delegated to the Scottish Kennel Club.

22. Definition of Stakes, Eligibility and Exercises.
The detailed Regulations for the Definition of Stakes, Eligibility and Exercises are given in Annex A.

23. Specific Regulations for Working Trial Rallies and Matches.
The Specific Regulations for Working Trial Rallies and Matches are given in Annex B.

24. Description of Exercises and Guidance for Judges.
The Description of Exercises and notes for the Guidance of Judges are given in Annex C.

(A)

DEFINITION OF STAKES, ELIGIBILITY AND EXERCISES

1. When entering for Championship or Open Working Trials, wins at Members Working Trials will not count.

2. No dog entered in P.D. or T.D. Stake at a Championship Trial shall be eligible to enter in any other Stake at the meeting.

3. All Police dogs shall be considered qualified for entry in W.D. Championship Stakes if they hold the Regional Police Dog qualification 'Excellent', provided that such entries are countersigned by the Senior Police Officer I/C when such entries are made. Dogs holding this qualification are not eligible for entry in C.D. or U.D. Open or Championship Stakes, nor in W.D. Open Stakes.

4. No Working Trial Stake shall be limited to less than 30. If a limit is imposed on entries in any Stake, it shall be carried out by ballot after the date of closing of entries. Championship T.D. or P.D. Stakes shall not be limited to numbers.

5. Open Working Trials.
   a. Companion Dog (C.D.) Stake – For dogs which have not qualified C.D. Ex or U.D. Ex or won three or more first prizes in Open C.D. or any prize in U.D. Stakes, W.D. Stakes, P.D. or T.D. Stakes at Open or Championship Working Trials.
   b. Utility Dog (U.D.) Stake – For dogs which have not been awarded a Certificate of Merit in U.D., W.D., P.D., or T.D. Stakes.
   c. Working Dogs (W.D.) Stakes – For dogs which have been awarded a Certificate of Merit in U.D. Stakes but not in W.D., P.D. or T.D. Stakes.
   d. Tracking Dog (T.D.) Stake – For dogs which have been awarded a Certificate of Merit in W.D. Stakes but not more than one Certificate of Merit in T.D. Stakes.
   e. Patrol Dog (P.D.) Stake – For dogs which have been awarded a Certificate of Merit in W.D. Stakes but not more than one Certificate of Merit in P.D. Stakes.

6. Championship Working Trials.
   a. Companion Dog (C.D.) Stake – For dogs which have not won three or more first prizes in C.D. Stakes or any prize in any other Stake at Championship Working Trials.

b. Utility Dog (U.D.) – For dogs which have won a Certificate of Merit in an Open U.D. Stake. A dog is not eligible for entry in this Stake if it has been entered in the W.D. Stake on the same day.

c. Working Dog (W.D.) – For dogs which have qualified U.D. Ex and have won a Certificate of Merit in Open W.D. Stakes. A dog is not eligible for entry in this stake if it has qualified WD Excellent twice in previous trials.

d. Tracking Dog (T.D.) Stake – For dogs which have been awarded two Certificates of Merit in Open T.D. Stakes and have qualified W.D. Ex at two Championship Trials.

e. Patrol Dog (P.D.) Stake – For dogs which have been awarded two Certificates of Merit in Open P.D. Stakes, and have qualified W.D. Ex at two Championship Trials.

7. Members Working Trial.

Restricted to the members of the Society holding the Working Trial, otherwise eligibility for Stakes is as for Open Working Trials.

8. Schedule of Exercises and Points.

a. COMPANION DOG (C.D.) STAKE

	Maximum Marks	Group Total	Minimum Group Qualifying Mark
Group 1. Control			
1. Heel on Leash	5		
2. Heel Free	10		
3. Recall to Handler	5		
4. Sending the dog away	10	30	21
Group II. Stays			
5. Sit (2 Minutes)	10		
6. Down (10 Minutes)	10	20	14
Group III. Agility			
7. Clear Jump	5		
8. Long Jump	5	20	14
9. Scale (3) Stay (2) Recall (5)	10		
Group IV. Retrieving and Nosework			
10. Retrieve a dumb-bell	10		
11. Elementary Search	20	30	21
Totals	100	100	70

b. UTILITY DOG (U.D.) STAKE

	Maximum Marks	Group Total	Minimum Group Qualifying Mark
Group I. Control			
1. Heel Free	5		
2. Sending the dog away	10		
3. Retrieve a dumb-bell	5		
4. Down (10 minutes)	10		
5. Steadiness to Gunshot	5	35	25
Group II. Agility			
6. Clear Jump	5		
7. Long Jump	5	20	14
8. Scale (3) Stay (2) Recall (5)	10		
Group III. Nosework			
9. Search	35		
10. Track (95) Article (15)	110	145	102
Totals	200	200	141

c. WORKING DOG (W.D.) STAKE

	Maximum Marks	Group Total	Minimum Group Qualifying Mark
Group I. Control			
1. Heel Free	5		
2. Sending the dog away	10		
3. Retrieve a dumb-bell	5		
4. Down (10 Minutes)	10		
5. Steadiness to Gunshot	5	35	25
Group II. Agility			
6. Clear Jump	5		
7. Long Jump	5	20	14
8. Scale (3) Stay (2) Recall (5)	10		
Group III. Nosework			
9. Search	35		
10. Track (90) Articles (10+10=20)	110	145	102
Totals	200	200	141

d. TRACKING DOG (T.D.) STAKE

	Maximum Marks	Group Total	Minimum Group Qualifying Marks
Group I. Control			
1. Heel Free	5		
2. Sendaway and Directional Control	10		
3. Speak on Command	5		
4. Down (10 Minutes)	10		
5. Steadiness to Gunshot	5	35	25
Group II. Agility			
6. Clear Jump	5		
7. Long Jump	5	20	14
8. Scale (3) Stay (2) Recall (5)	10		
Group III. Nosework			
9. Search	35		
10. Track (100) Articles (10+10+10=30)	130	165	116
Totals	220	220	155

e. PATROL DOG (P.D.) STAKE

	Maximum Marks	Group Total	Minimum Group Qualifying Marks
Group I. Control			
1. Heel Free	5		
2. Sendaway and Directional Control	10		
3. Speak on Command	5		
4. Down (10 Minutes)	10		
5. Steadiness to Gunshot	5	35	25
Group II. Agility			
6. Clear Jump	5		
7. Long Jump	5		
8. Scale (3) Stay (2) Recall (5)	10	20	14
Group III. Nosework			
9. Search	35		
10. Track (60) Articles (10+10=20)	80	115	80
Group IV. Patrol			
11. Quartering the Ground	45		
12. Test of Courage	20		
13. Search and Escort	25		
14a. Recall from Criminal	30		
14b. Pursuit and Detention of Criminal	30	150	105
Totals	320	320	224

SPECIFIC REGULATIONS FOR WORKING TRIAL
RALLIES AND MATCHES

1   A Working Trial Rally or Match may be a competition between Club Members or an inter-Club competition between Associations, Clubs, Societies or Branches of Clubs.

2.   Only registered Associations, Clubs, Societies and Dog Training Clubs may hold Working Trial Rallies and Matches.

3.   A Club may hold up to 12 Working Trial Rallies and Matches per annum. In the cases of Clubs which have registered Branches, each Branch may hold up to 12 Working Trial Rallies and Matches per annum.

4. Application.   Applications for permission to hold Working Trial Rallies and Matches must be made in writing to the Kennel Club at least 28 days before the date of the proposed Rally or Match accompanied by the relevant fee. The application must be signed by the Club Secretary and countersigned by the Chairman who shall act as guarantors to the Kennel Club that the Rally/Match will be held in accordance with the Regulations.

5. Regulations.
    a. No exercise at a Working Trial Rally or match shall vary from those contained in the Kennel Club Working Trial Regulations.
    b. A dog must, at the time of competition, be registered at the Kennel Club. Exhibits must be the property of Members of one of the Associations, Clubs, Societies or Branches competing in the Working Trial Rally or Match.
    c. The Committee of the organising Club may reserve the right to refuse any entry on reasonable grounds.
    d. Dogs under 18 calendar months of age are not eligible for competition at Working Trial Rallies and Matches.
    e. If a dog competes which has been exposed to the risk of any contagious or infectious disease during the period of six weeks prior to a Working Trial Rally or Match and/if any dog shall be proved to be suffering at Working Trial Rallies or Matches from any contagious or infectious disease including contagious

results of inoculations against distemper, the owner thereof shall be liable to be dealt with under Kennel Club Rule 42.

f. Not more than 52 dogs may compete at a Meeting.

g. Prize cards, diplomas or other printed awards may be awarded at Rallies and Matches provided such awards are clearly overprinted, 'WORKING TRIAL RALLY' or 'WORKING TRIAL MATCH'.

h. Not more than 5 Special Prizes shall be awarded at Working Trial Rallies or Matches.

i. The organising Club shall keep a list of the names of all competing dogs with awards and the names and addresses of their owners for a period of 12 months from the date of the Working Trial Rally or Match.

(C)

DESCRIPTION OF EXERCISES AND GUIDANCE FOR JUDGES

1. Method of Handling.   Although implicit obedience to all orders is necessary, dogs and handlers must operate in as free and natural a manner as possible; persistent barking, whining, etc. in any exercise other than location of articles, person or speak on command should be penalised. Food must not be given to the dog by the handler whilst being tested.

2. Heel Work.   The Judge should test the ability of the dog to keep his shoulder reasonably close to the left knee of the handler who should walk smartly in a natural manner at normal, fast and slow paces through turns and among and around persons and obstacles. The halt, with the dog sitting to heel, and a 'figure of eight' may be included at any stage.

Any act, signal or command or jerking of the leash which in the opinion of the Judge has given the dog unfair assistance shall be penalised.

3. Sit (2 Minutes).   Dogs may be tested individually or in a group or groups. The Judge or Stewards will give the order 'last command' and handlers should then instantly give their final commands to the dogs. Any further commands or signals to the dogs will be penalised. Handlers will then be instructed to leave their dogs and proceed to positions indicated by the Judge or Steward until ordered to return to them. Where possible, such positions should be out of sight of the dogs but bearing in mind the short duration of the exercise this may not be practical. Dogs must remain in the sit position throughout the test until the Judge or Steward indicates that the test has finished. Minor movements must be penalised. The Judge however may use discretion should interference by another dog cause the dog to move.

4. Down (10 Minutes). Handlers must be out of sight of the dogs who may be tested individually or in a group or groups. The Judge or Steward will give the command 'last command' and handlers should then instantly give their final commands to their dogs. Any further commands or signals to the dogs will be penalised. Handlers will then be instructed to leave their dogs and proceed to positions indicated by the Judge or Steward until ordered to return to them. Dogs must remain in the 'Down' position throughout the test until the Judge or Steward indicates that the Test has finished. No dog will be awarded any marks that sits, stands or crawls more than its approximate body in length in any direction. The Judge however may use discretion should interference by another dog cause the dog to move. The Judge may test the dog by using distractions but may not call it by name.

5. Recall to Handler. The dog should be recalled from the 'Down' or 'Sit' position, the handler being a reasonable distance from the dog at the discretion of the Judge. The dog should return at a smart pace and sit in front of the handler, afterwards going smartly to heel on command or signal. Handler to await command of the Judge or Steward.

6. Retrieve a Dumb-bell. The dog should not move forward to retrieve nor deliver to hand on return until ordered by the handler on the Judge or Stewards' instructions. The Retrieve should be executed at a smart pace without mouthing or playing with the dumb-bell. After delivery the handler will send the dog to heel on the instruction of the Judge or Steward.

7. Send Away and Directional Control. The minimum distance that the Judge shall set for the Send Away shall be 20 yards for the C.D. Stake and 50 yards for all other Stakes. The T.D. and P.D. Stakes shall also include change of direction or directions of a minimum of 50 yards. When the dog has reached the designated point or the Judge is satisfied that after a reasonable time the handler cannot improve the position of the dog by any futher commands the dog should be stopped in either the stand, sit or down position at the discretion of the handler. At this point in the T.D. or P.D. Stakes the Judge or Steward shall instruct the handler to redirect the dog. In all Stakes, whilst the Judge should take into account the number of commands used during the exercise, importance should be placed upon the handler's ability to direct the dog to the place indicated.

8. Steadiness to Gunshot.   The most appropriate occasion of testing this exercise is in the open country. The dog may be either walking at heel free or be away from the handler who must be permitted to remain within controlling distance whilst the gun is fired. Any sign of fear, aggressiveness or barking must be penalised. This test shall not be carried out without prior warning, or incorporated in any other test. The Judge will not provoke excitement by excessive display of the gun, nor should the gun be pointed at the dog.

9. Speak on Command.   The Judge will control the position of the handler in relation to the dog and may require the handler to work the dog walking at heel. If the dog is not required to walk at heel, the handler may place the dog in the stand, sit or down position. The dog will be ordered to 'speak' and cease 'speaking' on command of the Judge or Steward who may then instruct the handler to make the dog 'speak' again. 'Speaking' should be sustained by the dog whilst required with the minimum of commands and/or signals. Continuous and/or excessive incitements to 'speak' shall be heavily penalised. This test should not be incorporated with any other test.

10. Agility.   The descriptions below should be followed for Agility:
    a. No part of the clear, long jump or scale equipment to be traversed by the dog shall be less than three feet wide nor be in any way injurious to the dog. The tests shall be followed in any sequence decided by the Judge, including Clear Jump, Long Jump and Scale, but always commencing with Clear Jump.
    b. The Clear Jump should be so constructed that it will be obvious if the dog has exerted more than slight pressure upon it. The rigid top bar may be fixed or rest in cups and the space below may be filled in but the filling should not project above the bottom of the top bar. Appreciable pressure exerted by the

dog on the clear jump shall be considered to be a failure. Casual fouling with fore or hind legs may be penalised.

c. The construction of the Long Jump shall be as follows: The front element to be a minimum of 3 ft wide graduating over 5 elements (4 for small dogs), to a back element of a minimum width of 3 ft 8 ins. The front edge of the front element to be 4 ins high rising to 7 ins at the back edge. Each element thereafter graduating in height by 1 in – the back of the last element being 11 ins high. The minimum width (front to back) of each element to be at least 6 ins and clearly visible to the dog.

d. The handler may either approach the clear and long jumps with the dog or send it forward or stand by the jumps and call the dog up to jump. At no time should the handler proceed beyond any part of the jumps before they have been traversed by the dog. Once the dog has cleared the obstacle he should remain on the other side under control until joined by the handler.

e. The Scale should be a vertical wall of wooden planks and may have affixed on both sides three slats evenly distributed in the top half of the jump. The top surface of the scale may be slightly padded. The handler should approach the scale at a walking pace and halt within nine feet in front of it at his discretion and in his own time order the dog to scale. On reaching the other side the dog should be ordered to stay in the stand, sit or down position, the handler having previously nominated the position to the Judge. The Judge should ensure that the dog will stay steady and may indicate to the handler where he should stand in relation to his dog and the scale before ordering the dog to be recalled over the scale. A dog which fails to go over the scale at the second attempt shall be excluded from the stay and recall over the scale. Failure in the recall over the scale does not disqualify from marks previously gained.

f. Failure or refusal at any of the three types of jump may be followed by a second attempt and any one such failure shall be penalised by half the marks allotted to that part of the exercise in which the dog is given a second attempt.

g. Jumping heights and lengths:
   (1) *C.D. and U.D. Stakes:*
      (a) Clear Jump– Dogs not exceeding 10in at shoulder 1ft 6in
                     Dogs not exceeding 15in at shoulder 2ft

Dogs exceeding 15in at shoulder   3ft

(b) Long Jump – Dogs not exceeding 10in at shoulder 4ft

Dogs not exceeding 15in at shoulder 6ft

Dogs exceeding 15in at shoulder   9ft

(c) Scale   – Dogs not exceeding 10in at shoulder 3ft

Dogs not exceeding 15in at shoulder 4ft

Dogs exceeding 15in at shoulder   6ft

(2) *W.D., T.D., and P.D. Stakes*

(a) Clear Jump 3ft

Long Jump 9ft

Scale   6ft

11. Search. The Companion Dog (C.D.) Stake Search shall contain three articles and all other Stakes shall contain four. In all Stakes fresh articles must be placed for each dog who must recover a minimum of two to qualify. The Judge should choose articles in relation to the nature of the ground and the Stake which he is judging. The time allotted shall be four minutes in the C.D. Stake and five minutes in all other Stakes. The articles should be well handled and placed by a Steward who shall soil the ground by walking in varying directions over the area. Each competitor shall have a separate piece of land.

The C.D. Stake search area shall be 15 yards square, all other Stakes being 25 yards square, and shall be clearly defined by a marker peg at each corner. The handler may work his dog from any position outside the area, but must not enter it. In the C.D. Stake a maximum five marks should be alloted for each article and a maximum five marks for style and control. In all other Stakes a maximum seven marks should be allotted for each article and a maximum seven marks for style and control.

12. Track. The descriptions below should be followed for the Track:

a. The track should be plotted on the ground to be used for the nosework by Stewards previous to the day of commencement of the Trials. An area of ground which has had a track laid over it must not have another track laid over it until the following day. Wherever possible the ground used for a tracking Stake shall be as similar as possible to the ground used at that Trial in that Stake. The Judge should choose articles in relation to the nature of the ground and the Stake which he is Judging.

b. The track shall be a single line and may include turns. It shall be approximately half a mile long and should be laid as far as possible by a stranger to the dog. The article(s) should be well scented.

c. There shall be a marker left by the track layer to indicate the start of the track which must be far enough from the search square to allow the square to be worked without interfering with the track. The track layer will indicate to the competitor the line he took to the pole. There shall be no back track. In the U.D. Stake a second marker should be left not more than 30 yards from the start to indicate the direction of the first leg.

d. When the Judging is in process the track layer shall be present at the side of the Judge to indicate the exact line of the track and the position of the articles.

e. Unless the Judge considers the dog to have lost the track beyond recovery or has run out of time allotted for the completion of the track a handler may recast his dog at his discretion. The Judge should not at any time indicate to the handler where the dog should be recast except in exceptional circumstances.

f. Tracks for specific stakes shall be as follows:

(1) The U.D. Stake track shall not be less than half an hour old and shall include one article at the end, recovery of the article not being a requirement for qualification.

(2) The W.D. Stake track shall not be less than one and a half hours old and shall include two articles one of which must be recovered to qualify.

(3) The P.D. Stake track shall be not less than two hours old and shall include two articles one of which must be recovered to qualify.

(4) The T.D. Stake track shall be not less than three hours old and shall include three articles two of which must be recovered to qualify.

g. In all Stakes the last article shall indicate the end of the track. No two articles should be laid together.

h. A spare track additional to requirements should be laid but the opportunity to run a new track should be given only in exceptional circumstances.

i. The area used for tracking is out of bounds to all competitors for practice tracks and exercise from the time of the first track and any competitor found contravening this instruction is liable to be disqualified by the Judge and or Trials Manager from participating in the Trial in accordance with the provision of Regulation No: 7.C.

j. The dog must be worked on a harness and tracking line.

13. Quartering the Ground. The missing person should be protected consistent with safety, should remain motionless out of sight of the handler but should be accessible on investigation to the dog when 'winded'. The Judge should satisfy himself that the dog has found the person and has given warning spontaneously and emphatically without being directed by the handler. Once the person has been detected and the dog has given voice, it may be offered meat or other food which should be refused by the dog. If the dog ignores the food it may be thrown on the ground in front of the dog. A dog which eats the food and/or bites the person must be heavily penalised.

14. Test of Courage. This is a test of courage rather than of control. Dogs will not be heavily penalised in this test for lack of control. Handlers must be prepared to have the dog tested when on the lead by an unprotected Judge or Steward, and/or when off the lead by a protected Steward. The method of testing is at the Judges discretion.

15. Search and Escort. The 'criminal' will be searched by the handler with the dog off the lead at the sit, stand or down position. The Judge will assess whether the dog is well placed tactically and ready to defend if called to do so. The handler will be told to escort the 'prisoner' at least 30 yards in a given direction, he will give at least one turn on the direction of the Judge. During the exercise the 'criminal' will turn and attempt to overpower the handler. The dog may defend spontaneously or on command and must release the 'criminal' at once, either when he stands still or when the handler calls him off. The handler should be questioned as to his tactics in positioning the dog in both search and escort.

16. Recall from Criminals. (Exercise 14(a)). The 'criminal', protected consistent with safety, will be introduced to the handler whose dog will be free at heel. After an unheated conversation the 'criminal' will run away. At a reasonable distance the handler will be ordered to send his dog. When the dog is approximately halfway between handler and the 'criminal' he will be ordered to be recalled. The recall may be by whistle or voice. The 'criminal' should continue running until the dog returns or closes. If the dog continues to run alongside the 'criminal', the 'criminal' should run a further ten or dozen paces to indicate this.

17. Pursuit and Detention of Criminals. (Exercise 14(b)). The 'criminal' (a different one for choice) and handler should be introduced as above, and the dog sent forward under the same conditions. The 'criminal' must continue to attempt to escape and, if possible, should do so through some exit or in some vehicle once the dog has had a chance to catch up with him. The dog must be regarded as having succeeded if it clearly prevents the 'criminal' from continuing to flee, either by holding him by the arm, knocking him over or close circling him till he becomes giddy. If the dog fails to make a convincing attempt to detain the 'criminal', it shall lose any marks that it may have obtained under exercise 14(1) or alternatively, it shall not be tested on exercise 14(1) if that follows exercise 14(b).

(The use of the singular throughout this Annex may, where appropriate, also apply to the plural.)

APPENDIX H

KENNEL CLUB OBEDIENCE SHOW REGULATIONS
1st July 1988

GENERAL REGULATIONS

1. **Eligibility.**
   a. Obedience Show licences will be issued to registered or affiliated Societies only, with the exception of Exemption Show licences which will be issued to unregistered organisations only.
   b. Dogs entered at Kennel Club licensed Obedience Shows, with the exception of Exemption Shows, must be registered at the Kennel Club in accordance with Kennel Club Regulations for Classification and Registration B.
   c. Only dogs of six calendar months of age and over are eligible for entry at Kennel Club licensed Obedience Shows.
   d. If, in the opinion of the General Committee, a dog is of a savage disposition it shall be ineligible for entry at any Show held under Kennel Club Regulations.
   e. Persons disqualified or suspended under Kennel Club Rules are not eligible to take part in any Kennel Club licensed event.

2. **Licensed Obedience Shows.** Licensed Shows held under Kennel Club Rules and Regulations are those held under licence granted by the General Committee of the Kennel Club and are:
   a. Championship Obedience Shows – Open to all competitors, except where a qualification for entry has been approved by the General Committee of the Kennel Club, and at which Kennel Club Obedience Certificates are offered.
   b. Open Obedience Shows – Open to all competitors.
   c. Limited Obedience Shows* – Where entry is limited to members of the Show Societies or to competitors resident within specified areas or otherwise subject to the approval of the General Committee of the Kennel Club.
   d. Sanction Obedience Shows* – Where entry is limited to members of Show Societies.
   e. Matches – Where entry is limited to members of the Societies.

f. Exemption Shows* – at which registered and unregistered dogs are eligible to compete.

* – Dogs which have won an Obedience Certificate or obtained any award that counts towards the title of Obedience Champion under the rules of any governing body recognised by the Kennel Club are not eligible for entry at these Shows.

3. **Permission to Hold Shows.**

a. The General Committee shall have the power to grant, withhold or cancel permission to hold any licensed Obedience Show.

b. Any cancellation or abandonment of a Show without prior permission of the General Committee must be reported in writing to the Kennel Club without delay.

4. **Guarantors.**

a. Licensed Obedience Shows require Guarantors who shall undertake jointly and severally to hold and conduct the Shows under and in accordance with the Rules and Regulations of the Kennel Club, to guarantee the due payment of any prize money, and to abide by and adopt any decision of the General Committee or any authority to whom the General Committee may delegate its powers subject to the conditions of Regulations 13.

b. Such undertaking shall also be taken as an agreement by such guarantors and each of them, that any decision given against them or any of them, under Rule 41 of the Kennel Club Rules may be communicated by the Secretary of the Kennel Club to the Secretaries of Dog Shows, Field Trials, Working Trials and Societies affiliated with the Kennel Club, and may also be published in THE KENNEL GAZETTE, the official publication of the Kennel Club together with a report of the proceedings in the matter, including names, addresses and descriptions.

c. Any notice sent by registered post to any such Guarantors at the addresses given by them on the licence application shall be deemed full and sufficient notice on the part of the Kennel Club to them, or any of them, of any proceedings, matters or decisions of the General Committee, or any authority to whom the General Committee may delegate its powers, or in regard to anything arising out of the Show Licence or to the conduct of the Show, or in respect of any other matter whatsoever arising out of or in connection with the same.

5. Application. The application for a licence to hold a Show must be made to the Secretary of the Kennel Club, 1-5 Clarges Street, London, W1Y 8AB, on the official form which must be properly completed, together with the appropriate licence fee:
   a. Championship Shows. At least nine calendar months before the proposed date of the Show.
   b. Open, Limited, Sanction Shows. At least six calendar months before the proposed date of the Show.

6. Documentation. At every Obedience Show the following documents must be available:
   a. The licence for the Show, which must be clearly displayed.
   b. A copy of Kennel Club Rules and relevant Obedience Regulations.
   c. A copy of the Schedule and Catalogue for the Show.
   d. The completed entry forms for the Show.

7. Disqualification of Dogs. A dog shall be disqualified and removed from the Show if it is:
   a. A bitch which is in season.
   b. Suffering from any infectious or contagious disease.
   c. Interfering with the safety or chance of winning of an opponent.
   d. Of such temperament or is so much out of hand as to be a danger to the safety of any person or other animal.
   e. Likely to cause suffering to the dog if it continues competing.

8. Objections.
   a. An objection to a dog must be made to the Secretary of the Show in writing at any time within seven days of the last day of the meeting upon the objector lodging with the Secretary the sum of £25.00. The deposit may be returned after the General Committee of the Kennel Club has considered the objection. Should any objection be made other than under Regulation 7 the dog should be allowed to compete and a full report made to the Kennel Club.
   b. When an objection is lodged the Secretary of the Society must send to the Kennel Club:
      (1) A copy of the objection.
      (2) The name and address of the objector.
      (3) The name and address of the owner of the dog.
      (4) All relevant evidence.

c. The objection will then be dealt with by the General Committee of the Kennel Club whose decision shall be final.

d. No objection shall be invalidated solely on the grounds that it was incorrectly lodged.

e. If the dog objected to is disqualified, the prize to which it would otherwise have been entitled shall be forfeited, and the dog or dogs next in order of merit shall move up and take the prize or prizes.

f. No spectator, not being the owner of a dog competing, or his accredited representative has the right to lodge any objection to a dog or to any action taken at the meeting unless he be a member of the Committee of the Society or of the General Committee of the Kennel Club or a Steward of the Show. Any objection so lodged will be disregarded.

9. Fraudulent or Discreditable Conduct at Obedience Shows.

The Secretary of an Obedience Show must immediately report to the Secretary of the Kennel Club any case of alleged fraudulent or discreditable conduct, or any default, omission or incident at or in connection with the Show which may come under his notice, even where parties concerned have indicated that they intend taking no action, and at the same time forward to the Secretary of the Kennel Club all documents and information in connection therewith which may be in his possession or power. If evidence is placed before the General Committee to its satisfaction that undue influence has been exercised by any person(s), or that any improper means have been used to influence the appointment of a Judge or to interfere with the exhibition of a dog at any Show held under Kennel Club Rules and Regulations, the General Committee may require all correspondence and evidence in connection with the case to be produced in order that it may deal with the offender(s) under Kennel Club Rule 42.

10. Penalty for Infringement of Kennel Club Rules by Obedience Show Management.

The General Committee shall have power to fine the Guarantors of a Show who have broken Kennel Club Rules and Regulations in the conduct of the Show.

11. Unlicensed Obedience Shows.

Notwithstanding the provisions of these Regulations, certain events which are not licensed by the Kennel Club may from time to time be recognised by the General Committee of the Kennel Club.

The General Committee shall have power to grant permission for

Kennel Club registered dogs to be entered for such events. A judge, exhibitor or promoter will not be prejudiced by participation in these special unlicensed events.

12. Obedience Certificates.
 a. The Kennel Club will offer an Obedience Certificate (Dog) and an Obedience Certificate (Bitch) for winners of First Prizes in Class C Dog and Class C Bitch at a Championship Show, provided that the exhibits do not lose more than 10 points out of 300, and provided also that the Classes are open to all breeds.
 b. Judges must also award a Reserve Best of sex provided that the exhibit has not lost more than 10 points out of 200.

13. Obedience Championships
 a. The Kennel Club will offer at Crufts Dog Show each year the Kennel Club Obedience Championship – Dog and the Kennel Club Obedience Championship – Bitch. A dog awarded one or more Obedience Certificates during the calendar year preceding Crufts Dog Show shall be entitled to compete.
 b. The Tests for the Championships shall be those required for Class C in these Regulations: If the winning dog or bitch has lost more than 10 points out of 300 the Championship award shall be witheld.

14. Schedule
 a. The Show Society must issue a Schedule for the Show, such schedule to follow the layout of the specimen schedule provided by the Kennel Club and conform with Kennel Club Regulations. No modifications may be made to the schedule, except by permission of the Kennel Club and such modifications must be advertised.
 b. *Submission of Schedules*
  Two copies of the schedule must be lodged with the Kennel Club when published; in the case of Championship Shows this must be three calendar months before the date of the Show.
(Above amendments to Paragraph 14, effective from 1st January 1990.)
 c. *Contents of Schedule*
  (1) On the front outside cover or title page, the name of the Show Society, the type, venue and date of the Show as described on the licence and any additional title for

which prior permission has been given by the General Committee of the Kennel Club; the names and addresses of the Guarantors of the Show, and the Secretary's name, address and telephone number where appropriate, and the name of the Chief Steward.

In the case of events where classes are provided for exhibits other than dogs, the names and addresses need only be printed at the head of the dog section.

(2) The names of the Judges(s) with the name of each Class.

(3) The words 'Kennel Club Obedience Certificate Dog; Kennel Club Obedience Certificate Bitch'. For Championship Class 'C'.

(4) The definitions of all classes and conditions of entry must be inserted in the order of Annex A of these Regulations 'Eligibility and Schedule of Classes'.

(5) All offers of sponsorship or donations with the names of the sponsors.

(6) The date of closing of entries.

(7) The amount of entry and other fees.

(8) The amount of prize money, where offered.

(9) The date for estimating the number of awards won.

(10) The time of opening of the Show.

(11) The latest time up to which dogs will be received and after which no dogs may be received except under exceptional and unforseen circumstances and by special permission of the Show Management; or notice to the effect that dogs will be received at any time.

(12) A statement that the mating of bitches within the precincts of the Show is forbidden.

(13) A statement that no bitch in season is allowed to compete.

(14) A statement that the Committee reserves to itself the right to refuse any entries.

(15) A statement that should a Judge be unable to fulfil the appointment to judge the Committee reserves the right to appoint another judge.

(16) A statement that should circumstances so dictate the Society, in consultation with the Judges, may alter arrangements as necessary. Such changes and the circumstances surrounding them must be reported to the Kennel Club.

(17) Notice of Kennel Club Obedience Show Regulations
paragraphs:
1 (c)
7
15 (a)
17 (c), (d), (f), (h), (i)
20 (a), (d), (g), (h)

15. Entry Forms.
a. An entry form shall have wording which must be in accordance with that approved for the time being by the Kennel Club.
b. All entry forms must be preserved by the Show Committee for at least twelve months from the closing date of entries and must be forwarded to the Kennel Club if requested, together with any other documents.

16. Catalogue.   The Show society must publish a Catalogue for the Show containing:
a. On the front outside cover or title page, the name of the Show Society, the type of Show as described on the Licence, and any additional title for which prior permission has been given by the General Committee of the Kennel Club; the names and addresses of the Guarantors of the Show, except in the case of Shows where classes are provided for exhibits other than dogs, where the names and addresses need only be printed at the head of the dog section.
b. The classes for each test, the numbering of which must follow that of the Schedule.
c. Championship Obedience Shows Only – Classes with Obedience Certificates on offer must be specified.
d. The names of the judges of each class.
e. Championship Obedience Shows – an alphabetical index containing the names and addresses of exhibitors, the number and name of each exhibit must be given in each class for which it is entered.
f. Open Limited and Sanction Obedience Shows – names and addresses of all exhibitors and full particulars of each exhibit as given on the entry form by the exhibitor.
g. Championship Open and Limited Obedience Shows only – the number of the ring in which each judge will officiate must be given.

Within fourteen days of the close of the Show, two copies of the official Catalogue for the Show, containing a full and correct list of all the entries, with all the awards correctly marked, must be submitted to the Kennel Club.

17. **Management.** Societies are responsible for the following:

   a. Judging rings shall not in any circumstances contain less than 83 square metres (900 square feet) of clear floor space and shall not be less than 6 metres (20 feet) in width except that for Championship Class C the ring must contain not less than 148 square metres (1600 square feet). Ring sizes should, where possible, be considerably larger.

   b. Classes may be scheduled in any order but this order must be followed at the show except that a Society, by publication in the schedule, may reserve the right to vary the order of judging when the entry is known.

   c. The maximum number of entries allowed in any class is 60. If the entry received exceeds 60, except for Championship Class C, the class shall be equally divided by a draw and each division judged separately. Prize money for each division shall be the same as that offered for the original class.

   d. Where classes are divided, competitors entered therein shall be notified of all changes and timed stay exercises must not be held earlier than advertised for the original class.

   e. The maximum number of dogs a person may judge on one day is 60. Reserve judges may enter dogs for competition at the show but may not compete if called upon to judge. Show Committees should appoint sufficient judges for the expected entries.

   f. Where the entry for Championship Class C exceeds 60, it will be reduced to 60 by a ballot based on a system of merit conducted by the Kennel Club.

   g. One judge only may officiate for each sex of Championship Class C and must be present when dogs are under test.

   h. A draw for the running order in Championship Class C at Shows must be made prior to the Show and exhibitors and judges notified of the running order before the day of the Show. The Kennel Club will ballot for the running order for Championship Class C and Show Secretaries must forward the names of the dogs and handlers by recorded delivery or registered post to the Kennl Club for ballot within seven days after the closing of entries. Where a complete draw for the running order of Classes other than Championship Class C is not made, Show Managements must ensure that at least ten competitors/dogs are available, by means of a ballot for judging in the first hour following the scheduled time for the commencement of judging of that Class, and these competitors must be notified prior to the Show. All competitors must personally report to the Ring Scoreboard Steward and book in within one hour of the scheduled time for the commencement of judging for the Class. Those reporting late will be excluded from competition unless they have reported previously to the Chief Steward that they are actually working a dog entered in another Championship Class C, or in the Stay Tests of another Class. Where a complete running order is made, all competitors must be notified prior to the day of the Show, and they must book in on arrival at the Show. Published orders of running must be strictly observed. When a draw makes provision for reserve competitors, they should not be substituted before 12 noon.

i. Where timed stays will take place it must be announced in the Schedule that they will take priority over other tests. The times of such tests to be published at the Show and in the catalogue. In the case of Championship Class C, stays must not be judged before 12 noon. In all other cases, timed stays must not commence before one hour after the published time for the commencement of judging.

j. The Show Executive shall appoint a Chief Steward whose name must be announced in the schedule, and who must not enter or work a dog or act in any other capacity at the Show. The Chief Steward alone shall be responsible for the control of any running order and for the smooth running of each Class and his decision in such matters shall be personally conveyed to the judge and shall be final.

k. Should a Judge be prevented from completing a Class which has commenced, the Chief Steward shall decide what action is to be taken.

l. The Show Executive shall ensure that 'Caller' Stewards are appointed for each Class scheduled who must not work a dog at the Show.

m. Neutral scent cloths must be provided by the Show Executive for all classes.

18. **Approval of Judges.**
    a. Show Societies must apply to the General Committee for approval of all judges for Championship Obedience Shows, at least 12 months before the date of the Show on the form provided.
    b. The following minimum conditions apply for the nomination of Judges for Championship Shows:
       (1) For Class C at Championship Shows judges must have at least five years judging experience and judged at thirty Open Obedience Shows at which they have judged Class C not less than fifteen times. Judging experience of other Classes must include at least two each of the following at Open or Championship Shows: Beginners, Novice, Class A and Class B.
       (2) For all other Classes, to have at least three years judging experience at Open Shows and have judged two each of Beginners, Novice A and Class B.
    c. Judges at Open Shows on first appointment must satisfy the Show Committee that they have two years experience judging at a lower level, have won out of Beginners at a Licensed Open Obedience Show and have acted as a Caller Steward or Marker Steward on six occasions at Licensed Shows.
    d. Intervals between judging appointments.
       (1) Judges of Obedience Certificates will only be approved to judge an Obedience Certificate for Dogs and or Obedience Certificate for Bitches once in each year calculated from 1st January to 31st December.
       (2) There is no minimum interval between appointments to judge classes, other than Obedience Certificate Class 'C', at Championship Obedience Shows.

19. **Judging.**
    a. Judges at Kennel Club licensed Obedience Shows must judge in accordance with Kennel Club Rules and Regulations.
    b. Variations to tests are not allowed.
    c. In any test in which Judge's articles are used, none should be injurious to the dog, and must be capable of being picked up by any breed entered in that test.
    d. In the event of dogs obtaining equality of marks, 'Run Offs' to decide the winning dogs will be judged one at a time by normal scheduled tests.
    e. In all tests the points must be graduated.

f. A Judge of Class C must record each dog awarded 290 points or more in the Judging Book. The Show Secretary will record these in the official marked catalogue.

20. Competing.

a. Any dog which is not presented for stay or scent exercises when called for testing will be considered to have withdrawn from the class.

b. In all Tests, dogs must compete in the same order but the judge may relax the running order where necessary in the Scent Tests. These must not be carried out during the main ring work but will take place as a separate test at the judges discretion.

c. In all Classes the handler may use the dog's name with a command or signal without penalty. All tests shall commence and finish with the dog sitting at the handler's left side except in Stay Tests and Distance Control and in Beginners, Novice and Class A Recall Tests when the dog may be left in either the Sit or Down position at the handler's choice.

d. Food shall not be carried or given to a dog under test.

e. Dogs may only wear a slip chain or smooth collar when in the ring.

f. Imperfections in heeling between tests will not be judged but any physical disciplining of the dog by the handler in the ring or any uncontrolled behaviour of the dog such as snapping, unjustified barking, fouling the ring or running out of the ring even between tests must be penalised by deducting points from the total score and the judge may bar the dog from further competition in the Class.

g. No person shall carry out punitive correction or harsh handling of a dog at any time within the boundaries of the Show.

h. No competitor shall impugn the decision of the Judge or Judges.

21. Delegated Powers of the Scottish Kennel Club.

a. For the purpose of paragraphs 2 and 3 of these Regulations the power to grant, withhold or cancel permission to hold any licensed Obedience Show in Scotland, other than a Championship Obedience Show, shall be delegated to the Scottish Kennel Club.

b. For the purposes of these Regulations, all powers of the

General Committee relative to Shows held in Scotland and licensed by the Scottish Kennel Club are delegated to the Executive Council of the Scottish Kennel Club. Applications for licenses, objections and allegations of fradulent or discreditable conduct relative to Obedience Shows licensed by the Scottish Kennel Club must be made to the Secretary General of the Scottish Kennel Club, 6b Forres Street, Edinburgh, EH3 6BJ.

22. Eligibility and Schedule of Classes.
The detailed Regulations for Eligibility and the Schedule of Classes are given in Annex A.

23. Specific Regulations for Obedience Matches.
The specific Regulations for Obedience Matches are given in Annex B.

24. Explanatory Notes for Obedience Test.
The Explanatory Notes for Obedience Tests are given in Annex C.

25. Instructions as to the Duties of Obedience Ring Stewards.
The Instructions as to the Duties of Obedience Ring Stewards are given in Annex D.

(A)

ELIGIBILITY AND SCHEDULE OF CLASSES

ELIGIBILITY

1.   In the following Definitions of Classes First Prize wins in Limited and Sanction Show Obedience Classes and Open Shows confined to one breed do not count for entry in Open and Championship Show Obedience Classes.

2.   Dogs are ineligible to compete at Limited and Sanction Shows which have won an Obedience Certificate or obtained any award that counts towards the title of Obedience Champion, or the equivalent thereof under the rules of any governing body recognised by the Kennel Club. Obedience Champions are only eligible to compete in Class C at Open and Championship Shows.

3.   A dog must be entered in the lowest class for which it is eligible and may also be entered in another class if desired, one special class excepted, with the exception of Championship Class C for which only dogs qualified may be entered. (Note the qualifications for Championship Class C and Obedience Warrant.)

CLASSES

4. Pre-Beginners.
   a. Pre-Beginners Classes may only be scheduled at Limited and Sanction Obedience Shows.
   b. To compete in Pre-Beginners an owner, handler or dog must not have won a First Prize in any Class.
   c. Handlers will not be penalised for encouragement or extra commands except in the Sit and Down tests. In these tests, at the discretion of the Judge, handlers may face their dogs. Judges or Stewards must not use the words 'last command' except in the Sit and Down tests.
   d. The detailed tests will be:
      (1) Heel on lead   15 points
      (2) Heel free   20 points
      (3) Recall from sit or down position at handler's choice. Dog to be recalled by handler when stationary and facing the dog. Dog to return smartly to the handler, sit in front, go to heel – all on command of Judge or Steward to handler. Distance at discretion of Judge. Test commences when handler leaves dog.   10 points
      (4) Sit one minute, handler in sight   10 points
      (5) Down two minutes, handler in sight   20 points
      (6) TOTAL   75 points

5. Beginners.
   a. To compete in Beginners an Owner or Handler or dog must not have won a total of two or more First Prizes in Beginners Class, or one First Prize in any other Obedience Class.
   b. Handlers will not be penalised for encouragement or extra commands except on the Sit and Down tests. In these tests, at the discretion of the Judge, handlers may face their dogs. Judges and

Stewards must not use the words 'last command' except in the Sit and Down tests.

c. The detailed tests will be:

(1) Heel on lead	15 points
(2) Heel free	20 points
(3) Recall from Sit or Down position at handler's choice. Dog to be recalled by handler when stationary and facing the dog. Dog to return smartly to handler, sit in front, go to heel – all on command of Judge or Steward to handler. Distance at discretion of Judge. Test commences when handler leaves dog.	10 points
(4) Retrieve any article. Handlers may use their own article	25 points
(5) Sit one minute, handler in sight	10 points
(6) Down two minutes, handler in sight	20 points
(7) TOTAL	100 points

6. Novice.

a. For dogs that have not won two First Prizes in Obedience Classes. (Beginners excepted).

b. Handlers will not be penalised for encouragement or extra commands except in the Sit and Down tests. In these tests, at the discretion of the Judge, handlers may face their dogs. Judges or Stewards must not use the words 'last command' except in the Sit and Down tests.

c. The detailed tests will be:

(1) Temperament Test. To take place before heel on lead. Dog to be on the lead, in the Stand position, handler to stand by dog. Judge to approach quietly from the front and to run his hand gently down the dog's back. Judge may talk quietly to the dog to reassure it. Any undue resentment, cringing, growling or snapping to be penalised. This is not a stand for examination or a stay test.	10 points
(2) Heel on lead	15 points
(3) Heel free	20 points
(4) Recall from Sit or Down position at handler's choice. Dog to be recalled by handler when stationary and facing the dog. Dog to	

return smartly to handler, sit in front, go to heel – all on command of Judge or Steward to handler. Distance at discretion of Judge. Test commences when handler leaves dog.   10 points

(5) Retrieve a dumb-bell, handlers may use their own dumb-bell   15 points

(6) Sit one minute, handler in sight   10 points

(7) Down two minutes, handler in sight   20 points

(8) TOTAL   100 points

7. Class A.

a. For dogs which have not won three First Prizes in Class A, B and Open Class C in total.

b. Simultaneous command and signal will be permitted. Extra commands or signals must be penalised.

c. The detailed tests will be:

(1) Heel on lead   15 points

(2) Temperament Test. Will take place before Heel free. Dog to be in the stand position and off the lead. Handler to stand beside dog. Conditions as for Novice Temperament Test, except that the test will commence with order 'last command' and end with order 'test finished'. Extra commands will be penalised. This is not a stand for examination or a stay test.   10 points

(3) Heel free   25 points

(4) Recall from Sit or Down position at handler's choice. Dog to be recalled to heel by handler, on command of Judge or Steward, whilst handler is walking away from dog, both to continue forward until ordered to halt. The recall and halt points to be the same for each dog and handler. Test commences following handler's last command to dog.   15 points

(5) Retrieve a dumb-bell. Handlers may use their own dumb-bell.   15 points

(6) Sit two minutes, handler in sight   10 points

(7) Down five minutes, handler out of sight   30 points

(8) Scent discrimination. Handler's scent on

cloth provided by Judge. There must be six cloths set out in a straight line with the handler's scent on one cloth with no decoys. 30 points
(9) TOTAL 150 points

8. Class B.
a. For dogs which have not won three first prizes in Class B and Open Class C in total.

b. One command by word or signal except in the Send Away, Drop and Recall. Extra commands or signals must be penalised.

c. The detailed tests will be:

(1) Heel free. The dog shall be required to walk at heel free and shall also be tested at fast and slow pace. Each change of pace shall commence from the halt position 40 points

(2) Send Away, Drop and Recall. On command of Judge the handler to bring the dog to the place indicated, set up the dog and stand upright. On further command, the handler will send the dog in the direction indicated by the Judge. After the dog has been dropped, handler will call the dog to heel whilst walking where directed by the Judge and both will continue forward until ordered to halt. No obstacle to be placed in path of dog. Simultaneous command and signal is permitted but as soon as the dog leaves the handler, the arm must be dropped. (N.B. an extra command may be simultaneous command or signal but must be penalised) 40 points

(3) Retrieve any one article provided by the Judge but which must not be in any way injurious to the dog (excluding food or glass). The article to be picked up easily by any breed of dog in that Class and to be clearly visible to the dog. A separate similar article to be used for each dog. Test commences following Judge's or Steward's words 'last command' to handler 30 points

(4) Stand one minute, handler in sight 10 points
(5) Sit two minutes, handler out of sight 20 points

(6) Down five minutes, handler out of sight   30 points
(7) Scent discrimination. Handler's scent to be
    on cloth provided by the Judge. There must
    be ten cloths with handler's scent on one
    cloth with one decoy.   30 points
(8) TOTAL   200 points

9. Class C.

a. At Championship Shows, dogs must have won
   out of two novice Classes, two Class As and two
   Class Bs and have won Open Class C on one
   occasiojn and have been placed not lower than
   third on three occasions under different Judges.

b. At Open Shows, open to all dogs.

c. At Limited and Sanction Shows, open to all dogs
   except Obedience Certificate winners and dogs
   which have obtained any award that counts
   towards the title of Obedience Champion or the
   equivalent thereof under the rules of any governing body recognised by the Kennel Club.

d. One command by word or signal, except in Send
   Away, Drop and Recall where an extra command may be simultaneous command and
   signal. Extra commands or signals must be
   penalised.

e. The detailed tests will be:

(1) Heel Work. The dog shall be required to
    walk at heel free, and also be tested at fast
    and slow pace. At some time during this test,
    at the discretion of the Judge, the dog shall
    be required, whilst walking at heel at normal
    pace, to be left at the Stand, Sit and Down
    position in any order (the order to be the
    same for each dog) as and when directed by
    the Judge. The handler shall continue for-
    ward alone without hesitation, and continue
    as directed by the Judge until reaching the
    dog when both shall continue forward
    together until halted. Heel work may include
    left about turns and figure of eight at normal
    and/or slow pace   60 points
(2) Send Away, Drop and Recall as in Class B   40 points

(3) Retrieve any one article provided by the Judge but which must not be in any way injurious to the dog (excluding food or glass). The article to be picked up easily by an breed of dog in the Class and to be clearly visible to the dog. A separate similar article to be used for each dog. Test commences following Judge's or Steward's words 'last command' to handler   30 points

(4) Distant Control. Dog to Sit, Stand and Down at a marked place not less than ten paces from handler, in any order on command from Judge to handler. Six instructions to be given in the same order for each dog. Excessive movement, i.e. more than the body length of the dog, in any direction by the dog, having regard to its size, will be penalised. The dog shall start the exercise with its front feet behind a designated point. No penalty for excessive movement in a forward direction shall be imposed until the back feet of the dog pass the designated point   50 points

(5) Sit two minutes, handler out of sight   20 points

(6) Down ten minutes, handler out of sight   50 points

(7) Scent discrimination. Judge's scent on a piece of marked cloth. Neutral and decoy cloths to be provided by the Show Executive. The Judge shall not place his cloth in the ring himself, but it shall be placed by a Steward. A separate similar piece to be used for each dog and the total number of separate similar pieces of cloth from which the dog shall discriminate shall not exceed ten. If a dog fetches or fouls a wrong article this must be replaced by a fresh article. At open-air Shows all scent cloths must be adequately weighted to prevent them being blown about. The method of taking scent shall be at handler's discretion but shall not require the Judge to place his hand on or lean towards the dog. A separate similar piece of cloth approximately 6 inches by 6 inches but

not more than 10 inches by 10 inches shall be
available to be used for giving each dog the
scent. Judges should use a scent decoy or
decoys. Dog to be sent on Judge's command   50 points
(8) TOTAL   300 points

(B)

SPECIFIC REGULATIONS FOR OBEDIENCE MATCHES

(to be read in conjunction with Kennel Club Obedience
Show Regulations)

1. An Obedience Match may be a competition between club
members or an inter-Club competition between Associations, Clubs,
Societies or Branches of Clubs.

2. Only Registered Clubs, Societies and Dog Training Clubs may
hold Obedience Matches.

3. A Club may hold up to 12 Obedience Matches per annum. In the
case of Clubs which have registered Branches, each Branch may hold
up to 12 Obedience Matches per annum.

4. Application. Application for permission to hold Obedience
Matches must be made in writing, to the Kennel Club at least 28 days
before the date of the proposed Obedience Match accompanied by
the relevant fee. The application must be signed by the Club
Secretary and countersigned by the Chairman, who shall act as
guarantors to the Kennel Club that the match will be held in
accordance with the Regulations.

5. Regulations.
   a. A dog must, at the time of competition, be registered at the
   Kennel Club. Exhibits must be the property of Members of one
   of the Associations, Clubs, Societies or Branches competing in
   the Obedience Match.
   b. The Committee of the organising Club may reserve the right
   to refuse any entry on reasonable grounds.
   c. Puppies under six calendar months of age are not eligible for
   competition at Obedience Matches.

d. If a dog competes which has been exposed to the risk of any contagious or infectious disease during the period of six weeks prior to an Obedience Match and/or if any dog shall be proved to be suffering at Obedience Matches from any contagious or infectious disease, including the contagious results of inoculations against distemper, the owner thereof shall be liable to be dealt with under Kennel Club Rule 42.

e. Not more than 52 dogs may compete at an Obedience Match Meeting.

f. Prize cards, diplomas or other printed awards may be awarded at Obedience Matches provided such awards are clearly over printed 'MATCH'.

g. Not more than two Special Prizes shall be awarded at Obedience Matches.

h. The organising Club shall keep a list of the names of all competing dogs with awards, and the names and addresses of their owners for a period of twelve months from the date of the Matches.

(C)

EXPLANATORY NOTES FOR OBEDIENCE TESTS

1. **General.**
   a. In all Classes the dog should work in a happy and natural manner but should not impede the handler and prime consideration should be given to judging the dog and handler as a team. The dog may be encouraged and praised except where specifically stated.
   b. Instructions and commands to competitors may be made either by the Judge or the Steward by delegation.
   c. In all tests the left side of a handler will be regarded as the 'working side' unless the handler suffers from a physical disability and has the Judge's permission to work the dog on the right hand side.
   d. To signal the completion of each test the handler will be given the command 'test finished'.
   e. It is permissible for handlers to practise their dogs before going into the ring provided there is no punitive correction; this is similar to an athlete warming up before an event.
   f. Time-table of Judging – to assist the Show Executive the following guide time-table is issued:

    (1) Class C .... 8 dogs per hour
    (2) Class B .... 10 dogs per hour
    (3) Class A .... 12 dogs per hour
    (4) Novice .... 12 dogs per hour
    (5) Beginners .... 15 dogs per hour
    (6) Pre-Beginners .... 18 dogs per hour

g. The dog should be led into the ring for judging with a smooth collar or slip chain lead attached (unless otherwise directed) and should be at the handler's side.

h. Competitors in Championship Class C who have lost more marks than would enable them to qualify with 290 marks at the conclusion of the judging may withdraw from the Class with the Judge's approval. The decision to withdraw is entirely at the discretion of the competitor and Judges must not compel such competitors to withdraw.

2. Tests.

a. Heel on Lead – The dog should be sitting straight at the handler's side. On command the handler should walk briskly forward in a straight line with the dog at heel. The dog's shoulder should be approximately level with and reasonably close to the handler's leg at all times when the handler is walking. The lead must be slack at all times. On the command 'Left Turn' or 'Right Turn' the handler should turn smartly at a right angle in the appropriate direction and the dog should keep its position at the handler's side. Unless otherwise directed, on the command 'About Turn' the handler should turn about smartly through an angle of 180 degrees to the right and walk in the opposite direction, the dog maintaining its position at the handler's side. On the command 'Halt' the handler should halt immediately and the dog should sit straight at the handler's side. Throughout the test the handler may not touch the dog or make use of the lead without penalty.

b. Heel Free – This test should be carried out in a similar manner as for Heel on lead except that the dog must be off the lead throughout the test. 'Left about Turns' in heelwork are only permissible in Class B and C at the Judge's discretion.

c. Recall – See specific Class Tests.

d. Retrieve a Dumb-bell/Article – At the start of this exercise the dog should be sitting at the handler's side. On command the handler must throw the dumb-bell/article in the direction indicated. The dog should remain in the Sit position until the handler is ordered to send it to retrieve the dumb-bell/article.

The dog should move out promptly at a smart pace to collect the dumb-bell/article cleanly. It should return with the dumb-bell/article at a smart pace and sit straight in front of the handler. On command the handler should take the dumb-bell/article from the dog. On further command the dog should be sent to heel. In Classes A, B and C the test commences on the order 'Last Command' to handler.

e. Stays – The Judge or Steward will direct handlers to positions in the ring. The command 'Last Command' will be given and handlers should then instantly give their final command to their dogs. Any further commands or signals to the dogs after this 'Last Command' will be penalised. Handlers will then be instructed to leave their dogs and walk to positions indicated until ordered to return to them. These are group tests and all dogs must compete together, but where this is impracticable at an indoor show, the Class may be equally divided but the Judging for the groups must be consecutive.

(1) Sit/Stay – Dogs should remain in the Sit position throughout the test.

(2) Stand/Stay – Dogs should remain in the Stand position throughout the test.

(3) Down/Stay – Dogs should remain the Down position throughout the test.

f. Scent Discrimination – On command the handler should bring the dog to the point indicated. The dog should be facing away from the cloths whilst the steward places the scent cloths amongst the other cloths. When directed the handler should face the cloths and after giving the dog scent, the handler should stand upright before sending the dog on Judge's command to find and retrieve the appropriate cloth. The dog should find the cloth and complete the test as for the Retrieve Test. In all tests, scent cloths are to be placed at least two and not more than four feet apart. If a dog brings in a wrong cloth or physically fouls any cloth (i.e. mouths it) this cloth will be replaced. Limiting the time allowed for this test is at the Judge's discretion.

(1) Class A – Handler's scent to be on cloth provided by the Judge. There must be six cloths provided by the Show Executive set out in a straight line with the handler's scent on one cloth with no decoys.

(2) Class B – Handler's scent to be on cloth provided by the Judge. There must be ten cloths with handler's scent on one cloth with one decoy.

(3) Class C – Judge's scent on piece of marked cloth. A decoy Steward should not handle a cloth for a period longer than the Judge.

(D)

INSTRUCTIONS AS TO THE DUTIES OF OBEDIENCE RING STEWARDS

1. **Authority/Responsibilities.**
   a. A Steward's responsibilities are at all times to assist the Judge in the course of his duties and to ensure the smooth and efficient running of the Ring.
   b. Stewards should always remember that the Judge is in overall control of the Ring and accordingly should follow the Judge's directives.

2. **Duties**
   a. Before Judging:
      (1) To ensure that all equipment has been provided in the Ring and that the score sheets and prize cards are available for each Class with a copy of the catalogue.
      (2) To report to the Judge on his arrival and acquaint himself with the Judge's tests and instructions.
      (3) To advise exhibitors that Judging is to commence after which the responsibility for dogs being brought into the Ring at the correct time is entirely the competitors'.
   b. During Judging:
      (1) To ensure that all commands are given in the same place and in the same manner for each dog and competitor.
      (2) To ensure each competitor has the correct Ring number for their dog when entering the Ring and that the number is prominently displayed whilst working.
      (3) To ensure that there is no interference with dogs being Judged.
   c. After Judging:
      (1) To complete the award slips and obtain the Judge's signature at the conclusion of the Class.
      (2) To mark the results of the Classes in the catalogue and hand the completed copy to the Judge.
      (3) To ensure that the Judge signs the Obedience Certificate, Reserve Obedience Certificate and any other awards.

GLOSSARY

AMBLING. A form of movement when both the fore and hind legs on the same side move in the same direction simultaneously.

ANGULATION. The word used to describe the construction of the hock and stifle joint, and the position of the foreleg and the shoulders.

ANUS. The posterior opening through which the contents of the bowels are eliminated.

APPLE HEAD. A rounded, or very domed skull.

AUSLESEGRUPPE. The selected 'Excellent' exhibits at the German Sieger shows.

BALANCED. No exaggeration anywhere, every part of the German Shepherd Dog in proportion to the other.

BARREL RIBS. Rib cage excessively rounded.

BITE. The meeting point of the front teeth.

BONE. References to 'light bone' or 'heavy bone' refer to the four legs.

BOSSY. A term occasionally used to describe heavy or loaded shoulders.

BREECHING. The profusely coated 'trousers' on the hind legs.

BRISKET. The chest, beneath the forelegs and beneath the withers.

BUTTERFLY NOSE. A black or liver-coloured nose, speckled with pink.

CANINE TOOTH. The long fangs, one each side of the jaw.

CAT FOOT. Round, thick, tightly closed foot, resembling that of the cat.

CHALLENGE CERTIFICATES. The awards, offered by the Kennel Club at Championship shows only, three of which, won under three different judges, entitle a dog to become a Champion.

CH. The abbreviation, most commonly used, of the above.

CHISELLING. The angles dividing skull and foreface.

CLOSE-COUPLED. Short in back and loin.

COBBY. Thick-set. Compact.

COUPLING. A word sometimes used to describe the act of mating.

COUPLINGS. The section of the body that joins with the hindquarters.

COWHOCKS. Hocks that turn inwards, weak hocks.

CROSSBREED. The result of a mating between two dogs of two different pure breeds.

CROUP. The extremity of the backline, and point at which tail is set on.

CRYPTORCHID. A male animal in which neither of the two testicles is externally visible or functional.

DENTITION. The arrangement of the teeth.

DEW-CLAWS. Extra 'toes', complete with claws, set well above the feet on the inside of fore and/or hind legs. Hind dew-claws should be removed from German Shepherd Dogs, front dew-claws are normally not removed.

DEWLAP. Soft, pendulous skin under the chin and neck.

DISH FACE. A concave muzzle.

DISTEMPER TEETH. Teeth pitted, decayed, discoloured brown, as a result of disease.

DOG. Any member of the species canine familaris.

DOUBLE COAT. A smooth, upper coat with a closer, woollier mat of hairs growing near the skin.

DRY. Neat, tight skin formation. Firm, hard muscles.

DUDLEY NOSE. A light brown or flesh-coloured nose.

ENTIRE. A male dog is 'entire' with both testicles normally descended in the scrotum.

EWE NECK. A think excessively arched, neck.

FANG. A large canine tooth.

FIDDLE FRONT. Crooked front legs, out at elbows, legs sloping inwards at the pastern joints, bent forearms, front feet turning outwards.

FLEWS. Pendulous lips.

FLYER. An outstanding specimen of any breed.

FOREARM. The long bone of the front leg.

FRONT. The chest and forelegs as seen from directly in front of a dog.

GAY TAIL. A tail carried very high or curled over the back.

GOOSE RUMP. An unusually sloping croup.

GRAND CHAMPION. The English term used to describe the German Sieger.

GD. CH. Abbreviation, frequently seen on pedigrees, of above.

HACKNEY ACTION. The exaggerated lifting of the front legs in the manner of a hackney horse, a motion which is not considered to provide an enduring gait or movement.

HARE FOOT. A long, oval-shaped, narrow foot.

HEIGHT. The height of a dog is measured from a spot between the shoulder-blades at the highest point where the neck joins the back, referred to as the withers.

HERDEN GEBRAUCHTSHUND. German working qualification for sheep herding.

H.G.H. Abbreviation for above.

HOCK. The lower joint of the hind leg.

INBREEDING. The pairing of closely related animals.

INTERNATIONAL CHAMPION. A dog which has won its Championship titles in more than one country.

INT. CH. Abbreviation of above.

KNUCKLE OVER. Forelegs with knobs which bulge forwards at the pastern joints are said to 'knuckle over'.

LINE-BREEDING. The pairing of animals with one or more common ancestors.

LIPPY. Lips looser, longer, fuller than desirable.

LOADED. Shoulders are said to be 'loaded' when they are disproportionately thickset or heavy in comparison to the rest of the dog.

LOINS. The party of the body between the hip-bone and the ribs.

MOLAR TOOTH. One of the smaller, grinding teeth towards the back of the jaw.

MONGREL. A dog of mixed ancestry, containing the blood of several pure-bred dogs of different breeds, or made up of dogs of mixed parentage themselves.

MONORCHID. A male animal with only one testicle descended in the scrotum. Monorchids are not eligible for exhibition under Kennel Club Rules.

MUZZLE. The foreface, extending from between the eyes to the nose.

OCCIPUT. The peak of the skull between the ears.

OUT AT ELBOW. Elbows turned away from the chest, uneven in appearance, loose.

OUT AT SHOULDER. Shoulder-blades loosely attached to the body, jutting out. Usually combined with loose elbows, and often with excessive width between the front legs.

OUT-CROSSING. The mating of wholely or partly unrelated animals.

OVERSHOT. A short lower jaw, or teeth arranged so that the upper set project forward over the lower teeth.

PACK. A number of hounds or dogs.

PAD. The sole of the dog's foot.

PADDLING. A faulty gait, whereby the front legs are thrown outwards in a loose, uncoordinated manner.

PASTERN. The small section of the front leg that joins the foot to the fore-arm.

PEDIGREE. A record of a dog's parentage and ancestry, usually for three or more generations.

PERIOD OF GESTATION. The length of time taken for a bitch to produce a litter – normally sixty-three days.

PIN-TOED. Front legs turned inwards.

P.D., P.H. Police dog, Politzei Hund (German). Working qualifications.

PREMOLAR TOOTH. The small teeth placed between the large canines and the molars or large back teeth. Premolars are sometimes absent, and this is a fault.

PREPOTENT. A dog is said to be prepotent when it transmits certain qualities to its progeny.

PUPPY. A dog not exceeding twelve months of age.

RICKETS. A disease of the bones caused by malnutrition, lack of vitamins, sunlight, fresh air. Also caused by dark, damp or cramped kennelling.

RING TAIL. A tail curled over the back or round in a circle.

ROACH BACK. An arched spine.

SCH.H. Sch.H. I, II, or III, German 'Schutz Hund' working qualifications, three different grades.

SCISSOR BITE. Teeth fitting correctly and closely, the upper set sliding down just in front of the lower set when the jaws close.

SECOND THIGH. The hind leg between the stifle and hock joint.

S.G. 'Sehr Gut' (German). The qualification 'Very Good'.

SHELLY. Lightly built, narrow, lacking bone, body, substance.

SICKLE HOCKS. Hocks bent, the upper joints inclining outwards.

SIEGER AND SIEGERIN. The German Grand Champion titles, dog and bitch.

SLAB SIDES. Very flat ribs and sides.

SNIPEY. Narrow, slight, pointed and sometimes overlong, muzzle.

SPLAY FOOT. A foot with loose, badly fitting toes with spaces between them.

STIFLE. The joint immediately above the hock.

STOP. The space between the eyes, dividing forehead and muzzle.

STRAIGHT HOCKS. Lack of hind angulation (generally causing poor propulsion and short, choppy movement), faulty proportion of hock bone to thigh.

STRAIGHT SHOULDERS. Many novices think that this term applies to the shoulder-blades immediately below the withers, but it is commonly used to describe the upper arms. If the position is too upright, the result is restricted forward reach of front legs while moving.

TAIL CARRIAGE. The correct position of the German Shepherd Dog tail is down, ending in a slight curve. The tail may be raised when moving but should never curve over the back.

TAIL FEMALE. The female lines in a pedigree, tracing back from the dam.

TAIL MALE. The male lines in a pedigree, tracing back from the sire.

THROATY. Possessing too much loose skin under the chin or round the throat.

TIMBER. The term 'plenty of timber' is sometimes used to indicate ample heavy bone.

T.D. Tracking Dog – Working qualification.

UNDERHUNG, UNDERSHOT. Prominent lower front teeth, the lower jaw extending beyond the upper jaw.

UPPER ARM. The section between the elbow and the point of the shoulder bone.

V. When used as part of a German dog's name, abbreviation for 'von' or 'vom', meaning 'of' or 'from'.

V. Vorzuglich. (Excellent.) German qualification.

V.A. Excellent, and included in the finally selected group. German qualification.

WEEDINESS. Lack of bone, substance, stamina.

WRINKLE. Small folds of loose skin on skull.

Z.P.R. Zuchtprufung. Elementary German working qualification.

BIBLIOGRAPHY

The German Shepherd Dog, von Stephanitz, Verein für Deutsche Schäferhunde, 1950.

The Complete Alsatian, Nem Elliott, Nicholas Vane, 1961.

The German Shepherd Dog in America, Geraldine R. Dodge and Josephine Z. Rine, The Orange Judd Publishing Co., 1956.

The German Shepherd Dog, G. Horowitz, Our Dogs, N.D.

The Alsation Owner's Encyclopaedia, Madeleine Pickup, Pelham Books, 1964.

Alsatians, Lilian Leonard, Foyles, 1958.

The Book of the Alsatian Dog, F. N. Pickett, Weald Press, 1950.

Modern Bloodlines in the Alsatian, Nem Elliot, Kaye and Ward, 1968.

All About the German Shepherd Dog, Madeleine Pickup, Pelham Books, 1973.

Index

faults, standard, 55
Fee (Bell), 29
feeding: adult dogs, 124–5; after
   whelping, 104; during pregnancy,
   101, 103; for eczema, 176;
   epilepsy, 177–8; and hysteria,
   181–2; puppies, 104–6, 121–4,
   129–30
feet: care of nails, 183; faults, 78–
   81, Figs. 15, 16; standard, 53;
   structure, 76–81, Fig. 79
Fenton of Kentwood, 34, 133
Ferdl v.d. Secretainerie, 59
films, 160–1
first-aid boxes, 165–6
fits see convulsions; epilepsy
fleas, 118, 126, 176
Flora Berkemeyer, 98
forehead, standard, 50
foreign bodies, swallowing, 170,
   176–7
forequarters: faults, Figs. 10, 11;
   standard, 52, 56
foster mothers, 103
fractures, 178
Franze v.d. Secretainerie, 33
Funk, Dr Werner, 22, 30

gait, 62–70, 115, Figs. 4, 5, 8;
   standard, 53–4
Galliard of Brittas, 32
garlic capsules, 167, 186
gastric illness, 106, 178
general management, 100–7
genetics, 86–99; defective genes,
   92–9
German Shepherd Dog League of
   Great Britain, 33, 36, 40, 42, 45–
   6, 180
Germany, shows, 60–1, 144–6
Gerold of Brittas, 29–30, 32
Gockel von Bern, 83
Godden, Mrs M., 34
Godden, Sonnica, 133
Gottfried of Coulathorne, 31–2
Governor, 162–3
Graf Eberhard von Hohen-Esp, 27,
   88–90
Greif v.d. Peterstirn, 98
grooming: bathing, 138–9; for
   shows, 138
guard dogs, 152, 154

guide dogs, 158–60
Guide Dogs for the Blind
   Association, 46, 158
gums: disorders, 178; teething, 188
Gundo v. Simplon, 36
Hahn, Count von, 20–1
hand-rearing puppies, 103
hard-pad, 128, 171, 172, 174, 179,
   183
Harding, Lyn, 160–1
'hare' foot, 78, 80, 183, Fig. 15
Harras v. Glockenbrink, 99
head, 76; standard, 50–1, 57
height, 74–6; standard, 55
Hektor v. Schwaben, 26
Hella Secretainerie, 34
Hendrawens Spartacist, 134
hepatitis, 171, 173, 179
heredity, 82–99
hernias, 179
Herold aus der Niederlausitz, 31
Hester, Mrs, 37
hindquarters: faults, Fig. 6; puppies,
   116; standard, 53, 56
hip dysplasia, 164, 179–80
history, 17–35, 36–48
Horand v. Grafrath, 26, 28, 36, 89
hormones, 93–4, 184
Horst von Boll, 98
house training, 126–7
Howard, Mrs, 22, 32, 36, 37
Hussan vom Haus Schütting, 29,
   32, 83
hybrid vigour, 85
hydrophobia, 180–1
hygiene, 106–7, 118, 126
hysteria, 181–2

impotence, 182
inbreeding, 23, 83–5, 87, 164
Ingosohn of Errol, 33
inoculations, 128, 174
insect stings, 187–8
intelligence, 162–3
intermate breeding, 85
Ireland, shows, 147–8
Irish Kennel Club, 147

jaundice, 182
jaws, 71, 76
Jet of Seale, 32
Jones, Mrs I., 157